SUGAR AND SPICE

Slugs and snails and puppy dog's tails

Sugar and spice and all things nice

Abi Austen

Sugar and Spice

Copyright © 2023 Abi Austen

All rights reserved.

No part of this book can be transmitted or reproduced in any form including print, electronic, photocopying, scanning, mechanical or recording without prior written permission from the author.

Sugar and Spice

"I'm no longer accepting the things I cannot change. I'm changing the things I cannot accept."

Angela Davis

"No one can make you feel inferior without your consent.'

Eleanor Roosevelt

"The best way to predict the future is to create it."

Abraham Lincoln

"Always be a first-rate version of yourself, instead of a second-rate version of somebody else."

Judy Garland

Table of Contents

WOMAN ... 1

THE PARACHUTE REGIMENT ... 2

LIFE ... 3

THIS MORNING ... 19

SURGERY ... 21

FIRST CREATION ... 27

FAMILY ... 42

BANGKOK, 2007 ... 79

STONEHAVEN, 1973 ... 97

BELFAST ... 111

BANGKOK, 2008 ... 141

ABERDEEN, 1976 ... 146

TWO YEARS LATER ... 162

BANGKOK, 2007 ... 186

ABERDEEN 1978 ... 188

DREAMING OF SOLDIERS ... 192

A COMBINED CADET ... 215

OFF COURSE ... 229

TRYING TO FIX THE ENGINE ... 236

BANGKOK, 2008 ... 241

HOME NO MORE ... 246

SANDHURST ... 255

US EMBASSY, SKOPJE, 40 YEARS LATER	267
BERLIN, 40 YEARS EARLIER	272
THAILAND, 2008	293
SCOTTISH TELEVISION, 1986	296
MAKING MOVIE MAGIC	304
TRAVNIK. BOSNIA, 1992	316
BLACKPOOL, 2006	333
GLASGOW, 1994	339
TELEVISION – THE END GAME	346
SURGERY NIPS AND TUCKS 2008	357
GRANADA END OF DAYS	360
LONDON 2007	366
THE PARACHUTE REGIMENT	370
'P' COMPANY	374
AMBITION ACHIEVED	386
WEARING THE MAROON BERET	390
WHAT'S THE POINT?	394
WOMANHOOD	400

Sugar and Spice

WOMAN

'An adult female human being.'

'An adult who lives and identifies as female, though they may have been said to have a different sex at birth.'

'A wife or sexual partner.'

'Women in general.'

Cambridge Dictionary, 2022

THE PARACHUTE REGIMENT

I am the only female Parachute Regiment officer, ever. Period.

I am the first female to pass Airborne selection – the fabled P Company. I did that over 20 years ago.

I look forward to the day another woman walks where I walked. It is long overdue.

This is my story.

LIFE

At birth, I was designated male by a midwife who summarily examined between my legs and pronounced judgement. I was to become many things, but I have never been male.

I am woman. I always have been.

Doubt me? Go back a page. I'm in the dictionary.

I was forced to live as somebody I am not for the first 44 years of my life. A rather grim prism through which to exist; I am sure you will agree. A life sentence awarded to the innocent.

My only offence was to be born female. I didn't ask for the medical accident of attached flesh, or the false midwife diagnosis. That error reverberating through my life has caused so much pain.

I turned that mistake around to find a life I could have otherwise never enjoyed. I became an officer in The Parachute Regiment. I passed the rigorous Airborne selection 20 years before the army said another woman was the first.

That is simply not true.

I am the first.

I became a paratrooper by adopting a disguise forced upon me by a midwife's designation. I didn't choose that. Having been forced to live with it, I turned it around to beat the patriarchy at its own game. Women were not allowed to join the Regiment. To achieve my ambition, I hid my identity. It was the only way to win. No other woman has ever achieved what I achieved.

I went all the way with The Parachute Regiment, commanding paratroopers in combat in Iraq and Bosnia. I went to the Special Air Service. I deployed multiple times with Special Forces in Afghanistan. I served in Cyprus, Kenya, Belize, Oman, Poland, Germany, Jordan, Kuwait, the United States and Northern Ireland. I packed in more in my decade with the Regiment than most do in a lifetime.

When I tired of hiding, I had my own 'voila!' that appalled them all. I revealed to the military who I really am. Now that truly was a moment... they said I'd betrayed them. I said you didn't think that when two British Princes of the Blood decorated me for my service. I stayed with the army just long enough to be confirmed by the army as the first female Parachute Regiment officer, therefore, the first female to pass Airborne selection.

Then I was gone.

The army made it clear women weren't welcome. Merely by becoming me, they rejected me.

I had worked my way round the regulations. All within the rules. They weren't expecting that. They couldn't then walk it back. I'd proved to one and all I was Airborne. They thanked me for my service, then told me I had to leave.

Women weren't allowed to serve in The Parachute Regiment. The army had found a stop sign I couldn't work around.

I have a letter from the Regimental Colonel that says exactly that.

No matter. The army can't deny I walked on their forbidden ground.

I have been female all my life. That is the rock that forms the foundation of my existence. There's a whole gaslighting epic about 'biological sex', but that's merely the last gasp of baby boomer bigotry.

The attached gonads I happened to arrive with were a mere medical accident. No different from webbed feet or any other paradox of gestation. When I could, I fixed that, and changed every aspect of my life accordingly. I'm an awfully happy person now, but continually unhappy at how society continues to persecute my right to self-determination.

I firmly believe that in decades to come, folks will look back on the way my community has been pilloried by society and view it as the same sort of aberration that once saw left-handed people condemned as evil. I think we've just about reached that tipping point over same-sex sexuality. I hope I may yet be alive when my people are viewed with the same relative tolerance.

It was logic and reason, not cultural discrimination, which gave me my answers. A sort of gender enlightenment, if you like. And it was science that provided me with my final, external solution. I was always me, always have been. I was female from the moment I was conceived and will be till the day I die. What society did was make me ashamed of my lived reality by teaching me I was evil. I was given no other option. Until now:

I will no longer accept the things I cannot change. I will change the things I cannot accept.

That, I think, deals with that…I'll not apologise for any of it, nor second guess myself anymore, nor allow you to second guess me either. It's taken me sixty years to achieve that self-belief. Society ranges every power it has against my community. Life remains a constant challenge.

None of this has been easy. I've been begrudgingly offered a form of legal identity by an English-based government. The Tory party still seek to destroy my identity. The right-wing press eagerly create completely fantastical scenarios of sexual debauchery in argument against any form of human progression for my people. We are still the persecuted.

I've got a female passport, but I get a ping every time I go through customs control. Nobody says anything, but then I get the nudge and the look from the border police. If I phone a government department and give them my social security number, there's a pause and a throat clear and the line goes on silent while I get put through to a 'special' helpline. I am now calling Orwell's Room 101. Somewhere, in some dark and dank office down a dark and dank corridor, behind a door and a sign marked 'special', there's somebody sitting with a list of 'special' people, ready to treat me in a 'special' way. No matter how apologetic, every engagement is beyond intrusive.

I've tried to find a partner, but there always comes the dreadful, hateful moment when I have the conversation. I rarely get beyond the look of shock and confusion. I live alone now. It just got too complicated.

The dichotomy is evident because that societal rejection has also been my greatest blessing. I had to learn to be somebody else. The foundation of my professional success was predicated on being enough of an actor to work the other side of the gender divide.

Without that midwife's error, I simply could not have enjoyed the career and the adventures I have had. As a woman, I would not have been allowed. Such is the patriarchy. Such is the paradox.

My life has been unique in its challenges and unique in its achievements.

I am my own superhero.

Being called a man allowed me to develop a confidence I would never have been permitted to enjoy had I always been openly female. The leadership skills I learned as an officer would never have happened for me, simply because women were barred from the Parachute Regiment.

Was I an imposter? Don't think so - I passed the same tests as everybody else and served my time in the same way everybody else did. I led soldiers. Everybody brings baggage to the parade square. I may have been different, but I met so many oddballs in the army, I am far from being alone in my difference. I had an awful lot of mental trauma bags to haul about, but I also had a blinding, OCD level, ambition that drove me onward.

It's not my issue that the army didn't see me for me.

The army recognised my talent and ambition and fully exploited it, so the institution was as complicit in my career as I was. I never lied about my identity, just that nobody in authority chose to ask me the question. When I did tell them, they fired me. I have no regrets about not mentioning it before.

I owe the Regiment and the army for the opportunities it gave me. In seeing me as a man, they opened Pandora's

Box for me to exploit. I did just that, picking up, examining, and loving every jewel on offer. Jewels that would have been forbidden to me, had they known me as the woman I am.

The army isn't the only career I've had. However, it is the only one that was so extreme in its rejection of women that I had to forge another identity to be allowed to participate.

Of the rest, I wouldn't change anything. I look back now with a strong and deserved sense of professional success. In spades.

That, believe me, is a real rarity for somebody with my background. Not many make it this far. Those that publicly do, tend to end up in entertainment, largely as a curiosity of parts, a sort of PT Barnum oddity. I am not sure whether folks are laughing with or at us. I'm not judging, survival is what it is. Whatever gets you through the night, right? I just wish there were more of us openly out there doing something different. We are just as diverse as any other group of humanity.

What all did I do to keep the bailiff from the door and my neck from the self-inflicted noose?

After my career in The Parachute Regiment, I became a police officer. Before all that, I had a highly successful career making television. I've written a best-seller, which is well on its way to becoming a movie. After moviemaking, the army, and the police, I built a new life as a diplomat advising presidents, generals, and government ministers. Since I openly became me, I've had more success than the rest of it put together. I wake up happy. That makes all the difference.

Important people – including many military generals - think I'm good at what I do. Many of whom have since become dear and deeply valued friends, my new family.

All of them respect me for me and I treasure them for that. They listen to what I have to say and then tell me I am wise, which always pleasantly surprises me. I'm not good at compliments. Comes from having had so many rejections. I find it hard to believe the good.

The establishment gives me medals, trophies, and for a while there, the rank of ambassador. The success comes from getting older. I've just seen a lot of stuff and experienced a lot of pain. The skill they pay me for is in my telling and sharing of those accumulated crumbs of knowledge so countries don't make the same mistakes twice. The understanding of life cannot be learned in a book. Wisdom is gained through losing, not victory, and I've had a lot of loss in my 60 years.

I'm now paid well for my failures and successes. Which is nice, because when I did march proudly out to change everything, the price of my journey ended up with me becoming homeless and jobless. Everybody in my life walked away, including the Regiment.

That came after 44 years of mostly silent but incredibly demanding and demeaning internal struggle. The loss of all that I once had has made me more compassionate for the deprived, more ruthless in my condemnation of the bigots, and more determined that nobody will ever hurt me that way again.

I enjoy my money. Materially, I turned it around by risking my life in war. I live in a stately house, with a posh car in the drive, posh furniture inside, and a cabinet full of champagne. I even own a Picasso. I don't absolutely adore the painting. I bought it because I had money, and it was a Picasso. Nope, the painting doesn't make me delirious, but telling people I own a Picasso does.

Go figure.

Coming back from the damned can have such joy but is still mixed with pain. As a woman, I face different struggles now.

I went for a contract appraisal last week. We were reviewing a year of work where I took a major international security program for an international organisation from nothing to something cool. I travelled all over the world to do it, all by myself. Nobody helped me get there. I built it all in my head and then sold it to male military stakeholders in fourteen different countries. The head of the whole shebang, a famous guy, told me that my work would become the model for future operations across the world. The President of a real country praised me for my work and gave me a medal.

For a minute there, I thought I'd broken through the pie crust.

There's a format for these appraisals – post, performance, personality, potential. The first two are the fluff, they always say nice stuff – it's the last two that are important. That's the bit that says what folks think of you and what they think you'll do next. This year, I've really tried to make it all click. Tried to hide my talent, to let others shine, be a team player. What women are expected to do – be empathetic, nurturing, consensual. I thought I'd nailed it this time.

In potential, they said I am a 'disruptor', which in management speak means somebody who rips up the consensus and creates waves, which may not always be positive. What happened to the bit where the author acknowledged that before I arrived there was no program? I disrupted it by saying nothing worked, held truth to power, and then made the dodo into something that could really fly. Less disruption, more honesty.

In personality, they said I had:

'Prodigious intelligence that challenges norms but which could intimidate in team settings.'

How do you make intelligence less intimidating? Speak slowly? Use less syllables? Sign language, perhaps? Or maybe I should have just made the tea and taken notes? Or left failure alone and told the men it was all fine?

As a woman, it's different.

What they're praising but criticising is my very being. The gender part: being a woman in a man's world. That's the intimidating part. All my colleagues were men. They didn't like that I wouldn't compromise and had the bright ideas. A man would be praised for that forth righteousness, single mindedness, and intensity.

Can't do that as a woman, though.

It was my background in a male workplace that gave me the experience and skills to put the security plan together. It was the male disguise part of my life that gave me entry to forbidden halls. I knew all the weapon types and the ammunition scales and the operating doctrine. I could not have learned that as a woman.

Women were not allowed to learn that.

Expressing that knowledge got me marked down for intelligent intimidation. You mean standing my ground and not accepting mediocre? Setting the program objective and delivering success? All good manly stuff – except, I am not a man.

I now know that no matter how hard I toil or how well I do, nothing I do will ever count for as much as it did when I was pretending to be a man.

I knew more than they did, expressed that knowledge better than they did, and the men are intensely jealous of that. I achieved my knowledge by subterfuge, but I'll lay you money that any number of women could have been just as successful as me. If only they had been given the chance by the men to participate.

Could I have just gone with the flow? Could I have lived an ordinary and unhappy life? Nope, I'll never be ordinary and unhappy. What is that? Be like my parents: mom, pop, apple pie, and a hidden life of booze, pills and wife beating? I don't think so.

My horizons have always been bigger than my environment.

I don't recall my family with any affection. I'll be up-front now and tell you they disowned me all those years ago when I told them I am a woman. After a lifetime of denial of what was literally in front of them, they turned away. Not once did they ever try to change that. I reached out a couple of times. All I got was hatred in return. In the end, they took their rejection of me to the grave. I had a lawyer tell me they were dead just so the estate could get wound up. I wasn't mentioned.

That level of hurt makes you a harder person. Well, I must be. Nobody - and I mean nobody - is going to come help me if I can't manage. Charlton Heston once said, 'there's nothing concentrates the mind like having to make the rent.'

Damn straight, Moses. Onwards, and don't spare the horses.

One of these days, I may find a spiritual home, but for now, I'll keep that middle finger up and do it my way:

The sense that there is always something out there. Something out there, just around the corner, down the hall, right beyond my fingertips, just waiting for me to touch it.

It's the hunt that keeps me in the game. I've always felt this life has promised me more than I have ever realised, or ever delivered. I've flitted from post to post, job to job, town to town, relationship to relationship, discarding my skin every time I have moved on, re-inventing, changing, evolving, hunting, searching, but never truly finding.

I learned early on in life that there is another way to confront life's challenges. Instead of living in the prism, change the optics. Renege, renew, realise. All my life, I've changed the unacceptable in a hunt for the extraordinary. It's a constant howl round loop of re-invention to find happiness. I had a therapist once who had a term for it; geographising.

My spell check is howling, and I think you'd end the Scrabble dinner party if you pulled that one out, but it is on the mark. I just keep on rolling when the life I am leading gets turgid.

Change it up. Move on. Self-realise.

So much of what I have achieved was done in another role, playing as another person. So much of my existence has been a performance piece, acting out a role to satisfy an audience, but which did not satisfy me.

It's a different kind of resume:

- I've been a woman masquerading as a man and a woman being a woman.
- I've worn a tuxedo, high heels, boxers, and a bra. When I was fully method man acting, often all at the same time.
- I've had sex with men and women as a man and a woman – I bet you don't hear that too often.

I view my former life as a fruitless boxing match against a suffocating blind of smothering sheets of voile that blew in the wind of my turbulent existence. I became very good at fighting them, but I could never win that battle if I lived in that body. I was barely alive, smothered by self-hatred at what society had decreed for me.

That was where war came into the equation.

My struggle to reconcile my outer appearance with a wholly different inner being became reflected in my desire to be part of conflict. War meant I could forget. When the fog starts to suffocate, you got to up-change the weather. So that was what I did, constantly charging onwards, taking ridiculous risks, a butterfly dodging the flame.

I went to eight major conflicts; I willingly went to every one of them, most I volunteered for.

I was drawn to war between peoples as a reflection of the war I fought within myself. Society rewarded my sacrifice in those terrible conflicts with awards and medals. The more I acted as a man, the angrier I got at the utter ridiculousness of my situation, the more decorations I was given. They gave me prizes for putting myself in a position where I could be killed. A form of release from my own torment. All I did as I got older was amplify the risk.

I nearly died on the battlefield many times, just as I nearly died in life fighting my own internal struggle for liberation. I fought my learned hatred of myself to the bitter end. To the stage where I could fight no more, and the only alternative was eternal darkness. I fought myself to a standstill before I capitulated. I stopped caring if I lived or died, and only just found my redemption in time.

I am resigned to death. I don't seek it, but if the fight becomes too much, I will happily end this life if I must. I've been so close so many times, mortal end fails to have any fear.

Those wars remain seared into my mind and contribute to making me the person I have become. I have spent 17 years on the forgotten frontlines of some forgotten war in forgotten countries. When the rest of the world was forming relationships and families, I was trolling over some battle-scarred landscape. Most soldiers count themselves lucky to see one war – I've seen far too many.

No one could be the woman I am without the mould being cracked just a bit. I am wary of humanity because my life has always been adversely judged. Now, I am very, very careful about who I let in.

It's a necessary carapace.

I found my own joy without others. It is simple; I live life as the woman I always have been. I revel in that joy every day as if it could be my last. A joy that took me more than half my life to find.

I don't need your pity; I chose this.

What I do ask for – nay, demand – is your acceptance.

I want you to know that I am a very, very, very happy woman. It could have been an easier road, but it is what it is. I found my grail – and I drink deeply from that battered cup.

This is how it all came to pass….

THIS MORNING

I feel the light prickle at my eyelids...It's time. Dreams diffuse as events temporal intervene. I sometimes dream as the person I used to pretend to be. That's fading now as the years pass, but there are moments when all that was revisits me.

I welcome the light.

As ever, my first conscious thought is to stretch my arm out before me, in a sweeping, languorous arc, bringing it into my field of vision, capturing the bone and sinew in shadow before the brightness of the sun sweeping in from my window. As ever, I marvel at my newfound construction - the narrowness of the forearm, the delicacy of my wrist. That's the power of my happy hormones.

I am reminded that what was is no more. I smile at the joy of that realisation.

My caress moves to the flatness between my legs and the curve of my breasts. They are all mine. They are me. Each waking is extra-ordinary. As it has been ever since that first day I woke in Thailand.

I thank my angels for the gift of female life – and the joy of the waking of every day. Nobody can take that away from me.

I am alive. I am happy. I am content.

I am woman.

SURGERY

It took stupendous medical effort to realise my reality; dozens of unconscious hours being amended.

My surgeries all took place in Thailand. I broke the bank to go to one of the world's greatest surgeons; Doctor Suporn. Thailand became my second home, Dr. Suporn's clinic my sustenance. Gradually, over ten years of successive operations, I changed myself, outside in, from the broken body I inherited, to who I really am and always was.

In total, I underwent thirty-six different surgical procedures, well over thirty hours on an operating table. I spent around £140,000 to achieve my dream, all earned by me, not a penny taken from the state. I am proud of that; I did it all by myself.

I carefully planned the work; the timescale less so, and the wherewithal to fund it least of all. The money came haphazardly. I was grateful for every increment. I risked my life returning to war to earn it.

The first session was on September 22nd, 2007. It was the most invasive. Dr. S sawed a large portion of my skull away, re-shaped my nose and re-structured my face. He returned my face to its female form; undoing the effects of the horrid hormones I had been subjected to for over four decades. He then gave me breast implants. That session, around eleven hours long, really, really hurt. It was ridiculously painful.

I went home, healed, got fit, and returned to have my genitalia realised on February 1st, 2008.

Realising is not the term most folks use for this operation, or rather, a series of operations. Today's term seems to be reassignment, which makes it sound like a journey and destination. It wasn't reassignment for me, it was an act of redemption.

I was female the day I was born. Being female was all I had ever wanted to be, an obsession that destroyed me every day I had to act as a man. The rest of it was nobody's fault *per se*, but an awful lot of folks made it a lot worse by sticking labels on me that I didn't believe in.

The societal gender post office had stuck the wrong postcode on my stork's package. In Thailand, I returned to sender and started again.

On the pain scale, the first lot had been a 'Spinal Tap' eleven. Down below was a nine and a half.

And then it was home to recover, and then back for more. Like that Tom Cruise movie, I lived, died, and repeated. On September 3rd, 2008, I had my body re-shaped a couple times, and my ass augmented. That was madly uncomfortable, but around a seven and a half compared to the other two.

After that, I was broken. By the physical, mental, and financial effort.

It took me three straight years in Afghanistan to raise the money for the rest, which was the comparatively simple stuff of having my nose re-done three times and my throat shaved. Plus, seven and a half thousand hair grafts, transferred from two very long and painful incisions to the back of my head.

I intimately know the inside of an operating theatre, and how to lie in a hospital bed. Along the way, I went full Elvis' prescription medicine overload, got morphine addicted, and tried to kill myself.

Surgery has been an adventure. An awful lot of blood and toil.

BANGKOK, FEBRUARY 1ST, 2008.

My attached genitals were gone. I'd never wanted them. They'd nearly ruined me.

During ten hours of surgery, the leading gender reassignment surgeon in the world had removed the testicles, scrotum, and penis.

At last, I was freed from them.

I now had a vagina, labia, and clitoris.

My body was finally female. I was complete.

The decision to be in Thailand could scarcely have been more profound. I had sacrificed everything, my marriage, my career, my life savings, my colleagues, and my family. I could not go on in that form. I could not make those compromises any longer.

I chose life. I chose happiness. I chose me.

I was euphoric.

My life was now finally my own. An entirely selfish and very personal act of survival. I owned my decision then. I still do, and I embrace it completely. I choose to be me. I gained the gift everybody else is given at birth.

I was re-born.

I earned that moment. My last and only real chance to find contentment. For the rest of my life, nothing would ever be the same again. You can't fish old Willy Pete out of the jar and stick it back on again. Nor would I ever want to; honest and true.

Society's discrimination had driven me to the edge of reason itself. I had fought for as long as I could for other people's acceptance, never for my own. Hoping against hope that the sure and certain knowledge I am female could be ignored.

I couldn't continue pretending to be a man. I never was one. I was done acting.

A television camera crew recorded my first waking moments. I cried, turned to the lens, and asked:

'Does anyone have George Clooney's number?'

It was the single most healing moment of my life.

Hater's footnote: I have never, not even for a second, ever regretted or even questioned my decision. I revel in the memory of that moment of realisation and the life it has given me since. And I genuinely don't care that you don't understand that.

It was never about you.

When this life hurts me, I recall that single, blinding realisation. The moment when I felt what the rest of the world takes for granted: comfort in my own reality.

When a body and a brain and a soul fuse into one.

Lying in that recovery room, I began to dream of all that was, and all I thought it could now be. Dreams and reality woven into a kaleidoscope of jumbled images. A life lived, a life forgotten, a life remembered. I was cosseted by a warm, all-embracing morphine blanket.

I began to fly...those dreams now fill these pages.

The nurses gently lifted me onto a gurney. I scarcely felt the movement. I floated on cotton-wool sheets of drug-enhanced softness. They took me down a long corridor, into an elevator, down another corridor, and back to the room I first vacated ten long hours ago.

The last act I had committed before laying down on that gurney of redemption had been to urinate standing up for one last time. I looked down at the lump of gristle between my legs and said goodbye to that part of me that I had never wanted. I had no regrets, no trepidation. I feared the surgery, the loss of control, the pain I knew I would have to overcome. I would not miss that thing between my legs.

I knew with absolute clarity and certainty that this was what I wanted.

Ten hours later, my genitalia were held together with nearly three hundred stiches. Between my legs, the entrance to my vagina was packed with thirty feet of surgical wadding. In my left arm, a plasma drip, in my right a morphine drip, in my groin, a catheter.

I was tethered while I healed, but my body belonged to me. What a stunning moment of self-realisation that truly was. A true Bodhisattva.

FIRST CREATION

The village of Stonehaven sits in a sheltered cove on the northeast coast of Scotland beside the icy and unforgiving North Sea. The ocean's moods provide the very rhythm of existence.

The sea provides a desolate beauty. The water is a cruel mistress. The North Sea is not a halcyon Mediterranean. In winter, the water is an arctic, grey expanse. In summer, the grey-green depths are little different. The wind that scuds inland from those endless waves is malevolently cold and freezing.

Stonehaven is a mirror for that dark, forbidding water.

The town is not an expression of soaring minarets and extravagant spires. It is a collective built of grey granite, rarely more than two stories high. Each dwelling sits squat, square and solid, straining against the ravages of wind, sea, and sand. In winter, it is hard to find the horizon. Water and sky are equally sombre and grey. No art deco splash of colour enlivens the homes there. No individual expression of creativity. The granite buildings are constantly dampened by a sea moisture that diffuses the stone's mica glint. Yet more grey to compliment the teal-grey ocean waves that crash within the bay.

It is that environment that shaped my childhood; I hated it. I've only once been back in adulthood, and I'll never willingly go back there again.

My family moved to Stonehaven as refugees from the war in Northern Ireland. I am Irish, raised in Scotland.

My mother and father had run from the bombs and the bullets of Belfast. They left behind one of the great cities of Empire for a cold, wet, grey, and inhospitable place where nobody spoke like me, and I knew nobody.

I grew up in Stonehaven, in a town whose people and destiny were governed by the tempestuous nature of the water and whose faith was shaped by the unforgiving evil eye of conservative Scottish Calvinism.

In my childhood, Stonehaven had an active small-boat fishing fleet. They are all gone now, fallen to the monster ships from Spain with their massive nets and deep-sea radars. Back then, though, the fleet was Stonehaven.

The fishermen were bred to be tough creatures. It is their hands I remember the most; big, tough, gnarled, strong, huge paws, the skin weathered and beaten. As a child, I watched them manhandle their catch, writhing within wooden boxes, onto the harbour front. Cod, halibut, crab, and lobster; to my terrified youthful eyes silver, wriggling, scaled creatures, raw with the intensity of nature.

The men that threw those boxes - scarred, wind-chapped, missing fingers, nails encrusted with scales and dirt - seemed to be warriors from another world to my immature eyes. Those fishermen were frightening Spartans who calmly matched their survival against the immoveable and unchanging depths, and publicly carried themselves with a physical pride and self-aware swagger. They hailed each other across the harbour, swearing with the fluency of raucous poets, laughing without inhibition, winking at me as I shyly avoided their eyes.

Their womenfolk would silently line the walls of the snug harbour, clustered in shawled groups, waiting patiently for the bows of the fishing boats to come around the head of the bay.

It was the sort of town where men were men and women were grateful.

Women stayed at home, the men went to sea. And that was that.

The only work opportunity for a female outside of gutting fish was in nursing or teaching or office admin; and that only for the educated. Regardless, it was expected that a female would only work until she was married, after which, she would raise children. For a woman to not be married by 30 was an oddity; a person to be pitied.

Men had different obligations. Stonehaven men did not cry. Nor did they openly express love. Men were expected to be strong and silent. As tough as the granite that the town was made of. They went to work, brought home the money, and expected their women to look after them: in the home, in their bed and in producing and raising their offspring.

Most of all, you were expected to conform.

Gender and socio-economic class dictated the path you would follow. Working class boys would follow their fathers onto the boats. Women would stay in their father's home until they left to be part of another man's married home. Before life had really begun, gender and class defined all that you were and all that you could ever be.

When and where I grew up, individuals didn't have a right of personal aspiration. Individuals had responsibilities; cold, logical, unavoidable, and irresistible responsibility.

My parents may have occasionally touched each other, but I have no active memory of them ever hugging or kissing – nor of hugging or kissing me. Emotional ostentation had no place in that society.

Fitting in, making do and mending, being invisible, conservative, and conforming was what mattered: being a part of a codified system of societal control.

Britain was dull, monotone, stifling and depressing. Stonehaven amplified those sentiments by its isolation. I have no great warmth for the good old days. Those times suffocated me.

Twenty years before, an entire civilisation had signed up and gone to war. When I was young, the bus conductors and the postmen and the park wardens all wore their medal ribbons. As children, we played with the detritus; in dis-used pillboxes and empty bombsites, reading comics filled with tales of caricature Nazis and plucky Tommys. Our schoolbags, army surplus small packs.

The cost paid by an exhausted nation still hung in the air.

The war suffused everything with a dread melancholy. The war lay like untreated mould in the dark corners of the country's collective ego.

Alcohol was the soporific, a leavening of the classes and a means of escape. Scotland has always had a tortured relationship with drink.

On Friday and Saturday nights, the town was a riot of drunken men. There was no room in Stonehaven for restaurants or theatres or art galleries. Trawler men lived a dangerous existence; survival concentrated the mind on the immediate. Food was not for enjoyment – food was for filling the stomach. The creative arts were for the bored and indolent rich.
Alcohol was an antidote for temporary oblivion. Booze was the binding ingredient for a shared adult experience.

Most drinking establishments - and there were many - operated a public and lounge bar. Females were only welcome in the lounge bar, in the chaperoned company of their menfolk. The lounge bar was considered female-friendly by the addition of seats. Women were barred from public bars. Public bars might have had a stool or two for the aged - but social etiquette dictated that a man stood to drink until he could stand no more. Quite often, there were no toilets for women at all, which discouraged excessive feminine stays. Several drinking saloons barred women, full stop.

A woman would never buy drinks. That was a man's job. Even when couples went out together, the women would be expected to stay seated at the back while the men gathered at the bar. Men would drink tankards of beer, or whisky, or both together. Women would drink petitely and demurely - a dry sherry or sweet vermouth. No woman would ever drink beer; pints, in a dimpled glass with a handle, were for men.

Public houses were forbidden and dangerous territory for children. By law, the selling and consumption of alcohol had to be hidden from public view. Bar windows were blacked out, hidden behind ornate stained glass. Bars were dens of mystery, a place where adults did unspeakable things together. My parents would enter largely responsible human beings and emerge incoherent and garrulous. To stand outside was to wonder at the machinations of a devilish conspiracy. Every now and again, the door would swing open, releasing a fetid smell

Sugar and Spice

of sweat, cigarette smoke and beer, while the raucous sound of baritone male laughter emanated from within the grimy and dark interior.

There was no such thing as closing time in a community like this. A bar stayed open until its patrons could drink no more or a fight broke out, each outcome being equally likely.

Stonehaven was a town of near primeval emotion, of strict divide and closeted community, with rules and unspoken regulations as carefully demarcated as any religious commune. The all-pervading Scottish Church issued its weekly edicts of disapproval over the depravity of alcohol and homosexuality. The Kirk Minister patrolled the streets; his black cassock billowed behind him as he balefully forbad the enjoyment of life. That was the path to sin. Only by righteous redemption and a scourging of mortal desire could humanity find our salvation.

I was not born into this. I am a child of Ireland. My mother came from Belfast. My father was the Scot. We moved to Stonehaven because we fled the Ulster war.

We moved to the outskirts of town, into a new build estate. Fifteen miles south of Aberdeen, Stonehaven was the epicentre of a commuter belt for the big city. There was a great divide between the traditional fishing and farming community and we foreigners. We were the outsiders.

It all seemed so aspirational and modern. I came to understand Stonehaven was the compromise my Scottish father had made with my Irish mother to persuade her to leave her native Belfast. The bombs may have been terrifying, but we were also economic migrants. My father could make better money on the mainland, and Northeast Scotland was short of labour. So off we went to vault the socioeconomic classes from a Belfast tenement to the pebble-dashed security of a cul-de-sac.

My parents bought into the big dream of becoming middle-class. Our home sat on the end of a promontory, which my mother, with her ever-acquisitive nature, would describe as, 'the best plot on the whole estate.' My parents, with an almost ironic lack of imagination, called their new palace 'Four Seasons'. Constructed on the edge of an exposed cliff, the North Sea, a most contrary neighbour, battered that house from the day it was built. Four seasons arrived every hour.

The howling Arctic gales made Four Seasons particularly prone to the cutting winds of winter. My father planted trees all around the edge of our property to mitigate the worst. Many years later, after we had moved, the new purchasers woke in the middle of the night to find half their garden had disappeared down the cliff-edge. The wind was so keen, it had undercut the roots of my father's trees. At a single swift stroke, half of our quarter-acre plot became a mere pile of dirt fifty feet lower down the hill from the house, earth jumbled with the wreckage of fallen trees.

Sugar and Spice

Stonehaven was a tough place to grow up – particularly tough if you were born different. I've always been jealous of the London arts school set and their insouciant self-confidence. That is bred from acceptance and tolerance. There was none in Stonehaven. David Bowie would have struggled there.

Try being an individual in Stonehaven: all it would earn you was a punch. That Calvinist upbringing is why I fought against my inner destiny for so many decades. Its lessons and punishments are seared into my consciousness. I was bred to conform. I was beaten until I complied. I wrapped myself in consequential guilt for decades.

Difference brought violence. Violence hurt. I learned to hide my difference. I learned to hate myself for my difference.

When I think back on my childhood, it is mostly about violence. Everybody hit everybody else. Sometimes it was your own peer group, but mostly it was about picking on somebody smaller, less aggressive, and less able to defend themselves. As a child, 'a cuff round the ear' could be administered by any participating adult – parent, teacher, bus conductor, the man walking past. Everybody was licensed to commit publicly accepted violence. To be different merely brought an added level of application.

My problem was I didn't understand how to frame the question of my tortured existence, let alone process a response. The gender debate, indeed, the very words, had not yet been invented. I knew I was different, but I had no words, nor lived example, nor cultural reference, to express that longing in any meaningful way.

It's hard now, in this diverse society, to imagine what life was like in Scotland in the '60's and '70's. I don't just mean the obvious things, such as the dearth of information caused by the non-existence of the internet, mobile phones, or even computers. I mean growing up in a society that was still dominated by the attitudes of the war years and the baleful gaze of the Kirk. Of putting up and shutting up, of making do and mending, of 'mustn't grumble', Dunkirk spirit and stiff upper lip.

Scotland then was a world where it was legal for a husband to rape a wife, where any expression of homosexuality, private or public, was punishable by jail. Where parents were expected to beat their children regularly; 'Spare the rod and spare the child.' Scotland was a world of deference to rank and age, ridden with mind-numbing formality that was inculcated by impressing a dumb acceptance of authority from the earliest opportunity.

My first school, Dunnottar Primary, had separate boys and girl's entrances and playgrounds. We sat in a gender demarcated class, on opposite sides of the room. The world map on the wall was coloured predominantly pink, to mark Great Britain and Northern Ireland's Empire and Dominions. I have never understood why pink was chosen as a map colour for Empire. I was taught that far-off lands with exotic names such as Canada, New Zealand and Australia had recently belonged to us. We looked wistfully at the pink triangle of India when we were told it had been part of our Empire but that it didn't want to be British anymore because of the war. We were taught to puff with pride when we learned those Dominions had been disproportionately conquered by Scottish soldiers and governed by Scottish civil servants. We were taught the war had ended those days, but we should still be proud of the Empire that had been maintained by the adults now set over us.

Classes together were very much taught by rote learning. There were over 40 in my year group, with a single teacher. We spent hours steadfastly repeating as a whole, 'two times one is two, two times two is four.' I can still repeat arithmetical catechisms to this day. Speaking out was not encouraged. School was for absorption, for learning. Your opinion as a child was not sought.

We stood each morning to ritually repeat the Lord's Prayer and sing the national anthem. Any disobedience would be met with either a ruler across the knuckles, or that particularly Scottish punishment, the tawse; a long leather belt serrated into many pieces at one end, the better to inflict pain. If a child was deemed to require punishment, you were expected to stand at the front of the class, hands out, palms upper-most, while the teacher took a run and a big over-arm swing to scourge your exposed hand. Jesus would have been familiar with such a technique at his crucifixion.

I was aged seven when I was first belted with a tawse.

Calvinist guilt was much encouraged. The general antics and exploration of youth, what social workers today would call 'self-expression', were discouraged as laziness, sloth, greed, and untidiness.

Homosexuality was a sin so severe that the word was never mentioned without shame in the very utterance. The rooting out of it hung in the air with the verve of the Inquisition.

I was actively told that being left-handed was a mark of the Devil. It was never explained to me why writing that way was evil; merely that to do so was satanic. If caught writing with my left hand, I would be beaten with my teacher's ruler. At a time when copperplate scribing was much valued, my writing remains to this day a doctor's prescription of illegibility. I am thus coherent with neither hand, a hangover of my confusion at being prevented from fulfilling what is a logical and natural function.

The subjects taught were indicative of the life role gender ascribed. Boys were taught metalwork and woodwork, while girls were taught needlework and 'home economics' – cooking and the art of managing a household on a budget allotted by a husband.

I was assigned to sit with the boys and proved singularly useless at construction. I did manage to produce a pipe rack, even in the early '70's something of an anachronism. In metalwork, I made a setsquare, achieving the seemingly critical angles by complete mistake, watched over by an exasperated master. Neither of these skills has been of the remotest use to me in later life. My only real memories of hammering and sawing are of utter boredom and a fear of big, spinning machinery.

Many years later at Sandhurst, I was to envy the seeming self-confidence of English public-school boys as they casually offered their opinions with verve, panache, and languid self-assurance. We Scots just did not possess that kind of overt self-belief. Speaking up was showing-off in the Scotland I remember. Scottish society promoted homogeneity of identity; to articulate an individual opinion would have been regarded as overbearing. Scotland was, and to a large extent still is, a collectivist, socialist community. We are all Jock Tamson's bairns.

Individual silence didn't mean we weren't as bright. Much later, at Army Staff College, I achieved the highest mark of my entire syndicate in the final, written exam. I was then written down to the middle third for 'not verbally contributing to classes.' Speaking up hadn't occurred to me. I had been brought up to believe the classroom was where you listened, not offered your own opinion. My mistake.

We did have one brave soul at Dunnottar, a Dutch boy, whose father worked on the then nascent oilfields off Aberdeen. He asked to study home economics with the girls. He wanted to cook. He obviously didn't come from Stonehaven. Women cooked in Stonehaven society: no man would be seen near a saucepan. How we laughed at his innocent desire. Even the teacher laughed. He left the school soon after. I clearly remember the hurt on his face as we all smirked at him. How I secretly wished, even if I did not understand why, that I could have shown the same resolve. The peer pressure of youth can be a cruel mistress.

No, Stonehaven was not a town to be different. For my mother and father, it must have been quite familiar territory.

My family would be what is now known in the US as Scots Irish. Vigorously Presbyterian evangelical, white, conservative, hardworking, emotionally, philosophically, and culturally blinkered; the menfolk are Masons. A masculine ability to hold one's drink and one's feelings in check is very much prized.

I only ever remember seeing my father cry once, the day his father died. When he was given the news, he locked himself into his study. My mother sent me in to see him, against my own wishes, for I feared him. Too often, a meeting with my father resulted in violence. He had a volcanic temper and was not afraid to express it physically towards his children. I did as I was told and was shocked to see him sitting with his head in hands. He lifted his tear-stained face and told me to leave him alone. I was six. He rejected me because he was embarrassed to be seen crying. I was quite distraught at his rejection. The lesson was there for me to absorb - Scottish men do not cry. Crying is for women. Crying was weakness: therefore, women, by their tears, prove themselves weaker.

Except when Scotland loses at football. Then men will cry, the loss enhanced by alcohol. It is probably a good thing for the sake of the Scottish nation that the football team loses regularly, for then there is at least a moment where pent-up emotion can be released in a manly fashion without that passion turning, as it regularly otherwise does, to violence.

That's what I remember the most. The being hit, or the constant street urchin struggle to avoid being hit. Violence pervades every aspect of my childhood.

FAMILY

My father's family hail from Ayrshire on the West coast of Scotland, from a small mining village called West Kilbride. My paternal grandparents lived all their lives in a terraced council-owned house, in what was known as a 'two up, two down'; rented social housing being the norm for that economic class and generation. There was one living room downstairs, a kitchen to the rear, with two bedrooms and a tiny bathroom upstairs. In a small plot out back, my grandparents had a vegetable patch and a garden shed.

In her old age, my grandmother Liza was very proud to have central heating installed. All through my childhood, my father's family relied on a coal-fire in the front room. When I was young, she taught me how to clean the grate and set a fire, with newspaper and kindling, gradually feeding coal onto the fire. I was fascinated to watch the coal burn, first with great coils of sooty smoke, then to slowly burst into flame.

There is an attraction to a naked flame for a small child. I would sit and watch that fire for hours at a time. When we visited, I slept on a fold out sofa in the lounge, my parents having the spare bedroom. I would try to stay awake at night to watch the fire finally go out, a battle perpetually lost. Once, I leaned out to touch the flames,

Sugar and Spice

hurriedly withdrawing as the flame blistered my skin. My grandmother taught me to put a burn under a cold-water tap to anesthetise the wound. Before she died, she told me she had watched me move to put my hand in the fire. I asked her why she had not tried to stop me, she replied; 'If I had, you would not have learned that fire will burn you.'

My grandfather worked on the railways, literally on the rails. He was part of a gang that walked the line, from West Kilbride to Kilwinning, the next town on the main line south from Glasgow, clearing the rails of debris. His crew would then turn around and walk back again. The same stretch of track, every day of his working life. Come rain or shine, each morning my grandmother would make him breakfast before he set off in his blue overalls, lunch pail swinging from his belt.

His midday meal in his billycan was porridge, which he also ate for breakfast. Spooned into a bowl, it would set hard as a brick. I was fond of porridge, but only with sugar and milk. My grandmother would berate my father for allowing me this howling indignation. She regarded such sweet softness as an English habit.

My grandmother was a Scottish nationalist. We were brought up that way. On the wall in her kitchen, she hung an embroidered tea towel, proclaiming all that was great about Scotland and its people, the inventors of golf, penicillin, and television. She viewed the English with great suspicion, and retained a romantic love of tartan, shortbread, and bagpipes until she died.

She also remained relentlessly Luddite in her views on technology. She did not agree with television, as much as she was proud of its Scottish inventor. My father gave her an old back-and-white set, but it was rarely used. She was very upset by much of the content. I remember her being in a massive fizz for days after watching David Attenborough's series on 'The Birth of Man.' An old-time Church of Scotland Christian, she was adamant in her revulsion of Darwin; 'There is no way I came from any ape!' She exclaimed, before writing to the BBC to demand a retraction.

I am the oldest child begat by my parents. I had two younger brothers, neither of whom will have many recollections of either of their father's parents. My middle brother was little more than a baby when my grandfather died. He was long dead before my youngest brother was born, and my grandmother would pass on before my youngest sibling was five years old.

To me, though, my paternal grandparents were special. I caught them at an age in life where they had mellowed. They doted over me. West Kilbride was one long street, and my grandfather was well known there. I remember him as a huge man, with enormous hands which fascinated me with their working roughness. He used to put me up on his shoulders, introducing his grandchild to one and all. My treat on these trips was to be bought a bar of milk chocolate, which I was not strong enough to break. I would bang it off the top of his head in my eagerness to get a piece, an outrage he suffered with great humour.

My grandfather loved nothing more than digging in his garden. Our summer visits were always marked by a salad grown by his own hands. Iceberg lettuce, radishes, cucumber, and salad onions were produced in profusion, grown under homemade cloches of old polythene bags and chicken wire. Tomatoes were a bought-in luxury, being far too delicate for a Scottish garden climate. Each week, my grandmother would make a great cauldron of Scotch broth soup, which took two days of simmering to soften the lentils and barley. She would bargain at the butchers for a ham hock to make stock, where she also bought the liver and flat sausage she fed us to help our bones grow. Ever one for a bargain, she would buy all the 'four for the price of three' offers going. Her cupboards were filled with row upon row of tinned peaches and Spam. She told me she did so in preparation for the next war, as she knew from bitter experience that fruit and meat would be rationed.

Our diet then would frighten today's nutritionists. Offal, plus vegetables or salad covered in salt, were followed by such treats as a sugar sandwich - white bread, butter, and a large spoonful of white, granulated sugar. During the war, this had been greatly prized as sugar had been another rationed good. Each morning, to encourage healthy brain growth, we were forced to swallow a dessert spoon of cod liver oil and another of malt extract that glued our jaws together, doled out from a huge, evil-smelling bottle.

Later, when American police shows, such as 'Kojak', became national obsessions, I would marvel at such exotic foods as peanut butter and jelly sandwiches. I had no idea jelly was an Americanism for jam. Jelly, to us, was a dessert made from concentrated, flavoured gelatine, mixed with hot water, refrigerated until it had hardened. Peanut butter was unheard of – I don't remember ever seeing it at all in the UK until the '80s. Instead, I buttered white bread, sprinkled it with my father's salted peanuts and added our dessert jelly to emulate my television heroes, and pretended I enjoyed it as much as Telly Savalas did. How I wondered at the apparent strangeness of Americans.

My mother's family came from Belfast. I'd been born there and spent my early years there. Each summer, my father would load up the car and we would set off, first to West Kilbride, then to Belfast, on the ferry from Stranraer to Larne, then back again 2 weeks later. Travel then was not the routine it is now. The road from Stonehaven to the South was single lane, twisting and turning through small towns such as Montrose, Arbroath and Laurencekirk.

Much was made of preparing the car. Tyres pressurised, oil checked, petrol tank filled to the brim, the interior prepared with travel rugs, home-made sandwiches, and thermos flasks of hot, sweet tea. Oh, and of course, the obligatory, mother ordained visit to the loo before we set off. Often, we would travel at night to avoid the constant distraction of being stuck behind farm tractors, caravans, or slow-moving lorries. There was no motorway or dual carriageway then. The main road South was little more than a country lane. I remember watching the sunset over the North Sea as we drove south, and asking my father; 'Where do the clouds go when it gets dark?'

Arrival in West Kilbride to visit my father's family was a variable feast, dependent on how long it took to transit the great, industrial city of Glasgow. This was long before the motorway was constructed that now bisects the city. Travel across Glasgow meant straight through the city centre. To my young eyes, it seemed such a dirty, dark, and frightening place, with six-story, soot-stained buildings that blocked out the light from its narrow streets.

My paternal grandparents always welcomed us with dinner. Scotch broth from the ever-bubbling cauldron, followed by ham sandwiches and iceberg lettuce salad. While the adults talked, I would be given a box of my father's old toys, real metal Dinky cars, with proper rubber wheels, and metal Meccano strips. My grandmother never threw anything out. I loved going into her garden shed – I still adore the smell of Creosote – where she kept my father's collection of 'Boy's Own' magazines, filled with stories of Dan Dare and Biggles, plus sensible articles on how to find your way out of the woods when lost and the best football boots for 1948.

Many years later, after she had died, my father found all his old schoolbooks in the loft, every jotter and textbook. As a child, I used to make model aeroplanes, which I often gave to her. She kept them all, the years being identifiable by the clumsiness of their assembly. As I got older, less glue got spilled, the decals better applied to the right part of the wing.

They were generally delighted to indulge me and pleased to see their son. My father was an only child. My father's character - overly quiet, introverted, and internally self-sufficient - was shaped by the experience of being an only child.

In so many ways, he was different from his own family.

Growing up in West Kilbride was, I think, as suffocating an experience for him as growing up in Stonehaven was to prove for me. He spent a large part of his youth doing everything he could to leave it behind. My father was a pre-war baby, born in 1938. Don't ask me what date. I never knew his birthday, nor ever celebrated it.

His father, my grandfather, did not fight in the war as he had a reserved occupation on the railways. It never bothered him, either. He told me of the men who had been Territorials before the war, how they had spent their part-time wages on drink and women and then lost their lives fighting in far-off lands when the King had come to collect his shilling.

My grandfather was one of those solid, unambitious, and content men, supremely happy in his life and his work. He had a family at home, a set income, and a route to follow every day. He stayed that way right up to the day he was forcibly retired at sixty-five. He was dead three years later, mostly of a lack of purpose to his life. British Rail had repeatedly tried to promote him to station manager, but he would have none of it. He was happy walking the line until the day they told him he could no longer walk the line. That sudden rip from all that defined him destroyed him.

I don't believe my grandmother ever worked for a salary. Toiling in the home was a full-time job for a generation of women bereft of the domestic technology of today. Hoover is, in many ways, the ultimate feminist enabler. She was one of an extended clan of nine brothers and sisters, spread all over the West coast of Scotland, except for a celebrated scion, who immigrated to Virginia, USA after the war. The only time she ever flew on a plane was to visit her American relations. She was in her seventies. The experience caused her much bemusement, and she swore she'd never do it again, family or not.

My grandmother's greatest ambition for her son was for him to work for the Post Office in West Kilbride, marry a local girl and settle down next door.

My father had different plans. He wanted to get away, to see the world. In some ways, he achieved his aim. Which made return West Kilbride visits an anachronism for him, even if my father retained some of the baggage of that tough upbringing.

The one remaining local bar from that period has a wall full of photographs from the 1940s. There's a photograph of my father on the wall, dressed and equipped as a drummer in the Boys Brigade. He was a handsome boy, with a shocking cow's lick of dark brown hair. His shyness is apparent, even then, and his face is downturned, with an almost diffident smile counter-acting the seriousness with which he is striking his side drum. There's a pride in his appearance, his part of being something in an organisation of worth. He is thin to the point of being gaunt – a result of the war years.

Educated at Ardrossan Academy, he excelled in mathematics and went on to study electrical engineering in Glasgow, getting the train north over the very line that his own father maintained. I wonder if the two caught the other's eye as the carriages trundled up to the city? He discovered he had a real talent for the infant technology of electronics. He was extremely practical with his hands. He made our family's first hi-fi amplifier from a kit of parts, with glowing valves and Heath Robinson dials.

Later in my youth, we lived next door to a wealthy lawyer's family, who were given a table tennis kit for

Christmas, of which my brothers and I were very jealous. My father made us one – out of an old leaf dining table he bought in Oxfam, topped by chipboard painted green and white. Only the ball and bat were real. The homemade effort had a crazy bounce, but we spent hours playing on his homemade gift. Not many fathers would have thought of that or had the patience to put it together.

My father's first job after college was back in West Kilbride, using his youth and strength to shinny up chimneys, putting the new-fangled aerials for television onto the roofs of the local gentry's mansions. Later, he told me he had worked with an older man, a paratrooper during the war, and 'one of the toughest men (he) ever met.' My father always had a respect for the physical – I think it was probably an admiration of his own father. His first gig can't have been a pleasant job, working in the dreich Scottish weather, but it did introduce him to television, which my father was to make his profession.

The big break from home for him came in the early 60s, when he was offered a job with Pye Electronics in Cambridge, England. The offer must have seemed like a dream for an ambitious young man from a working-class mining village.

Cambridge also turned out to be where he met my mother.

My mother was the dominant presence in my childhood. My relationship with her was as complex as it was fraught. She was extroverted, whereas my father was not. Loud, whereas my father was not, and very emotionally demanding. Where the two were united was in their ambition for change. They stayed together through it all for over 50 years. Whether those were happy years is a moot point, as I shall explain, but they did stay together; it was what was expected then.

My grandparents on my mother's side were both remarkable people. My maternal grandmother was one of the shrewdest, most intelligent, and hard-working people I have ever met. I never met my grandfather. He was a soldier. He died alone in a bed-sit in Swansea, estranged from his entire family due to his behaviour after returning from the war with profound PTSD.

Born one of thirteen in Wales, as a young man he immigrated to Canada after his mother remarried and he fell out with his new stepfather. His papers, which I recovered many years later as part of his military record, state his profession as labourer. Somehow, he ended up enlisting in the British Indian Army in the early thirties. The legend I have heard is that he worked his way across Canada as a lumberjack, before boarding a ship from Vancouver, bound for India. That part of his life is shrouded in mystery, for my grandmother never talked of him, my mother and aunt despised him, and the only record I have of him is as given in his army service papers.

I have a few yellowing photographs of him. He was certainly a handsome man and a very debonair dresser, with a Douglas Fairbanks moustache, cigarette languidly draped from his lips. Although he joined the army as a private soldier, it is not difficult to see that had the lucky silver spoon of birth been more amenable, he would have made a dashing officer.

My grandfather lived a life of relative privilege in Imperial India, as all *nabobs* did, irrespective of rank, serving on the North-West Frontier in what is now Pakistan. When he died, my grandmother gave me a photograph album of his from that period, together with his service medals. She had just returned from his burial in Wales. She hadn't wanted to go to the funeral, but she did want her widow's pension. So, off she went at the army's invitation. She told me later that he was buried with full military honours - but it was all she could do to pretend to play the devastated and bereaved wife. After a separation of decades, her lace handkerchief contained emotions of ironic amusement, not tears. Surely, though, there must have been some regret for days gone past and never recovered.

In my own lifetime, I have travelled up the Khyber Pass, into Afghanistan, through the now-restricted tribal areas. Engraved on the Khyber rock-face are massive reliefs of the crests of the British army's finest units. There is one there of my grandfather's regiment. The Khyber Road is still overlooked by the forts my grandfather's generation constructed, still linked by the single-gauge railway that connects the old main supply route from Peshawar. I have a photograph of him, standing sentry on a lonely rampart. Dressed in solar topee and over-sized shorts, sword bayonet fixed to his Lee-Enfield rifle, he looks like an extra from colonial-era central casting. I also have a photograph of him as part of the regimental cricket team, resplendent in striped blazer and cap, sitting on a tiger-skin rug. Although taken in the 1930s, you could just as easily caption the photographs the 1860s.

Soldiering at that time must have been unglamorous and demanding work, more akin to a paramilitary police force. The frontier, known as the Durand Line, constructed between Afghanistan and northern British India, has always been ungovernable. As the occupying power, Britain exercised rule by proxy, bribe, and judicious threat, while looking the other way to organised theft and smuggling. There is little that has changed there in hundreds of years. My grandfather would certainly have found the same norm he experienced in the 1930s, had he joined me on my own tours of duty in that unfortunate country nearly a century later.

It was the threat of war in Europe that brought my grandparents together. In 1938, he left the Indian Army, and returned home to enlist in the British Army, arriving in Belfast, Northern Ireland, where he met my grandmother.

My grandmother must have caused her family great shock when she took up with an itinerant soldier. Her family were all quite well-to-do, living in the posh part of Belfast, near Stormont Castle. Yet, she always had a rebellious, contrary streak to her, and grandfather was certainly a handsome man. They were not together for very long because he found himself sent to England after enlistment.

Somewhere along the line, they must have got physically together because my mother arrived in 1940. Again, don't ask me the date: I don't know the answer and I never celebrated that birthday either.

In 1941, my grandfather shipped out for North Africa.

While my grandmother did war service in Gallagher's tobacco factory in Belfast, his battalion saw active duty, chasing Rommel out of North Africa and onto garrison duty in Persia, modern Iraq. He must have been a good soldier as he rapidly climbed the ranks of the sergeant's mess, becoming a Warrant Officer. The Eighth Army then embarked for Italy, where he was destined to spend the rest of the war, slogging up the toe, the heel, and the boot, to finish the war in Trieste.

Somewhere amid this, my grandfather showed great bravery. He was mentioned in dispatches for storming a machine-gun post. He also showed a lack of control as he was busted back to sergeant for striking a soldier. I don't know the circumstance. He won his Warrant Officer rank back as he finished the war as the Provost Marshal for Northern Italy. That last year of war, on the Po, must have been horrific. The Regimental records show that his battalion was shredded three times, the final time being reduced from 650 all ranks to 65 still standing at armistice. He was extremely lucky to have lived through all six years of war service.

By now, he had been away from his family for many years. He sent for his wife and young daughter, my mother, to come to Italy to join him in 1947. A photo I have of that time shows my grandmother, bedecked in a very impressive fur coat, flanked by a handsome movie star husband in uniform, with my mother shyly hiding in her mother's skirts. They travelled to Italy on the requisitioned Blue Train, as befitted the conquerors of Europe. My grandparents hadn't seen each other in years. They must have been near strangers.

It was then that my grandfather showed evidence of the condition that was to ruin his life. Given what he had been through, it is hardly a surprise that he had acute PTSD. I have had this myself and was counselled for it. In 1947, there was no counselling. You just got on with it. Or, in my grandfather's case, you didn't.

He drank heavily and became violent with it. My mother told me many times of her father forcing her to count from one to ten in Italian, and when she failed, through fear and youth (she was only seven at the time), he would beat her with his army belt.

Unlike most of his fellow-servicemen, he didn't de-mob. The army had proven his only education and his only real home. He remained enlisted in the peacetime force, being sent back to Wales and a training depot as an instructor. He must have regularly come back to Belfast on leave, though, where my grandmother remained rearing my mother and her newly born second daughter. My aunt later told me of arguing with her absentee father at a bus stop. He grabbed her and smashed her head into a lamppost.

The family estranged. My grandfather made one last drunken plea by throwing a brick through the front door, to be confronted by my terrified mother telling him, 'daddy, please go away.'

He did just that, enlisting in The Nigerian Rifles, where he spent the next six years as a sergeant major, before he was sent home, as a sergeant again, after getting caught in a brothel by the military police, putting two MPs in hospital as they tried to arrest him. His decline was swift then. The last regimental entries say he was discharged for refusing to wash himself. Something was obviously very much out of kilter.

He discharged after serving his twenty-two years before the British colours in 1954 and was given an exemplary testimonial. He went on to become a commissionaire. A proud and decorated former sergeant-major found opening doors hard to take. He became a postman, back in Wales, where he remained until he died. Somewhere along the line, he sired another daughter, whom I have never met. He had no other contact with my side of his family for the remainder of his life.

Undoubtedly, he was a flawed man, but a man who served his country nonetheless, and one who had been given no leg up in life. I often wonder how he would have fared had his condition been recognised. His behaviour left deep scars on my mother and aunt, which today could possibly have been mitigated. I also wonder how he would have felt, knowing that his grandchild would become the first commissioned officer in the family. He'd probably never have forgiven me for not joining his regiment.

My grandmother, all five foot three and seven stones of her, was left in the invidious position of being separated from her husband, with no income and two young daughters to bring up: a shameful position for a respectable woman at the turn of the 1950's. She, however, was made of very strong stuff.

She went to her two brothers and borrowed money to buy a boarding house, off the Crumlin Road in Belfast, where she took in sailors and shipyard workers for bed and breakfast. She ran that house as a single woman for nearly twenty years. Through those early years, my mother and aunt didn't know what bed they would be sleeping in. Where they laid their heads at night all depended on the volume of the passing trade. Too often, bed would be a rolled-up quilt by the kitchen fire.

When I was young, my grandmother still had the house. I remember it as a huge and scary, Dickensian sort of place, full of the heavy tramp of big, unwashed men, coming and going at all times of the day and night. The toilet was at the end of the garden. I remember tramping down there in the snow, to find squares of the Belfast Telegraph pinned to a butcher's hook hanging off the wall as extemporised paper. I spent my days in a small family room and kitchen, off the hall, where I felt safe; except for her Scottish terrier, which was old and bad-tempered and didn't take to exuberant children running around.

Many years later, I was stationed in a big army base called Girdwood, right next to my grandmother's old home on Clifton Park Avenue. I had remembered it as a vibrant street, with a corner shop where I was sent on errands. During my service at Girdwood, Clifton Park Avenue was decayed and desolate, dominated by the huge, grey slabs of concrete of my army base. My grandmother's house had gone, but the skeleton of her neighbour's remained, daubed with a huge mural of Bobby Sands, the IRA hunger striker. It was a sad demise for a colourful and united community.

She remained a scrimper and a saver until she died. Nothing was ever thrown out. Old sheets were sown into dust cloths, my school trousers darned and mended, much to my disgust as my peers were the beginning of the disposable generation. I remember her repairing a hole in my school shoes with a rubber patch from my bicycle repair kit.

My grandmother was the only member of my family to ever know about me. I don't know if she ever told anyone else, but I do remember the day she caught me in one of my mother's bras. I was sixteen when she walked in on me. All she did was tell me to take it off. She told me, 'You're a man and men don't wear those. If you choose to do that, you'll have a very difficult life.' That was it. It was never mentioned again, ever, until the day she died.

She was incredibly tough for such a tiny woman. When my brother and I were watching television, she asked him to come and help her dry the dishes. He shouted over his shoulder, in an irritated and casual way, 'I'll be there in a minute.' The next thing my brother felt was a frying pan heavily connecting with his head. I think she had seen quite enough of men taking advantage of her in her lifetime to take it from her grandson. Grandmother whacked me a couple of times too, clenched fist, right hook. She bloodied me good and proper.

As a small child, I was quite the fidget, always wanting to wander off on adventures. She put me into restraining reins and would leave me tied to a lamppost while she went in shopping. In those days, it was seen as bad manners to bring a child into a shop. Lines of prams were left outside shops, quite safely. A small child tied to a lamppost would elicit wry smiles of amusement, nothing more.

When I misbehaved on a bus, she gave me to the conductor, told him I was his, and got off the bus without me. She abandoned me to my new owner with a hidden wink and a nod. I was only left for a few hundred yards, as far as the next stop, where she walked along to gather me up. I learned my lesson, though. Today, I suppose, she would be reported to social services.

I think there was always an underlying competition between our side of the family and the rest of her relatives. On our visits, we used to make a courtesy trip to see my second cousins, who lived in a very large house, with a cabin cruiser yacht set ostentatiously on a trailer in the driveway.

At the time, home chemical sets were quite the in-thing to give as Christmas presents. It sounds bizarre now, but back then, small children were freely given test-tubes of carcinogenic chemicals to play with as gifts. You could set iron filings alight or make saltpetre with your own methylated spirit burner. They even contained a sample of raw mercury to play with. It was quite possible to make explosives with the contents. I once blew off my eyebrows with one concoction, leaving a large, sooty stain on the ceiling. Nobody had heard of safety goggles or gloves. You just experimented with making stuff go 'bang!'

These kits ranged from one, the beginners, to seven, the ultimate, which came with all sorts of strange substances and test tubes. My cousin had kit six. I was devastated as

I only had kit two. Then, my gran bought me kit seven. I wanted to go straight round there and tell my 2nd cousin I had one better. My gran counselled otherwise. She told me to wait until the subject of presents came up. Then, when my cousin said he had kit six, I should just casually opine that was nice. Only when I was asked what I got, should I casually say – and she coached me in this:

'Oh, just a chemical set. Kit seven...'

Nothing more, nothing less; smart lady, my gran. I think my telling of that revelation to her relation's family gave her much satisfaction.

She remained whip-thin until the day she died. In part, due to an enormous tapeworm that she had ingested by drinking water direct from the tap. Although the worm was later removed, it had permanently damaged her digestive system. In her old age, she ate little but tomato sandwiches, covered in salt.

Always immaculate in her fur coat and fascinator, I loved her very much and was quite devastated when she died. I was in the army at the time, and they flew me to Belfast for the funeral, my first ever trip in a Hercules, an army transport plane. She had died peacefully, in her armchair, with my aunt by her side. She lay in her home before she was carried out of her terraced house and down her street, with all the neighbours standing in silent homage.

A singularly working-class tribute to an outstanding human being, who, like so many of her generation and time, could have been so much more had she not been born female and without the then obligatory succour of the protection of a man.

My mother wanted to be different. She had some of the same wanderlust as my father, but as a female in the 50s, her options were much more limited. She decided to become a teacher and made what would have been the extraordinary decision to go to England to study. Together with two friends, as travelling as a woman on your own without suitable chaperones would have been too scandalous, she went to teacher training college in Cambridge.

It is there, in Cambridge of 1962, that my parents met. My father was always impenetrable about his past, not a man of many words or expressive imagination. My mother, however, told me that she went to the local hop, where a handsome young Scot swept her into his arms exclaiming, 'Dance with me!' My mother always had an overwrought sense of the theatrical.

The young couple had no money to spare, once digs and food were paid for. A night out was a nursed pint of beer, a dry martini, and a shared packet of crisps. I used to have a photograph of my mother being punted along the Cam River by my father, his trousers rolled up over skinny legs, my mother imitating Grace Kelly in headscarf and over-sized sunglasses, both earnestly playing the glamorous couple. When they disowned me, I threw the picture away.

Later, my mother was to eulogise those days as the hungry years. For all its supposed happiness, I think the divide between town and gown reinforced their hunger to succeed. Both strived to improve their lot, both coming from disadvantaged backgrounds, both having achieved technical qualifications against the odds. For all that, as an engineer and a trainee teacher, they were scarred by the feeling of inferiority next to the privileged students at Cambridge University, with their exuberant Brideshead pretensions that only wealth and status can encourage. That lesson - on money, class, and power - was one that remained with them.

My mother constantly obsessed over her status in life, often quoting the socio-economic order. Her greatest pride came from having gone from 'Group E', unskilled labourers, to 'Group B', professional white-collar workers. It was her oft-stated ambition for us that we would make it to the top of the tree, 'Group A': defined as ministers, lawyers, other professionals - and commissioned military officers. I never forgot that stated ambition of hers when I eventually did become an army officer.

To today's ears class obsession might sound a little preposterous, but in British 20th Century society, there was very little social mobility. The class structure was incredibly rigid. My father, as an engineer, would never manage to penetrate senior management. There was something a little distasteful about the idea of promoting somebody who made things work.

That sense of inferiority led to a near-obsession on their part that I become a lawyer, despite my having neither any interest nor aptitude for the nuts and bolts of the law. Perhaps characteristically, this feeling of inferiority manifested itself when I did show some interest in becoming an advocate, to please my parents. The show-business part of presenting to a packed court appealed to my artistic side. They persuaded me that that was 'too risky' and I would be better in 'something safe', like conveyance. How dull contracting to buy and sell houses sounded to my young ears. It still does.

To my parents, being a lawyer would mean entry to the forbidden palace where all those posh Cambridge kids who looked down on them had come from. Which, in 1963, studies finished, was exactly the palace gate they intended trying to open.

Cambridge was left behind. The young couple moved to Belfast, where they were married, and my father got a backroom job in Ulster Television. I was conceived while they were all living with my grandmother in Clifton Park Avenue. My mother was delighted to be home, having that strong Celtic sense of family and home territory. My father was marking time.

I was born in Belfast Royal Infirmary at four in the morning. The Beatles were Number 1 in the charts,

'From Russia with Love' was playing in the movie houses, America had just lost a President and the Profumo scandal was the gossip of the day.

My earliest years were in my grandmother's boarding house. My parents took over the front room, while I slept in a cot in the kitchen. I remember shyly peeking round the door to see the ever-changing cast of sailors and itinerants come and go. I remember helping my grandmother and mother change the sheets on the single beds, packed six to an upstairs room. I remember the smell and the sounds of grown working men – the sweat and the beer breath, the heavy tramp of their feet, the deep bass and baritone of their conversations. I remember their diversity, the African American and Caribbean men, and the Asian men. I've never noticed racial difference in my entire life. Children are taught to hate by adults. It may have been economic necessity that brought them into my life, but diversity of race was core to my childhood. They were also my primer that the world was just over the horizon. Those men were living proof of somewhere else.

Discrimination in Belfast came in a different form. That of religion. The war hadn't yet started, but the social divide between Catholic and Protestant was very much entrenched. The North of Ireland was
Protestant and Unionist, overtly and aggressively so. Harland and Wolff shipyards didn't employ Catholics, neither did Gallagher's tobacco factory. The police had barely a Catholic in their number. That division of the

socioeconomic levers led to socioeconomic inequality which led to civil rights and, in only a few years, to British soldiers patrolling the streets to keep the peace.

There was, however, one unifying factor between the religions. And my introduction to a man who has been my boyfriend throughout my life.

He is Elvis Presley.

Yes, I know it sounds bizarre, but The King was the one discussion you could have, no matter the religion, and free of consequence. Go to a Protestant house like ours, and you'd see a picture of the Queen on the wall – next to one of Elvis. Go to a Catholic house and you'd find a picture of The Pope – next to a picture of Elvis.

Everybody loved Elvis. It wasn't just the music from his '50s trail blaze, barely finished, it was his movies. As dated as they may seem now, Elvis' early '60s output was to me a regular carousel of glamour, style, Cinemascope scenery, pretty girls, dancing, and The King himself - one of the most handsome and charismatic human beings ever born. Two hours of escape from the rain-soaked, dirty, terraced streets of Belfast.

We all knew his story. How he had dragged himself from abject poverty to becoming the biggest rock and roll star in the world. We all knew his songs, how they had broken the mould. When you come from poverty, Elvis proved it didn't have to always be that way. He was as much role model as inspiration. When you grew up surrounded by socio-economic devastation, Elvis spoke deeply to us of another life.

Belfast was like any of the great European port cities; devastated by world war. Poverty was rife, although we didn't know it because a lived communal experience is impossible to compare. We just took it for granted that every row of terraced houses had a gaping hole from Hitler's bombs and that an outside toilet was the norm. Showers? I didn't know what one of those was until I started school. We bathed daily in a bowl of water and in a bath once a week. Everybody lived like that.

Except Elvis. He lived in a fantasy land called Hawaii, where the sun always shone, and he beat up the bully for stopping him singing his songs to beautiful girls before they drove off in enormous cars with seats like beds. There was nothing else like him at that time. Sure, Merseybeat had taken the world by storm, but The Beatles were us, with the same bad, British teeth and the same port city background as us.

Elvis was akin to a God.

America as a global superpower? It had all the tanks and guns and aircraft carriers. But I'd contend superpower status was as much about Elvis as the 82nd Airborne. He represented the essential dream of America. Where a working-class kid could do anything, go anywhere, just through talent and hard work. When I was young, everything great came from America.

I still remember the visceral thrill of going to Saturday morning kid's film club and cheering as Elvis won his fight and kissed the girl. I loved his clothes, his hair, the way he moved, his irresistible smile.

None of that has ever left me, to this very day. And in dark childhood days soon to come, Elvis became more than a picture. I used to talk to him as if he were next to me, and pray that he would protect me, as he did all the girls in the movies.

I was allowed to love Elvis because everybody did, but I saw him as my first boyfriend. That was my difference. I have a very real love of that man. And it all came from lying in my cot in the back kitchen of a Belfast tenement as I gazed at his picture hanging on the wall above my grandmother's cooker and dreaming of Elvis holding me safe.

Real life in Belfast then was quickly taking a terminal turn for the worst.

The Catholic population rightly wanted their fair share of rights, their fair share of wealth. The Protestant population panicked at what began as a faith-based reflected repeat of the US struggle for racial Civil Rights, and then over-reacted to those peaceful protests with a hugely aggressive police response. In short order, the British army was called in to keep the two sides apart as society fell apart.

Clifton Park Avenue is just off the Crumlin Road, where the courts and prison are. It was a natural choke point for protest. Made much worse by the army requisitioning the cricket ground across the road and basing a battalion there. Every morning, I'd hear the rumble of the Saracen armoured cars passing our front window. Every night, I'd hear the screams and the dull report of rubber bullets and the reflected flash of petrol bombs in the window.

My daily task was to go to the corner shop for bacon, bread, cheese, butter, and milk. One day, I stepped over my gran's holystoned front step to be startled by a British soldier lying in her front rose bed. I'd never seen a soldier close-up before, nor a gun. He wore a camouflaged jacket, different from the green the other soldiers wore. Just in the way he exuded competence at violence, he was different. He turned to smile at me, amused by the terror in my small face. On his head, he had a maroon beret, jauntily worn, on his face an enormous moustache. He probably said something to me, I can't recall. I was transfixed by him. It was his sense of purpose, strength and vitality that struck me. My gran was shocked by the man in her garden. She told me he was a 'Para', the toughest of the tough, and warned me to stay away from them. From that time onwards, I've always judged men by that image in my head. That moment formed the root of why I was so desperate to be a paratrooper myself when I needed answers to my life.

I've never forgotten the first time I saw a British paratrooper.

Conflict in the streets outside was matched by the conflict within our walls. My father chafed at the restrictions of sharing his home with a wife and a mother-in-law, crammed into a front room with a succession of sailors in the hallway. He was now part of that exclusive closed shop made up of unionised technical tradespeople. He worked in the engineering department of the brand-new Ulster Television. Commercials were brought to air via massive, analogue tape machines that fed content via 30 second tape cassettes. To ensure continuity, a whole row of these behemoths needed to be exquisitely synched, mechanically, and electronically. It was very niche work, but the basis of the profitability of the station. No commercials, no money. The entire industry was a closed shop, totally controlled by the technical unions. My father's profession was akin to the print setters in the newspaper industry. Their much specialised skill gave them enormous leverage to set their own pay scales.

As a result, he was catapulted in very short order from the poverty of a shared bag of crisps with my mother in Cambridge to making an awful lot of money.

It's little wonder he wanted a roof of his own, command of his family, and away from the chaos he saw on the streets. Belfast wasn't his home, he didn't have the close sense of attachment to community my mother had, nor the network of friends and shared experiences. And it was getting very dangerous.

I was also displaying what were to him very worrying signs of effeminacy. I was much taken with borrowing my mother's lipstick and jewellery. I loved to dance and twirl, adored being with my grandmother in the kitchen. At that time, the women (and the visiting sailors) of the house just laughed and indulged me, but I can remember the look of anger on my father's face.

He tried to change me. Instead of a doll, I was given a present of a toy oil tanker. I smashed it against the wall the same day. He gave me a present of a toy garage. I turned it into a playhouse the same day. It mysteriously disappeared the next.

I was just being me, but looking back, I can see the beginning of the rage that would come to overwhelm him. As an only child, he was used to control. In Belfast, he had none.

His solution was to take his family from Belfast to Scotland. His homeland, his society, his life, his control. He didn't want to go to the Central Belt, where he came from. He wanted a clean start, on ground familiar to him, but where he wouldn't have to face his own working-class roots.

Stonehaven was his solution.

Much as my father's progress bought relative material riches, it came at a huge price. My mother did not want to leave her family and home behind. My father gave my mother an ultimatum – you follow me as my wife, or we divorce. With a young child in tow, me, she chose to go with him. Such was the completely patriarchal society of those days. I think she was determined not to relive the chaos of her own parent's divorce.

In quick order, he left Ulster Television to move to Aberdeen for a promoted post with Grampian Television. Still in engineering, but with more money and more union protections. This was where the money came from for 'Four Seasons' at the end of the Stonehaven cul de sac. We moved fifteen miles south of Aberdeen, to commuter land, as a realisation of his dream of self-betterment.

Moving to Scotland was a decision that would form a cancer at the root of my parent's marriage that never healed. They spent the remainder of their lives in Aberdeen and Stonehaven. My mother permanently isolated from her culture and heritage. She was made for shared community and the *craic*. She never adapted to the cold insularity of Northeast Scotland. My father's uncompromising demand remained an unresolved tension that formed the foundation of all the unhappiness to come.

I don't remember being asked my opinion on the move, but I do remember waking in Stonehaven to absolute silence. No more armoured cars, no more shouting. Towards the end in Belfast, it had got so dangerous, my mother would phone the police to see if it was safe to go outside. Northern Ireland truly was violent then. Folks forget now, but the British Army lost as many dead and wounded in those early years of The Troubles as they did in Helmand, Afghanistan. My family were far from alone in leaving.

I went to Dunnottar Primary to learn to make my pipe rack. My father went off to work, revelling in his new life. For my mother, though, who was a smart and intelligent woman, it quickly became an unbearable bore of an existence. I remember trolling around with her on our own, a never-ending parade of walks round the park, walks round the reservoir, walks to town. She had literally nothing to do, no friends to share a life with. Just a small child who sensed her unhappiness but was powerless to help. A second son arrived, a brother for me, a temporary, but turgid repetition of child-rearing and nappy washing. Then a third son, a repetition of the same; another child to give a life going nowhere a purpose.

Those were the days of 'The Valley of the Dolls' when a doctor could prescribe a simple pill to solve the frustrations of a housewife. I didn't know the cause then, but I could see my mother's behaviour changing. They put her on lithium and diazepam.

She hadn't wanted to leave Belfast; she didn't want to live in a Scottish fishing village and was inherently not suited to bringing up children. She had real ambition, and she resented my father breezing off to have fun with the grown-ups, while she pushed buggies and burped babies.

The pills took the edge off, but they made her irascible, difficult to deal with, and prone to physically taking it out on me. I learned to be careful around her, in what I said and did.

Her favourite weapons were a hairbrush, or to whip me with the dog's lead. I felt beholden to try to protect my brothers from whatever issue was at the root of the day's dis-temper, so I bore the brunt of her abuse. But at that stage, I loved her deeply and was deeply distressed to see her upset.

Out of frustration, I asked her why she had had children at all. Quite a profound insight for a nine-year-old. I remember her answer, for it cut me to the quick:

'To perpetuate the species...'

Not that we were an act of love, or that we were a family united in love, no mention of love at all. I can see with hindsight she was being blunt and honest. But that bluntness came at a price. The price was her children's happiness.

Her general pill-buzzed malaise affected my father. He came home from a great day at work, usually after a few drinks down the club, feeling no pain, to be regaled with angry stories of how life had fallen apart at home in his absence. While my mother used a hairbrush, my father used his fists. I remember those days as being filled with real fear at the sound of his return. I'd hear the shouts and the slammed doors of the blame game as I sat in the kitchen with my brothers. Then that door would fly open, and in he'd come, looking for me. I became pretty good at running, but he'd always catch me. His favourite trick was to hold me against the wall by the neck and punch me in the face. He'd encourage me to 'take it like a man.'

As a single child, he was used to control. It's why he'd taken the family to Stonehaven, to ensure total control. Whatever it was my mother said to him transferred that sense of loss of control onto my nine-year-old shoulders. Beatings, punches, casual violence, those were the result.

I can say with certainty that I never loved my father, but from that age, I started to positively dread him. This was the era when Sean Connery said it was alright to slap a woman. My father did the same to my mother. And then hit us for good measure.

When my father couldn't physically impose his dominance, the rows ended with my mother dramatically filling a suitcase and departing down the driveway. I vividly remember running after her, wrapping my arms around her legs to stop her leaving, and begging her to stay.

Sometimes, I colluded in her disappearances. I remember going with her to Belfast when it got too much, going back to Clifton Park Avenue. When my grandmother had listened to my mother's sad story of unhappiness and stark loneliness, she asked her daughter of her marriage:

'Does he beat you? Does he give you money? Does he put a roof over your head?'

When my mother replied she had a roof, she had an allowance, and was currently mercifully free from bruises, my grandmother then asked her exactly what the problem was? My mother returned to Stonehaven. In those hard, post-war years, this country was a very different place. A woman's expectations remained entirely fixated and determined by her marital status and the dominance of her husband.

Every child wants to feel loved, to feel secure. I never did. Instead, I got wrapped around the axle of trying to secure my mother's approval while receiving violence in return, compounded by a miasma of gender confusion that turned to self-loathing. I was beginning to understand my difference. I knew I liked what society called girl's things more than boys. I knew I loved being with the girls at school. I knew I hated my body. I knew that those feelings were wrong because that was what I was taught at school, by constant application of the tawse. I knew that I was evil because that was what the Church taught me every Sunday. I came to realise that my father's beatings were infinitely worse after he looked with disgust at my expression of who I am.

What resulted quickly became very toxic.

I learned not to displease my mother because that would result in my father beating the crap out of me. Yet, she missed female company. I remember when the laundry hadn't been done, she would give me her knickers to wear (which I loved), and she would laugh when I danced with her, or we sang songs together from the radio that reminded her of her youth. Those were happy memories, but memories always set on a knife edge. I never knew when she would slip off the other side and joy would turn to rage and bruises would be the next reward.

Perhaps most heinous of all, she tried to get me into her drug routine. I remember her asking me if I wanted a lithium, another time a sleeping pill. I was nine. Even then, I knew this was wrong. I always refused, and I'd do a dance to change the subject, or put my hair into bunches, which always amused her.

Ah, you say, you are who you are because of a Freudian unresolved mother relationship? I'd agree with you that I never did make it work with my mother. But I was the child, not the adult. I wasn't the one in charge. I'd contend my relationship with my mother was fucked-up because it was truly irredeemably and criminally fucked-up.

I'm not fucked-up.

I was surviving.

BANGKOK, 2007

I awoke to a familiar voice. Dr Suporn was gently shaking my shoulder. Dr S: my real father, one of the world's leading gender surgeons. I owe Dr S my life.

He heads a remarkable institution. Based in Chonburi, about forty-five minutes from Bangkok, Dr S works alone. He has dedicated his own life to creating life for others. Resolving women out of those assigned as men, providing birth for thousands like me, who come from all over the world for his healing skill.

Chonburi is an unlikely destination. It is an unremarkable industrial suburb. The Suporn Clinic, a three-story townhouse, butts straight onto the main dual carriageway between Bangkok and Pattaya. Outside, the roar of traffic never stills. On the pavement, street vendors cook grasshoppers in oil and motorbike taxis embark *cheong-sam* wearing Thai women, who elegantly sit side-saddle across the panniers. Outside, it is chaos.

Inside, the clinic is sensually quiet, with tinkling waterfalls and bamboo encased walls.

Dr Suporn is a tiny man. He is barely 5'3" tall. He has a broad face, and a flat nose, with highly intelligent eyes set above a square forehead and short, wiry black hair.

Like all Thais, he bows elegantly on meeting, palms steeped closely together.

Thailand has long had a permissive attitude towards sex and gender. It is a legacy of faith grounded in the teachings of Buddha. In Buddhism, our bodies are seen as mere temporary vessels for our souls. Nothing is ever lost in the Universe. The physical form is less important than the spirit within. Buddha teaches that yin and yang must meet in perfect harmony to achieve happiness. Life itself is subject to change, in an ever-moving river. Cause and effect, or karma, can only be sorted when an individual strives for happiness. If you are not happy in yourself, you cannot make anybody else happy.

For a Buddhist, the constant quest for knowledge, for change, to pursue betterment of the human spirit and experience, is all entirely natural and correct. Buddhism is going to the doctor. I acknowledge I need help; I find out what is wrong and what can be done about it and administer the necessary poultice. Happiness cannot be achieved by materialism.

Happiness is a spiritual search that never ends. The journey of life is a journey towards enlightenment of the spirit. Life is not defined by the accumulation of material wealth for material wealth's sake. It is finding oneself within.

My parent's values, forged in that crucible of wartime Calvinist values, would not recognise such a conceit.

The last ever conversation I had with my father when I told him of my choice ended when he asked, why was I doing this to myself? I told him I wanted to be happy. My father replied:

'What is happiness? You have obligations.'

Because of that fixed immobility of supposed values I inherited from my parents, I spent a large part of my life believing I was warped and twisted from birth. Because I had all these feelings of displacement, I genuinely believed I was cursed. No matter how I tried to express the person within, I was thwarted by the role I had been assigned and the obligations that my family and society placed upon me. Rather than seek enlightenment by looking within myself, I judged my worth to the universe on other's opinions of my difference.

No-one can make you feel inferior without your consent.

When I found the strength to show that inner light to the world, my journey began, and I have never stopped revelling in its wonderment.

What Dr S does is act as agent for the final moment of revelation. It is medical intervention to achieve enlightenment. Profoundly Buddhist, profoundly human. He made the outer casing that fits my inner being. In doing so he brought yin and yang together. No longer opposites but joined in unity. Broken parts made whole.

The first day I met Dr Suporn, I knew I would be OK. I realised I had found a spiritual home. His clinic is part medical facility, part clinic, part healing curative. Over the years, Dr S has realised over three thousand women. We call ourselves 'Supornistas.' We are The Supremes to his Berry Gordy.

We even look the same. Dr S does one type of nose reconstruction. Put us all side-by-side and we are physical sisters, with the same cute 'Bewitched' turn-up and ski-slope proboscis.

Making women live is all Dr Suporn does: and is all he will ever do. He has no deputy. Everything he does, he does himself. The man is a human whirlwind of energy. He operates six days a week, then holds clinics into the late evening.

His patients are a worldwide mix of races, sizes, builds, temperaments, and outlooks. The one characteristic we all share is a profound sense of dis-location in the physical form we occupy. Because it is not our form. Dr S is the answer to our prayers and our aspirations.

Sitting in his clinic is to come home. For so long, I believed I was alone. Dr S has hundreds of similar lost souls visiting with him every week. I quickly realised I was anything but alone, and that those lucky few who I did meet are the winners of the lottery: those with the wherewithal, the money, and the drive to reach the end of the beginning of the journey. So many never make this stage, lost forever on their own sea of pain.

We all sought happiness, to be secured through Dr Suporn's care and kindness. If anybody should ever doubt that gender dysphoria is an integral part of the human condition of suffering, itself a key teaching of Buddha, then they should go visit Dr S. One glance into that global sea of humanity seeking redemption and succour would be enough to show that there is nothing imagined or pretended about this condition. It is too universal for that. Dr S' children come from all countries, of all ages, creeds, religions, and beliefs.

He has cured us all.

In the '60s and '70s, if you'd mentioned the term transgender, there would have been many furrowed brows. It was a concept yet to be created. There were pantomime dames. Danny la Rue, essentially a cross-dressing gay singer and comedian, was a big TV and stage star. In fact, rather paradoxically for a country so obsessed with a heterosexual binary norm, our Danny was Britain's highest-paid entertainer. Yet sexual identity is not gender identity. My own condition could not be explained away with stifled sniggers. Danny's whole act, in many ways his only *raison d'etre*, was that he knew he was a gay man in women's clothes, and he let the audience in on the gag.

He didn't want to be a woman. I am a woman, I desperately wanted to be openly female. I was not attracted to men as a man, but I am attracted to men as a woman, even when my appearance did not reflect who I am. So where did I fit in? Danny may have raised the roof, but the cultural inference was clear: gender dysphoria meant homosexuality. And to most people's minds, same-sex sexual orientation was wrapped up with being sexually deviant and illegal. If being a 'poofter' was not a good thing in Scotland, then my own complaint would have been unthinkable, one step further on the road to societal abjuration. I literally had no definition at all. Nor, because we were all criminals in the eyes of the law, was there anybody I could ask.

While there have been physically externally similar people like me throughout recorded history, Victorian sensibilities firmly pushed public and open discussion of the pan-sexual condition under the carpet. Not to say that the Victorians were any less sex-obsessed than any other generation of humans, they just decided it wasn't Christian and moral to openly talk about it all. Indeed, when I changed, I was forced to leave three churches before I found a community that would accept me.

That isn't exactly the gospels as I remember them.

When I cured my conflict through Dr Suporn's good offices, I was merely part of a long line of generations who have submitted themselves to medicine and science to solve the conundrum of accidental genetics. There is still much to discover there, and the process is evolving, but leaving the past behind must come with compromise. I will never have children. I had to willingly lay that aside. Just as the generations before me have.

The knowledge to castrate has been known for thousands of years. Eunuchs traditionally held high posts of responsibility within the Ottoman Empire, being entrusted with the smooth administrative management of the whole vast edifice.

There was an entire, intricate caste structure to define those roles, and parents were known to volunteer their children for the operation, carried out in horrifically crude circumstances, just for the opportunity of advancement. In Europe, castrati - boy singers who were castrated before puberty - were highly prized for their unique singing voice, much higher than a female soprano. Many of these individuals became internationally famous, the opera stars of their day. It is why so many scores, when performed today, are confusing. The female operatic soprano parts were often originally scored for a male castrati lead.

Eunuchs were marked by their abnormal physical development. The absence of hormonal flows meant they developed unnaturally long limbs and large heads. They were also to live short life spans, their body engines devoid of any hormonal control. Testosterone withdrawal did not mean the development of other female characteristics. It must have been a life of extraordinary sensual deprivation.

I am appalled by the concept. I chose my destiny. To have that forced upon you is unforgiveable.

Although I have been very willingly castrated, I am not a eunuch. I am much more than that. Eunuchs remain men. To compare me to a eunuch is to compare a tomato to a potato.

It was the discovery of the sex hormones, and a means to artificially re-create them that have allowed people like me to live in their true lives. Initially, the female hormone, oestrogen, was produced in horrific circumstances, from the urine of pregnant mares, which were tethered and catheterised to collect their body fluids. Called Premarin, it is a product that is still available, albeit now artificially created. The development of surgical re-assignment also has uncomfortable roots, being practised by the Nazis through medical experiments in the death camps to devise a permanent process that would allow the neutering of occupied Europe's homosexuals.

By the 1950s, the combination of hormone development and a new surgical technique, allowing the creation of a vagina from the skin of the penis, meant that the world would see the first women like me. Ironically much of the pioneering work was done to prolong the lives of the profoundly war injured.

The first publicly well-known female, and probably the most famous, was Christine Jorgenson. As a former GI, who had served during the Battle of the Bulge, Miss Jorgenson had her operation carried out in Norway and created an international sensation. Small and petite of frame, Christine was fortunate. Her body had not been excessively influenced by the male hormone, testosterone.

None of this is easy. Do not doubt the stark reality.

Over the years, I have been accused as everything from having made the whole thing up to being psychologically damaged to being a pervert. I can assure you that every memory I have of those first forty-four years, trapped in that body, is of acute personal dislocation and a constant battle to keep that reality at bay.

Not a day went past where I did not have to consciously battle those emotions. From the sight of a woman applying her lipstick, to a well-dressed mannequin in a shop window, to a young mother with her child. They all brought feelings of despair and regret – and anger at why I could not be the same.

I came to hate the way I had constructed my life, the male image of rugged dependability and physical strength I portrayed to the world. I just could not let the mask slip for fear of the consequences – and I only eventually did so when I could not keep the pretence any longer. I made a life for myself that I could not have enjoyed had I not maintained that masculine profile. Society forced that compromise on me. I had no other choice if I wanted to avoid the inside of a jail cell.

I can attest, though, that since I brought Abi to the world, I have woken every day with joy in my heart. I am complete now. Of course, the world is not perfect. I cry a lot more now. I certainly use an awful lot more toilet tissue. But the feeling of being, the wholeness of being Abi, a woman, is a perfection that sustains me through everything.

My condition is not a matter of confused sexuality.

While I have many gay friends, and have unsuccessfully tried gay sex on many occasions, I have never considered myself to be homosexual. I was then what you could casually describe as 'receiver' rather than 'pitcher'. But my issue was that the parts never matched. My body in those days belonged to somebody else.

I never had any desire to take charge of the appendage attached to me. I was delighted to get rid of it and have been an extremely happy and content individual since the day it was willingly taken from me. No man, gay or otherwise, could ever relate to that. I am not gay.

In evidence, I hold up Alan Turing. He made possibly the single greatest individual contribution to winning the Second World War for the Allies. Yet, he died in disgrace and penury, a convicted criminal, because he was gay.

Turing was a brilliantly gifted mathematician who by his own abilities, insight, intuition, and sheer graft was a prime mover in decoding the German Enigma machine, a seemingly impenetrable random mechanical cipher. His mathematical genius allowed the Allies to intercept and read Hitler's strategic messages to his troops in the field. He did this in an age before computers had been constructed. That intelligence gave the Allies an unsurmountable advantage.

Turing happened to be gay, in an age where homosexual acts were defined as 'gross indecency.' In 1952, he was convicted of physically enjoying the company of another man. To mitigate his sentence, he agreed to be injected with oestrogen, the female hormone. Quite what the authorities expected from this treatment is beyond me. Turing showed no evidence of gender disorder. He was a man who liked being a man. He just happened to be physically attracted to other men.

Turing's body, not surprisingly, developed female breasts. As an international class runner (he once ran a marathon in two hours, forty-six minutes, only eleven minutes slower than the then world record), Turing was emotionally and physically devastated. His life was effectively ended by the social disgrace he faced. His own body no longer belonged to him. In 1954, he took his own life. He died a convicted criminal.

In this century, British Prime Minister Gordon Brown publicly thanked Turing for his war-changing efforts. His homosexuality was not mentioned, nor his 'offence.' Brown refused to pardon him. It took a groundswell of public opinion for the government to finally change its mind in 2013.

This is the difference between a gay man, a eunuch, and me. It is hormonal.

Hormones are the oil of our human engines. Their effects drive our very existence. They regulate not just our bodies, but the function of our brains. Just as with a car engine, the wrong oil will cause it to seize, so the same is true of the application of hormones.

To Turing, oestrogen therapy was akin to feeding him arsenic. To me, oestrogen caused almost overnight euphoria.

Testosterone, in the quantities I endured, very nearly destroyed me. All my life, until I became Abi, I suffered constant asthma and eczema. Depression was my closest friend. Oestrogen cured that. Since I started on this part of my life, I have never suffered from either complaint. Not once.

I loved the sensation of growing breasts, watching my skin become softer - the opposite of the desperately misunderstood Turing. Most importantly, my brain started working properly. Hormones literally lifted a fog from my mind. Those same hormones led to Turing's suicide. What was done to him was a drastic travesty. For me, it was salvation.

The first real work on this condition in the west was done in the early twentieth century by a German psychiatrist, establishing concepts more fully explored in the forties and fifties in the US by a New York psychiatrist named

Harry Benjamin. He established the rule for gender re-assignment that is still internationally recognised: the Benjamin Standard. It was Dr Benjamin who coined the term
'Transsexual' and who stated that gender re-assignment should be ethically allowed if the subject had lived in their chosen gender role for at least two years under psychiatric evaluation. He arbitrarily decided on two years.

How little he could really have understood the desire to change. When the need to change comes, it comes as a tsunami of pent-up desire. Two days of waiting is a lifetime of agony, let alone two years.

All through his work, Dr Benjamin ascribes this condition as being psychosexual. In other words, people like me desired gender surgery as expression of a sexual desire, what would be described as an extreme form of body-fetishism.

Speaking with some authority on the matter, I can assure the casual observer that there is nothing fetishist or sexual about gender realisation. It is a bloody, long, painful, one-way escalator to redemption. I had no choice when I undertook this journey. The only other option was to give up on life itself. The prize has been sheer joy and happiness. I have yet to find another thrill of any kind that comes even close. Whatever the price, I willingly and happily paid it before it was too late to do anything about it at all.

I didn't let my womanhood fully live until I was in my mid-forties. Testosterone had wreaked a terrible price on my body. It took more than a weekly oestrogen patch to change my body into something the world would see as female.

In my case, my features had long hardened into a masculine face. Service in The Parachute Regiment had broken my nose twice. It took twelve hours of agonising sawing and suturing to change my skull and features into that of a female. It continues to take constant fasting to keep my frame as small as my bones will allow me. I am 5'10", at the outside of what would commonly be seen as the usual height range for women. My voice broke 50 years ago. I've learned to modulate my pitch, but I still live at the bottom of the range for a female voice. Dr Suporn used all his powers on me, but I will always have to live with the consequences of a testosterone development I didn't choose or want.

Legally, in the UK, transgender people face a long and difficult battle. Throughout celebrated court cases, the law has long refused to recognise the right of a transgender person to marry. A person like me was, until 2004, not even recognised in their true gender. When I became Abi, I was forcibly divorced by the State. Ten years ago, if had been arrested, I would have been sent to a male prison. While sense would now probably prevail, I am still denied the right to a female birth certificate. Until 2014, I could not marry a man – I could only enter a civil partnership. The law in Britain still sees me as a man – and there is nothing I can do about it.

Our first real rights in the UK came in 1999, with the changes to the Sex Discrimination Act that prevents discrimination on gender grounds. I don't think this legislation specifically set out to protect us, but it was the first time that the term 'transsexual' appears in legislation. In 2004, the Gender Recognition Act set out a convoluted legal process to allow us to legally define our gender. It lays out guidelines for transition from one gender to the other, which allows, after two years, the production of what is known as a Gender Recognition Certificate, which will allow a birth certificate to be changed. It is deeply flawed and intrusive legislation, but it did, for the first time ever, allow us hope that we could live a normal life.

The process still ascribes a psychosexual diagnosis. You are required to have constant monitoring by an approved psychiatrist. I am not mad. I don't need to see a shrink. I have been through over thirty different operations and openly lived, worked, and loved as a woman for a decade and a half. After decades of longing to do so. There's little a psychiatrist could add to that debate; I have answered all my own questions.

I have twice been refused a Gender Recognition Certificate.

Although Dr S is a world-renowned specialist re-assignment surgeon, the UK government does not recognise his work because he works and operates under a Thai license in Thailand. To receive a Gender Recognition Certificate, I am obliged to be under-go an intimate physical examination by a UK doctor to confirm his work. I am further required to visit with a UK-approved psychiatrist to obtain a UK-approved diagnosis of gender dysphoria.

I refuse to do that; what is a psychiatrist going to tell me that months on a hospital bed and years as a woman have not already confirmed? The price I pay for my recalcitrance is rejection by the state.

As far as the UK is concerned, I am still a man.

If I lived in France, the fact that I have undergone transition surgery would automatically legally change my gender. In the UK, the influence of the church on the legislative process prevented that.

Tory stalwarts and ardent Christians, such as Norman Tebbit and Anne Widdicombe, successfully argued that I am a travesty of scripture, and successfully had the law amended to refuse complete recognition of gender reassignment as a medical, not a psychosexual, process. I struggle to describe this as Christian, but it's what the Tories did.

Even having a piece of paper doesn't indicate equality in society. As a community, we are still massively misunderstood, persecuted, and reviled. There remains something incredibly deep-seated in the human condition that my community challenges. I cannot define it, although I have long tried. Perhaps it is that we set aside the ability to naturally create life? We cannot, as a species, get away from the fact that men procreate, and women conceive. Our very existence and our most base level recognition and behavioural systems are all premeditated on our sexual urges.

Nonetheless, the dial is slowly turning. My community is visible now. We have some rights; we now have a voice.

Such debate as exists nowadays was impossible in my youth.

It seems strange, looking back now, at how insular our world was. There was no internet, no satellite TV, no mobile phones. The only television channels broadcast were the three channels of BBC1, BBC2 and ITV. The outside world was not our world. My geographic confines were defined by the valley in which my small fishing village sat. My intellectual confines were defined by the contents of the local library. My moral confines by the tawse my teachers wielded on our palms and the strictures with which I was berated by the minister.

Later in life I was to meet urbane, sophisticated, elegant, well-travelled individuals who grew up in several different countries, spoke several languages and who were intellectually curious about a world they had already traversed.

I never had that. Any of that. But I knew it was out there. Elvis lived there. It had to be real. And from my earliest years, I resented that I wasn't already there, and I determined that as soon as I was able, I would be off to find it.

STONEHAVEN, 1973

As I watched the girls in my class, I could not help but notice the way they hung their hair in bunches or gathered their skirts up when they left school. How their lips would be pouted or the way they rolled their hips as they walked. My attention was not sexual. I knew I wasn't regarded as one of them. I couldn't yet explain it, but I felt a deep-seated affinity.

As other boys lusted in an immature way, I longed to be one of the girls I went to school with. My mother was the only female I had contact with. I looked to her for my inspiration, or to be precise, I looked to her clothes. I can't really say there was one day when I had my 'Eureka!' moment and started stealing her clothes to wear but my kleptomania grew over the years. I knew the theft was wrong but, just as my sense of displacement felt wrong, so my sense of contentment felt right when I wore her clothes. Dressing as a girl made me whole as a person. I felt normal, natural, happy, content, and complete.

I developed hidden stashes of jewellery, underwear, dresses, shoes, and everything I could get my hands on. I hid these in bags in the garden shed, in the loft, buried in the garden, anywhere I could get privacy for a few fleeting seconds. I took to keeping magazine pages of glamorous women – movie stars like Monroe and Russell.

Who could I share this with? I had learned that any expression of who I was would be met with stark horror and a beating. I became incredibly careful in my behaviour. I withdrew from all the regular relationships you would expect of a child. I didn't want to play football or sit in tree houses. Equally, I didn't want to tell anybody. I learned to take off on my own.

I was developing a schizophrenic existence, all underpinned by stark loneliness.

Although I never fully discussed my condition with my parents, they must surely have known I was different. My behaviour, my insularity, being so withdrawn, was not normal. Just as my mother must surely have noticed that her wardrobe was steadily diminishing. Above all, I developed a growing conviction that I was not right: I just couldn't define why I was not that normal child my parents so desired. I didn't fit any of the social contexts that filled my life. Slowly but surely, I came to believe I had been cursed.

My father attempted to intervene by trying to turn me into him. His favourite saying to me was 'just give yourself a shake and sort it out' – as if that was panacea for my increasing paralysis and depression. When that homily didn't work, he would use his fists. He was a violent man, particularly when he had been drinking. Like a lot of Scottish men of his generation, he carried a permanent air of aggression. It was almost as if by being permanently on the tipping point of fury he somehow reinforced his own self-perception of Scottish masculinity.

Scotland was a very angry place in the 1970s. Homosexuality was a crime punishable by prison and even sectioning for mental health. Let alone what the ever-pervasive Church said about it being an immoral sin. Every Sunday, I had to sit on a wooden bench and be lectured about the sin of self-expression and enjoyment of life. Utter torture. When I showed even the slightest hint of extravagance or anything that did not meet my father's standard of strict, controlled, simmering manhood, I would be met with his closed fist.

He thought getting me to join the Boy's Brigade would be the cure. He had been in the Boy's Brigade. I had no desire to join a quasi-religious uniformed group of boys. Nothing was further from my own self-perception. I rebelled, hardly turned up, failed to reach the standard of religious fervour required. Which resulted in another beating and strained silence for days around the dinner table.

I said I wanted a doll. I was given an Action Man, in camouflage uniform. I cut that off and turned it into a tutu and crop top with some scissors, needle, and thread. End of Action Man – straight into the bin, more beatings for me.

I said I would like a dog to look after. I meant a wee small bundle of fluff like my grandmother's that I could put a ribbon on. Instead, my father came home with a very large golden retriever that he had picked out. She was a lovely dog, but was forever more his dog, not mine. I just wasn't interested. Although I was frequently beaten with the dog's metal chain.

All I had that I felt was mine was my stolen bin bag of paste jewellery and clothes that I hid under a tree in the park. I'd go down there after school and feel their touch, imagine myself wearing them, playing hopscotch with the girls.

The one place I did find relief was in my fantasy movie world. Stonehaven had a movie house of its own. On a Saturday it hosted a kid's movie club. For twenty pence, we could be inside there all day in the darkness watching images of another world flicker on the golden screen. I used to sit in the front row of the balcony, with a bag of boiled sweets, and dream. Every week, an Elvis movie, the Lone Ranger, Casey Jones, then something rubbish made in the UK (which always looked cheap and boring next to the American stars), followed by the main feature, when the adults were let in to sit beside us.

The theatre couldn't afford to rent new releases, so it played the classics from the great golden age of the late 1950s and 1960s; John Wayne, Doris Day, Rock Hudson, Gregory Peck, Kirk Douglas, Burt Lancaster, Marilyn Monroe, Elizabeth Taylor, Barbra Streisand,

Omar Sharif, Judy Garland, Gene Kelly, Cyd Charisse, Fred Astaire, Paul Newman, Robert Redford, Ava Gardner, Marlon Brando, Elvis Presley, Steve McQueen, Audrey Hepburn, Charlton Heston, Sophia Loren. All the American greats. It was a day I adored. To see Elvis beat the bad guy and fly off with the girl while he sang an amazing song in a palm tree filled wonderland was catnip to me. Those movies and the technicolour world where right always prevailed was a stronger reality to me than the horrid real world.

I just knew that in movie land I could be Elvis' girl, dance like Cyd Charisse, hold onto Rock Hudson's arm, and everything would all be alright. I'd only leave my fantasy life as the credits flickered and the lights came up. I'd step out into wet, grey Stonehaven and trudge home, still living on the embers of my sense memories of America and its wonderful, handsome, and beautiful people, just waiting to welcome me.

In this century, I would Google the internet: and a wealth of answers would be there, right in front of me. In the 1970's, in Stonehaven, there was nothing. Who could I possibly ask? Nobody.

I wanted sequins and I lived amongst fish scales.

Until the day I met Donald.

Donald was a terribly sweet young man, who lived in the council estate across the railway tracks. He was blonde, waif slim, and wore drainpipe trousers with white socks and an Adidas tracksuit top. He looked very much like a young Faces-era Rod Stewart, with an unruly shock of tousled hair and a cheeky smile. I first saw him striding confidently down a corridor in school, hands in pockets, chewing gum. I can't recall who spoke to the other first, but I do remember how my heart skipped when I first heard his voice. That first day, we found ourselves on the same road, heading home. For the first time in ages, I smiled my best smile. Donald wasn't just drop dead handsome; he was cool.

He had a portable record player in his father's shed, what was called a Dancette, with a built-in speaker. In its day, a Dancette was the iPod of my generation. You could pre-load it with six singles, stacked up above the turntable. Imagine; six three-minute songs in a row without doing another thing! All in a shed that smelled of the same re-assuring creosote and woodchip I recalled from my grandmother's home.

At the time, I listened to bubble-gum pop by teddy-boy pastiche bands. Donald, on the other hand, had records by T-Rex and David Bowie. Not just the singles, a mere seven inches of black vinyl, but the whole album. I had never seen a long-playing album before. Twelve inches of wonder, with multiple tracks! A platter you didn't have to change every three minutes that turned not at a busy forty-five revolutions a minute, but at a lazy and languorous thirty-three and a third. That seemed awfully mature and sophisticated to me. What an amazing invention. How slowly they spun!

As much as the music introduced me to strange rhythms and distorted chords, it was the cover art on the packaging of these vinyl pieces of wonder that rocked my world to its core.

David Bowie.

Utterly seminal for me and a whole generation of outcasts.

He looked amazing, completely other-worldly. I knew his name was David, so he must be a boy. But the way he looked. He looked like I felt inside. He did it with such surety and confidence. His face alone, angular, feminine, eyes closed, painted white, with a lightning bolt of colour down one cheek. Or standing with one leg bent, illuminated from above by a streetlamp, in a blue spangled jump suit, guitar slung over his back, blonde hair coiffed in an elaborate back-comb. Or stretched across a sofa in a dress, an enigmatic smile caressing his lips. Oh, I envied him – and how I stared at those album covers, praying that I could be just a little like him.

I desperately wanted to look like that, to be exotic, to be different, to be able to dress like the girls dressed, with creativity, colour, style, imagination. I knew that to attempt such rebellion in Stonehaven would be an invitation to be beaten. I'd seen the girls in their bangles and beads, but I knew that no man or boy could ever be allowed to be like that. My world was a suffocating blanket to my ambition and the reality in my head.

Donald and I danced in that garden shed to Bowie, in a sort of rambling, uncontrolled, young person's kind of way, an expression of our frustrations, Donald instinctively taking the lead, me instinctively following. When he closed that door and put on that music, I felt free of the trappings of Calvinist Scotland, of all the bigots who threw their eyes up in horror as I laughed or smiled in Church.

I slowly fell in love with Donald, for giving me the gift of self-expression, for respecting me as me.

I told him.

Not in an organised, thought-out kind of way. I was ten – thoughts don't follow logicality at that age. My confession just tumbled out. I took a bag of my mother's clothes with me and showed him how I liked to dress. I showed him how happy I could be – and how happy he made me. He didn't hold his hands up in horror, that wee, tough boy from the wrong side of the tracks. He hugged me in a way I never thought a man could hold me. I put my head on his shoulder and cried as we swayed to the strains of 'Suffragette City.'

Was Donald gay? I am not sure he would have understood the term. He was just a very sensitive and caring young man who had the extraordinary maturity to see me for who I really was. Perhaps later, we would have been a thing. I don't know, for I never got to find out.

Sugar and Spice

I was always made welcome at Donald's. I don't think his parents were really that bothered what Donald did or were bothered by me. They were part of that class who were happy with who they were and what they had. I was respectful towards them, and they were kind towards me.

My mother, on the other hand, heartily dis-approved. I had started wearing white socks like Donald, rolling my trouser legs up to show my slim ankles, turning my collar up, wearing my tie with an enormous knot inside my shirt like a scarf, slicking my hair with sugar and water, as I had seen the girls do. All against school rules. It just felt right to me. I enjoyed how that made me feel.

Donald gave me the licence to be myself. His family didn't seem to bother about the rules. Donald didn't seem to care whether he was singled out for approbation. He just smiled, chewed his gum, and walked back in again the next day in the same white socks to sit next to me.

I hated the petty bureaucracy and the draconian teachers who revelled in their power over us. I had begun what was to turn into a life-long rebellion against small-minded pettifoggers who thrive on their position and power to impose their rules as an enforced substitute for respect. I didn't want to end up like them, in their cheap tweed suits and pursed lips and wilfully constrained moral code of disapproval. I wanted colour, life, love, and freedom; I wanted it all. In Donald's company, I felt that thrill.

I kissed him then – and he kissed me straight back. It was wonderful and I adored him.

Donald and I stopped going to school lunches, bunking off to the local park. We were caught together in a close embrace by the Dominie, who wrote to my parents to complain about my 'unhealthy' behaviour. My mother was appalled. I remember her reading the letter I had been given to present to her. She read it over and over, looking between the written page and me and back again, revulsion written on her face. She made me go to the Head to apologise. I went sullenly to his office and asked to speak to him. He asked me if I had something to say to him. I replied:

'My mother has told me I have to apologise to you.'

My eyes said it all – I wasn't in the least apologetic and he knew it. He nodded curtly, and I left. It was the last conversation we ever had. My mother was livid when I told her what I had said. My parents were of a generation that had a very different relationship to authority. Even then, I knew the Head was a prick and I would soon outgrow his control. To them, I was insulting the system when my 'place' in society didn't give me the right to be disrespectful.

This is a battle that I have never resolved. There can be no compromise over who I am - and nor will I ever apologise for it. I felt that near inchoate rage to be me begin in Dunnottar.

My parents said I was to stop seeing Donald. I couldn't do that. Nor could he stop seeing me. We had become symbiotic, and I loved it. Stonehaven railway station had several sidings, where old rail carriages were parked up. One was an old guard's wagon, no longer in service. I took to meeting Donald there. I would steal plates and tins of fruit from my parent's kitchen – old tins of pears and peaches, exotic delicacies in those days.

I would go to the carriage early and prepare a luncheon for Donald, all dressed in my latest stolen outfit. I loved wearing a bra, it felt important to me that one day I might have breasts. We would laugh and sing, and Donald would stand on his hands, or we would sit together for ages, waiting to joyously scream out loud in time to the rumble of the tracks as the inter-city trains powered by, and talk of our dreams for a life together. Then, I would carefully change and hide my precious possessions, hiding my true self by closing and sealing the mental box that contained my girlhood, literally thinking my way back into being the person I hated.

One day it rained, and I forgot to hide the signs in my haste to get home. I don't remember why I forgot to fully change. I do remember I was soaked by the time I got home. My family were in the kitchen eating dinner. I wanted to rush by and change elsewhere. I could feel my mother's stolen knickers and bra burning my skin – my God, how could I have forgotten? My father told me to strip by the door, he didn't want wet clothing inside his house. I refused, he insisted, I refused, he insisted again, his temper fraying. What a bizarre request; to see his child strip naked in front of him. I feared him at the best of times, for he was never slow to hit me. I could see no way out.

How could I explain that I was wearing my mother's lingerie? I stripped to my underwear and stood there, hands in front of me, in shame and embarrassment.

I can still see the incredulity in my father's face, my mother's shock, my brother's lack of understanding. How could I betray them this way? I wanted to die, to shrivel up and disappear, to curl up in a ball, to throw myself at their feet and beg their forgiveness for being wicked and useless, for betraying them and all that they stood for. Yet, from somewhere, a voice within made me raise my chin and say:

'I am a girl.'

I expected to be beaten. My parents had a cane and a metal dog's lead that they chose between, depending on the severity of the crime. My father's favourite was to make me stand still and accept a closed fist to the face. He took pride in that, as he put it, 'To learn to take a beating like a man.' This time, though, he just sat there, dumb with shock. This was perversion beyond his ken. It was my mother who broke the silence:

'Go to your room.'

Sugar and Spice

The incident was never mentioned again, never spoken of, never even breathed, not for another 34 years. Instead, my mother and I got on a boat to Belfast, where amidst hushed conversations between my mother, aunt, and grandmother, I was whisked from boy's clothes shop to boy's clothes shop for a fancy grey uniform.

On our return to Stonehaven, my parents summoned me to talk to them. My mother said, in a clear and matter of fact way:

'I blame the school and that boy Donald. You have been going to the dogs. I took you to Belfast to enrol you in a boarding school there. You will be leaving with your father tomorrow.'

I didn't understand a word of it, except that I was to no longer see Donald. What was this? Another new school? Well, that was an adventure, wasn't it? And I could surely see Donald at the weekends? Nobody needed to know.

I didn't understand that my parents planned a one-way trip of banishment.

My father took me to Belfast, city of my birth, to the most expensive and exclusive school in the province, the Eton of Northern Ireland. Their resolution was excommunication. I was to live amongst the most privileged children of the land, the folks they had envied while at Cambridge. He made enough money in his union-protected job to afford it. I was to be inculcated with the most elite system of patronage and power my parents could muster to cure me of my supposed perversion.

I didn't ask for any of it, my opinion was immaterial.

BELFAST

Donald was gone. I never kissed him again.

I was back in Belfast. Where I was born, but a million miles away from nestling in my grandmother's apron, revelling in her scent.

Boarding school was such a searing event for me that I must set the stage, as that performance would set the circumstance for the rest of my life.

My new school is still so exclusive that nobody outside of its own closed community really knows where it is. To drive past it, all you would see from the outside is mile upon mile of hedgerow. It sits in grounds so extensive that to be there is to be in your very own microcosm, untouched by the passage of time. That is the atmosphere the place nurtures, where the only values are school values, the sort of virtues that built the British Empire.

It is built in Victorian Gothic splendour, all spires and nooks and crannies, long vaulted corridors, polished floors, and dusty display cabinets of youthful faces in sepia tint, next to battered trophies for 'School 1st XV' and 'Best Academy Shot'.

My despised alma mater is very, very expensive. Cost is the one defining entry characteristic. At a time when the rest of Northern Ireland's youth had their academic future decided by the 11+ examination, where a pass was a golden entry ticket to a grammar school and qualifications, my school ignored the system. Pupils did sit the exam; we had to, the 11+ was a legal requirement. In my school for gentlemen, though, a failure merely meant relegation to a lower stream. Where the only real difference was that you weren't required to start Latin and a foreign language for another year. Money, or rather the lack of it, was the only way you would be asked to leave.

Teachers were called masters, yet we were addressed as master too. I addressed my masters as 'sir' and they called me 'young master'. My title was used as a diminutive. When I grew up, I was told I may become an adult master too if I followed the path of tradition and respected the hierarchy my school would lay out for me. College logic, as a proving ground for ingrained deference to systemic authority, was flawless.

Masters wore a black cape and a cap with a flat mortarboard, adorned with a long black tassel. Their noir cloak undulated behind them when they walked, Darth Vader without the mask. They reminded me of our Kirk Ministers of doom.

We young masters had a complicated and varied set of uniforms - daywear, rainwear, sportswear, Sunday wear, blazer, tie, morning dress, and nightwear. We had everything except ordinary clothes. Everything we owned was a uniform, each item with my name neatly stitched inside. No expression of individuality was allowed. We all dressed the same, inside, and out, top to bottom. School had a system, and we were its victims. We were row upon row of entitled little Lord Fauntleroy, identical in our issued clothes, homogenised to fit the system. Very similar to prison, or the military. We were deliberately shorn of the ability to self-express. We joined the Borg, willingly or otherwise. Assimilation was unavoidable.

Young masters slept in dormitories, twelve to a room, on iron bedframes, with all our worldly uniform belongings in a trunk beneath the bed. We went to lessons 6 days a week, Saturday and Wednesday afternoons being for sport. Sunday morning was spent at the school chapel, followed by homework and letter-writing. This was obligatory – the minimum requirement, one written missive a week home to the family, to let proud parents know what had occurred. The 1970s equivalent of e-mail. Amongst ourselves, no-one used their own name, we acquired our own special identifiers. We were all 'Binky' or 'Jo-jo' or 'Peddie' or 'Buster'. Individuality was suppressed: school identity was all.

The entire place was like being in a junior version of the Officer's Mess. Which was, of course, consciously the plan.

Our headmaster was a ramrod straight ex-Guards officer, who had once been an Olympian. I remember this because he wore a blue blazer, with the British flag on the breast pocket, inscribed with 'GB Olympic Hockey'. Headmaster had a photograph of himself with his soldiers during the war on his desktop. He had snow-white hair, except for one dark yellow streak on the left temple. He was a heavy smoker and constantly smoothed his hair with nicotine-streaked fingers. The more upset he was with you, the more he stroked his hair, the more his fringe turned ochre.

His office lay at the end of a long wood-panelled corridor, his lair on the left, the staff room on the right, filled with leather recliners, smelling of cigar smoke, and resonating with deep, masculine baritones. The walls to his hidden domain were lined with paintings of previous heads, the artists painting their eyes so that they followed you wherever you stood. The only time as a pupil you entered the corridor of power was when you were being punished, to stand outside the head's office, awaiting your fate.

Corporal punishment was very much approved.

Headmaster used a variety of means to express it. During the day, he used a cane of varying thickness, which he would ostentatiously choose from a rack of the things cased behind his desk. At night, if you were summoned to his on-site apartment, he would use a leather slipper. Both means were applied to a bare backside, trousers pulled down, student bent over. His office contained a fireplace. An errant pupil was required to pull their shorts and pants down, face the fireplace, grab the mantelpiece, put your head in the flu, close your eyes and wait for the beastly sting. At night, you bent over the banisters outside his apartment, to stare into the inky stairwell, pyjama trousers around your ankles. Every time he battered me, he'd begin by intoning:

'This hurts me more than it will hurt you...'

Sanctimonious prick.

Boarding school was the gilded prison where my parents sent me.

I got on a plane from Aberdeen to Belfast with my father. We took a taxi across Belfast to the hallowed gates with no obvious entry sign. The school had helpfully sent a map with the joining letter. Otherwise, we would never have found the place. I had never been anywhere so grand. As our car tyres crunched on the endless gravel drive, past the miles of sports pitches, I thought I was going to a palace.

Headmaster met my father with an imperious handshake, then took my hand too:

'Good morning, young master.'

Nobody had ever shaken my hand before, nor called me 'young master'. I looked around me to see if I was being confused with somebody important. Headmaster looked

Sugar and Spice

so tall and elegant. He took my father and me on a tour of the vast building, through the dining room, with its serried benches and tables, along the wood panelled corridors, past the classrooms. It is the smell I remember – of wood polish and disinfectant - and the complete silence. Hundreds of boys lived here, yet life was conducted as if in a monastery.

Headmaster asked if would like to play football with the other boys. Another master led me to the playground. I turned to see my father, deep in conversation, and went to kick a ball. We played for half an hour before the master took the ball from us. It had been an interesting day out.

'Where is my daddy?' I asked him.

'He's gone. You are staying here now,' was the reply.

I didn't believe him. My father wouldn't leave me.

Even now, as I write these words fifty years on, I feel the pain of that separation. Later, I was to learn that new boys were asked to play football to take their minds off being abandoned by their parents. Had I known, nothing could ever have taken my mind off that separation, certainly not a dumb game of kicking a ball. I had just turned ten and found myself all alone in a foreign land, facing a strange man in a strange black gown who now controlled my very destiny.

I was taken to my dormitory, to meet 11 boys who had all been at the school for 3 years, since the age of 7. They knew each other intimately and were steeped in the ways and traditions of this strange place. Who spoke not with a Scottish accent, but with a deep Irish brogue. I was the outsider, totally alone, with no understanding of why I was here, a child who was a girl in the harsh world of a male only boarding school.

Boys can be very cruel.

The torment started that night. They laughed as I said 'hello' in my different accent. They laughed as I changed into my pyjamas, still fresh from the box, hiding my body in embarrassment. It's the small things that make the difference at that age. They wore plain, cotton pyjamas. My mother, in her mad dash to outfit me for school, had bought patterned fleece pyjamas, adorned with cartoon characters. How they smirked and pointed and giggled.

Although I had shared a bedroom with my brother, I had never slept in a room with so many other people. I was nervous of my near nakedness, turning my body away, while they flexed young muscle and called to each other. The beds were mattresses on wire springs. The merest movement started a creak. I lay, terrified to move, while all around they threw books and clothing at each other and spoke with that strange Ulster twang. One of the masters came by, stilling the noise with a peremptory command, before switching the lights off. We lay in silence until his footsteps disappeared down the corridor.

I have found that men must have a pecking order; there can be only one alpha male in any group. In adult life, it is possible to be the alpha by formal appointment. At boarding school, it is more primeval. The alpha is the one who is the most violent. It was not a game I understood or was ever capable of playing. The alpha in my dormitory was called Sam. I later discovered Sam had been a border-line hooligan and his father had sent him away. The fact that our parents had deliberately abandoned us was all we had in common. Sam wasn't intelligent in the classic sense - but he was very smart in working out that there was a new threat to his tribe:

Me.

He called me out that night, to play what the boys called 'tag'. The rules were simple. You stood toe to toe and had a free punch at each other. One hit, while the other stood, rinse, repeat. The loser was the first to flinch. Sam called me on it. He even offered to let me have first hit. Not initially, only after he sensed the fear in my eyes. I wanted to say:

'I'm here because I am a girl. My parents sent me away because I am different. I don't like these games, I don't want to be hit, and I don't want to be here.'

I didn't, though. In all my comics and war stories, I had read there is a moment when, as a man, you must stand up and be brave. So, I resolved to try my best. I stood toe to toe with him, with shaking hands and desperate fear in my eyes and took a half-hearted swing at his shoulder. Yes, his shoulder....

Somehow, I thought he was only kidding, that this was just a daft game. If I didn't hurt him, maybe he would just laugh it off. Sam smiled; I closed my eyes, and woke up on the floor, tasting the blood on my lips. Sam seemed happy – he was still the king of the castle. I crawled back to my bed and tried to still the snuffle in my throat and the tears in my eyes.

It was then I truly believed I was evil – why else would my parents have sent me to this place?

It got worse as the weeks went on. Sam called me out every night, the sadist in him knowing I didn't have the courage to fight him. I made every excuse, anything just so he wouldn't hit me.

Then the group punishment started. I would lie in my bed at night, listening to the master's footsteps disappear. Lying rigid, knowing it was only a matter of time. I would hear them get out of bed, quietly padding about the room, hearing the rustle of bed sheets and pillows. I would close my eyes and listen to them surround my bed, waiting for Sam to give the signal. Then they would hit me. They filled their pillowcases with their shoes and beat me, all eleven of them. Rhythmically, in unison, one overhead stroke after another, Sam urging them on and on. Then I would scream, and they would run back to their beds, but nobody came. School echoed with the sound of my sobs, but the masters had long gone.

After a time, it would begin again. For hours, until they grew too tired for the sport.

Nights became a time of dread: days, a time to let the bruises heal.

It was then that Abi came to help me. I had always been solitary, but I found another place when they hit me. I could literally feel my soul leaving my body and looking down on them, my saviour being my inner self, the girl I truly was, holding me safe. My body lay in my bed and absorbed the pain. It had no meaning, not the impact, nor the bruises. In my own world, I was safe.

The more they hit me, the less I reacted. Then they would get bored and leave me. It was all I wanted. I stopped communicating with any of them. I took to wandering the grounds by myself. I found an old tennis racket, with broken strings, and spent my time hitting a bald tennis ball against a wall. I had no desire to play a team sport. I wanted to be alone, for in being alone I could not be hurt.

One teacher was interested in me, my English mistress. She was the only female presence in the school. She was tall, willowy, and smelt of lavender, the way I wanted to smell. She saw I had a little talent at the written word, but I offered nothing, staying silent in class, deliberately ruining my assignments. She told me that I was lazy, that

I could do better. She was right in the second assumption but wrong in the first. Yet, she was interested in me.

She ran the amateur dramatics club. The school put on an annual play. She was a radical – she wanted to do something other than the usual Gilbert and Sullivan. School was going to do 'West Side Story.' Gang warfare? Inner-city poverty? Inter-racial sex? Edgy stuff for a boy's private school – particularly as the story is a doomed romance between a boy and a girl.

The girls' parts would be an exquisite challenge.

My English teacher challenged me. She asked me to audition. Nobody wanted to take part. Sam scorned the whole idea. Maybe it was his revulsion that provoked me to say 'yes.' To be the antithesis of anything Sam espoused. Maybe it was an innate love of stage and theatre that took hold of me. Maybe it was because West Side is set in New York, the land of my movie dreams. For whatever reason I went and for whatever reason she asked me to read for the female lead of Maria.

When I read those words, Maria's secret love for Tony, the way the men in her life refused her freedom, the way she was an outsider in a group of outsiders, it spoke to Abi within me, and my memories of Donald. I couldn't express my sense memories at first. The camouflage of my recent past was too strong, the feelings too deeply hidden.

Yet she saw it in me. From the first she guided me,

'No, sit upright, don't slouch, a girl doesn't slouch, keep your knees together.'

And how I responded. As the other boys sniggered, I sang:

'I feel pretty, oh, so pretty...' I wasn't a great singer but, boy, did I mean EVERY word.

I got the part. I was officially told I was a girl. That was the first time in my life it was OK to be me. Oh, joy…. My austere life at school attained meaning. Lunchtimes, evenings, break-times were spent in rehearsal. I immersed myself in Sondheim's words. How it came easily and naturally to me. I learned to paint my nails, to do my face, to walk, to talk, to express myself. My teacher brought me my costume, virginal white, with a red sash. We watched the movie on 16mm, in hushed silence. My costume matched Natalie Wood's.

How happy it made me.

I was left alone. I confused Sam. Here was a transformation that was beyond his ken. He could fight, he was good at it, but this was a challenge that was deeply unsettling to his psyche. For the sake of the part, I was allowed to grow my hair. I left the varnish on my nails, 'forgetting' to remove it: my outlandish behaviour excused by masters and pupils alike. Perhaps, at some primeval level, they all acknowledged I was different. Perhaps, they even came to like me. I started to get admirers come to watch rehearsal.

Sugar and Spice

I learned to flirt. I learned to laugh. I learned to live.

Many years later, I read James Clavell's 'King Rat', about a group of male POWs imprisoned by the Japanese. One character in the book plays the female role in the camp drama group. He remains in that role, full-time, providing a female talisman for men starved of female company, reminding them of the gentleness and beauty that women bring to this world. Maybe my amateur dramatic adventure was the same for me. School was certainly the same kind of enclosed society, answering only to its own, internal masculine cultural values.

I was proud of my achievements. I was popular. The play ran for three nights. To this day, I can remember each scene. The whole school, from junior to senior, every master, came to see it. Every parent was asked to make the effort, to pay to see the play, to support the school.

Nobody came to see me. I don't think my parents even knew I was in it. My aunt, who was in Belfast, and was invited, didn't come either. Another limb was hacked off. It didn't matter to me. I was used to their rejection. The school hadn't rejected me, though.

I was a girl.

For three performances.

We wore fake tan to play the Puerto Rican parts. The night the play finished, the matron ran baths for us all and ordered us to take it all off. I was ordered to scrub myself clean, to take off my varnish and make-up, to hand back my precious outfit. The spell was broken. I retreated into myself again.

As my reason for being was removed, so the bullying began again. My shield was gone. Except, this time it was worse because I was now a 'fag' as well, condemned as a sissy for playing a girl's role.

The day after the play finished, Sam walked up to me in the playground and slugged me straight in the mouth. As I lay on the ground, he kicked me in the head, splitting my brow. I was taken to see matron, who stitched my head and applied a bandage. I was held overnight in the school sick bay for observation. Headmaster came to see me.

He had been told what had happened. He told me that these things were to be expected, he had spoken to Sam about it, and he was willing to allow Sam and me have an organised boxing match to allow me to regain my honour. Even if I lost, which he thought was likely, the other boys could see that I wasn't, as he delicately put it, going to be 'queer'. He talked a lot about honour, sacrifice and courage, taking part being more than the winning or the losing, how 'going over the top' was what men did. I had no idea what he was going on about. I didn't know what he meant but I could tell he blamed my beating on my fixation with being a girl.

My God. Could he not see I was terrified of Sam? Could he not see I hated this place? Could he not see that all I wanted was to be Maria, forever, to be loved by my family, and be safe? I shrank from his words and turned my body away from him, hiding my tears. I could feel his dis-approval radiating from him. He muttered something about 'thinking about his proposal' and left me alone again, safe in the solitude of my hospital ward.

I kept the bandage on for three days until I could stand it no more. I tore it off in the bathroom, staring at my reflection. I had nowhere to turn, no route out. I had proved I could act, so I resolved to bury my girlhood where nobody would ever find her to hurt her again. I took on a new acting persona:

To become the same as Sam.

I started misbehaving badly. I took up smoking. I started smashing stuff up around the school, petty acts of vandalism, throwing stones at classroom windows, ripping up bedsheets and kicking doors. I started carrying a clasp knife, swearing, shouting, and yelling in class. Worst of all, I found the weakest and smallest boys and beat them, just as Sam had beaten me.

Sam approved. I was allowed to join his gang. That, in turn, gave me protection from the other boys. It was pure survival. All the while I let the real me wither.

Headmaster and I became frequent travellers together on his corridor of shame. By the time the year was out, I had been beaten by him on sixty-three separate occasions. I recollect this exactly because I was proud to be told I had smashed the college record for corporal punishment beatings. You could be caned or beaten with up to six strokes. My only regret at the time was that I never achieved five. I was whacked one, two, three, four and six times. Never five. I was disappointed. I really did try my best.

Each evening, we were required to have communal showers. These were watched over by a master. How strange, in these days of adult checks, that a male teacher, plucked at random, oversaw hundreds of pre-adolescent naked children, shivering under cold, communal showers.

There was a man who took us for classics. He was very thin, with a reedy voice and an impatient manner. He wore crepe-soled shoes that he used to silently sidle up behind you and seize you by the shoulders when you weren't expecting it, which always caused him great amusement. It pleased him to see how much he scared me.

I can write about this master because he is now dead. He died ten years ago, sacked from the school for a generation of child abuse. I won't write his name because this would give him the credence of identity he does not deserve. Some brave souls came forward and did something about him. They had more courage than me.

I, too, was abused.

I hid it for thirty-five years, telling nobody. I hid it because I was ashamed, embarrassed, and appalled. Not just at the act itself but because, after a while, it becomes normalised, and I became a participant. When I did, finally, tell my mother, she slapped me, saying:

'Is that the reward you give me for sacrificing to send you there?'

When I first learned about The Holocaust, I was publicly aghast. How could the Jews let themselves be slaughtered? Why did they not fight back? Yet, I knew. I had not fought back either. I didn't know how to fight back. Like the beatings, on an emotional level, I numbed myself to it. I convinced myself the memory would go away.

It never will.

Caning on a bare backside leaves a mark, a welt. Sometimes, the cane broke the skin. The beating takes time to heal. Six of the best equals six florid welts. Naked, in the shower, this master began asking to examine me, explaining he wanted to make sure I was alright. The dance of attraction began easily enough:

'Just turn around, let me see,' then a jovial comment that there were only six welts:

'At senior school, you can get twelve, you know.'

The shower stall quickly moved on to an invitation to his chambers. Then onto a more serious examination:

'Bend over for me to check, let me feel here, just in case the skin is broken. It might get infected... Perhaps you should stop by my room every night, just to be sure... Gosh, you are getting tall. I saw you in the school play. You were very good; you make a very good girl... That's right, just take your pyjamas down and let me see you are OK. Now turn around. My, you know we have the same parts. Let me show you. Yes, mine is bigger because I am a master. Let me tell you what to do to make it bigger still. Here, hold it, that's right, just there, and I'll hold yours...Would you bend over for me? Oh, I know it's a little strange, but it means I can check you're growing OK. That's it, just a little more. Oh, you are good. You know how girl's kiss? Would you like to try, just a little kiss, on my master parts. Oh, well done, you are a clever girl, aren't you? Would you like to be my girl, to be in our own play every night? Nobody else will know, just you and me, you can be a girl for me whenever you like...'

My nightly interlude became an insidious cycle that wound its tendrils of shame around me. In return for the care and attention he gave me, I gave him what he wanted. I knew it was wrong. Deep down inside me, I knew, but there was so much gay sex going on it seemed immaterial. Show me a man who went through puberty at a boarding school, and I will show you a man who has at least indulged in mutual masturbation with his fellows.

Sex is a natural human function. We all have urges. When there are no women, you do what you must do. Except, what this master did, this was not natural. Yet, I couldn't draw away, for the sense of protection, of a warped sense of love. Between Sam and this master, I acquired the protection I needed. My warped behaviour brought me a salvation: at the cost of my soul.

I was left alone.

I did try to break this cycle. I didn't like what was happening. The games of touch were becoming more physical, painful even. When I said I wasn't coming back to his room, my master (how that word could take on different meanings) told me he would tell my parents about my acting as a girl. I couldn't bear that, so I tried to find a 3rd way. I did everything I could to make myself less attractive, stopping bathing in the showers, mussing my hair, anything to minimise my physical attractiveness. I wasn't in control in any way, and he knew it.

School had occasional long weekend breaks. An aunt or other distant family member would take me in. I had nowhere else to go. Weekends away spent in strange beds in strange people's homes. Weekdays at school spent in a strange dormitory bed with strange people. My aunt told me years later that when he picked me up from school, I smelled so bad she would wind the window of the car down. I had stopped washing, cleaning myself, anything to avoid that horrid contact.

One weekend, sitting alone in her garden, she gave me my young cousin's toy cars to play with. I picked up the heaviest stone I could find and smashed them all. They were boy's toys – I didn't want them. I didn't want any toys. I wanted to be left alone. She was appalled at my behaviour, and I was duly punished, by being locked in my room alone. I didn't mind. I didn't want to be in her house. I wanted to be alone, in a place where I couldn't be hurt.

There were occasional moments when I connected to something other than the jail sentence imposed on me. Once a month, the Head would dig out a 16mm film projector and we would watch an old and faded copy of a western or an Ealing comedy. Nothing spectacular, but at least a lift in the dread monotony.

Except for the week he played David Lean's 'Lawrence of Arabia'. O'Toole was magnetic. I instinctively felt the struggle within Lawrence as my own, the torn sexual desire, the sense of difference, his need to be recognised. And of course, O'Toole's fragile beauty. My word, he was utterly gorgeous. That film lit a fire in my soul, to be in the desert, in charge of one's destiny, totally in control, facing extra-ordinary challenges simply because they were there to be done. Here was a gentle soul who excelled in the world of men. I would have followed O'Toole to Der'aa, and happily shared his bed. I remain entranced with that film – then, it was another sign that there was a world out there to find. I just had to find a way to get there.

In a grim world shorn of positive role models, I was finding my own.

My dear, sweet grandmother gave me a cassette recorder, with piano key buttons and a little, portable microphone. The machine came with a cassette of Elvis Presley. How I loved his picture on the cover, so protectively masculine and handsome. I adored his songs. I endlessly played, rewound, and replayed that tape. The man I had seen on my grandmother's wall and on the movie screen in Stonehaven, when I had dreamed that I could be happy wherever he was. There was a song on there, from his '68 special, that still speaks to me: of dreaming of a better land, where everybody lives in peace, and The King asks why that dream can't come true? The melody moved me, but even then, as a child, it was the words that brought me to tears.

I didn't know then that Elvis had sung that song as a response to the shooting of Martin Luther King, a man whose teachings were to become a profound influence on me later in life. I believed then that Elvis was singing to me, sympathising with my struggle, hoping, like me, the pain would come to an end. He gave purpose to my wanderings at school. I took my cassette recorder everywhere, started making recordings. I experimented with sound, created my own effects. I manufactured my own world where I was safe.

Elvis was my friend then, as he had been in my grandmother's house. Elvis is still my friend, to this day.

That cassette recorder and his songs were mine. It didn't have a school crest, or a regulation colour, or an ironed-on label. Nor did it follow a school bell, a threat of physical punishment or a bestial act of sexual congress. It was the first possession I ever felt was truly mine.

My English teacher, who had been so proud of me as Maria, despaired at this dirty ruffian before her. She saw my cassette recorder and its portable microphone as a possible redemption. She suggested I use it to do interviews around the school, which the class could listen to. I curled up into a ball again. I loved the idea. I loved to talk and to write, but not in public, not in that place. School was a place to disappear into the pack. Do not, under any circumstances, draw attention to yourself. I had explained my machine as having a love of music, but she had spotted me making recordings of sports games, of the gardener mowing the lawn. I was fascinated by sound; the rhythm of life being forever preserved.

She had given me a task in front of the class. I had to do it. I was to interview the music teacher. He was a fascinating man, who played live on the radio with the Belfast Symphony Orchestra, and was therefore as close to a pop star as the place could muster. He wore a flamboyant neck scarf and had impossibly long fingers. He played the piano as a tarantula would caress the keys, moving with incredible speed, dexterity, and finesse. In him, I saw something of a kindred spirit, but the confluence of talking to him, recording his life story in words, and then playing it back to the class was paralysing.

I blew the interview, mumbled a couple of questions about how long he had played the piano and what exams he had taken, and bolted out of the room. The whole thing had lasted 3 minutes. I played it back to the class. My teacher was aghast and asked, 'Is that it?' It was indeed.

I wanted desperately to disappear into obscurity again. My class laughed at my general uselessness and her attention moved to somebody else. I went back to acting a minor Sam mini-me and all-around bad 'un beyond redemption.

I was surviving in this prison by being deliberately bad. I was learning the game. My night-time visits were becoming less frequent. The master of the night had moved on to other prey. The constant threats were receding, excepting the regular beating on the ass for bad behaviour - but I was inured to that.

Then Sam and I fell out. I don't recall the reason exactly - Sam was such a volatile character. He just turned and hit me one day, without announcement, straight in the face, bloodying my nose again. Perhaps my foray into journalism after my public gender swap had made me too different for him. Perhaps he thought he was losing his grip over me. I didn't even think of going to the staff for support. I had run out of places and people to turn to. It was the start of another vicious cycle. Sam pulled a knife and slashed my bag and uniform, cutting the strap that held my recorder. He was smart – he knew what gave me my identity. He knew that he was reinforcing his hold over me. I existed through his rules, not my own. I hid the recorder away, stopped making my recordings, anything to blend in and not be noticed.

I started to really misbehave. I was quite uncontrollable then. The canings became near daily.

Christmas came, school broke up for the holidays - except for me. I watched all the cars arriving, filled with proud parents, come to collect their young. Nobody came for me. I spent that supposed happy, festive time with the headmaster and his family in an excruciating farce. The place was empty, apart from his own brood in their grace-and-favour pad. He couldn't leave me on my own in the long, echoing corridors during the day. He pretended to be happy to welcome me. I sat, sullen-faced and unruly, refusing to sing carols or join in with the forced seasonal jollity.

I don't know why I was left at school. My extended Belfast family all had their own to look after. I was abandoned to the headmaster, the only pupil left behind.

I slept alone in the dormitory, surrounded by my tears and the dark and shadowy halls. To this day, I find Christmas a difficult time.

Boarding school became too much for me. I had always had asthma as a child, now I developed eczema. It travelled all over my body. The emotional stress burned out of my skin into open welts and sores. I turned eleven in the school sick bay. Alone, frightened, unloved, the victim of physical and sexual abuse, rejected because I had loved a kind boy and told my parents who I am.

The matron – a stern Protestant lady with a thick waist and a collection of grey hair on her chin - told me that if I just stopped misbehaving and followed Jesus' commandments, I would get better.

I believed her. Not in the sense she meant of not doing dumb stuff, but in expressing my inner being. It was me that was causing all this. By telling my parents, I had forced them to reject me. By becoming Maria, I had encouraged Sam and that master to abuse me. It was my fault.

I was evil.

God had rejected me because of my sin. I had no reason to live - because the woman I am was a satanic curse.

I ran away from boarding school. I walked out the gates of a famous Protestant public school in my Protestant public school uniform and headed into sectarian Belfast.

Riven Belfast, during a vicious civil war, where bombings and shootings happened on a nightly basis. I walked for hours in the rain, with no money, no idea where I was or what I was trying to do. I just wanted away, to find a place where I wasn't an embarrassment.

I wasn't a victim. I was the accused.

The army picked me up, late at night, on the Springfield Road, in the centre of the city. They'd been looking for me, the school had told the police I was missing. They took me back to the place I'd been trying to escape from in the back of a Samson armoured car, all grinding gears, smelling of gun oil and exhaust fumes. Tense, edgy men with English accents, huge in body armour and helmets, carrying real guns. They talked in clipped phrases, the hiss of their radios squawking back at them.

Headmaster met me at his office. The sergeant in charge gave me a lecture about how much danger I had been in and left. Headmaster was strangely quiet. He didn't beat me that night. I think he had seen his career flash before his eyes after I disappeared.

The next day, I went to his office, where I prostrated myself once more in his fireplace. With venom in his stroke, he gave me six more of the cane on my naked ass and ordered me to write to my parents to tell them what I had done.

My father's reply came in the mail a week later. I read it in the toilet, three pages, crammed with his tight, precise script. He told me how appalled he was at my actions. At how much more shame I had brought on my family and the school after all the other shame. How I had thrown their sacrifice in sending me away to Belfast right back in their face. He told me I had to immediately apologise to headmaster, my classmates, and the other masters.

My father never once asked:

'Why? Why did you run away?'

Not once did he enquire, in all my life and his. His letter then only expressed shame and anger. I had little doubt that, had he been in Belfast, for my supposed crime he would have added to my beatings.

When I reached the end of his missive, I ripped his pages into tiny pieces, tearing the paper again and again as each act of destruction marked another slash to my heart. I dropped the confetti into the urinal and watched it flow to the drain: as my love for him flushed away to be replaced with anger at all he had done to hurt me.

I never apologised to the school. Not to anybody. Ever. Nor will I. Ever.

Headmaster sorted my fate. He wrote to my parents and told them he thought I was not suited to being at boarding school. He didn't explain why. The decision was made. I wasn't expelled, just 'let go', marked as 'unsuitable'.

I would come home and go to school in Scotland.

My parents never asked me about what had happened at boarding school, not a single question.

The entire year was swept under the carpet as another embarrassing episode in my increasing litany of failures; first Donald, then the expensive schooling. None of it was ever discussed. The shame was laid bare for me to bathe in and for them to revel in for decades to come. I had been offered all they had never had and thought important and I had failed at it all.

Now I am old, I don't see it that way. I think I was brave in the circumstances. As brave as a ten-year-old could be.

I forced a clean break by my own actions in running away. I proved to myself that I could influence hurtful events by just leaving it all behind.

I was learning fast. To hide the person I really was, to create a facsimile of myself, and when it became too much, to run, bury the past and start again. My rolling stone of a life had its genesis. I couldn't defeat society's revulsion of who I am, but I am in awe at how quickly I learned to defend myself by ducking out of the way.

My parents had sent me there. They had left me to Sam and the others. They had taken my precious Donald from me. I never trusted them again. As soon as I was legally able to, I was to be gone forever from their home.

For all that I have kept running, I have never been able to shrug off the shock and trauma of that childhood experience. I have never been able to let others into my life, nor ever again trusted another human being. Every relationship I have had has ended in failure – partly through my unspoken expectation that it will end that way. Sexual abuse is such a terrible burden to carry throughout life. I will always feel a sense of shame at what happened, a sense of betrayal from my parents, and a sense of anger towards those put in a position of power over me.

I do not take well to authoritarian managers. It is all wrapped up in what happened in Belfast, I know it, but I can only mitigate against that rage, I can never let go.

I have found the ability to try to understand my parents. It was one of the toughest conversations I have ever had with myself, not just because of Belfast, but because they were never interested enough to ever ask me 'why?'

I tried to understand them because they were simplistically inadequate to the job of parent. Secondly because, in their ingrained trust in institutions borne of their generational respect of class, they could never believe such a thing as abuse was possible. They trusted the masters over their own child and willingly gave me to them. They didn't plan for me to be abused, even though they must surely have known that Belfast was not the place for me.

No, what happened in Belfast was a level of evil beyond the comprehension of most and the connivance of none but a very few twisted individuals.

Still, they did send me there, and forever more refused to face up to what happened there. Nobody could have predicted in advance what happened, but in failing to address it, I cannot help but feel revulsion for them. I can try to understand, but I will never forget. The scars go far too deep for that.

BANGKOK, 2008

Dr. Suporn woke me to tell me my surgery had been a success. I barely took in the words. My body had gone into a deep healing mode. All my energy and my spirit were directed at the colossal wad of bandages between my legs.

I could see nothing of his work. My groin was covered with a mass of gauze and sticking plaster, from which protruded a catheter, filled with urine, leading to a colostomy bag hanging from the side of the bed. My world stretched as far as my arms would reach. The terrace I had walked along hours earlier was a cruel, inaccessible ten feet away.

Dr. S has a unique and singular process for this realisation. He calls it 'The Chonburi Flap'.

In other more commonly adopted procedures, the surgeon performs an orchiectomy, removing the testes and skin, hollowing out the penis, creating a space underneath the intestine and, inverting the skin of the penis, creating an internal sheath. So far, so good. Except, I knew of people where the skin of the penis had failed to adhere and had literally fallen out, like an empty sausage. Or of others who had zero sensitivity, and therefore, had robbed themselves of the ability to pleasurably enjoy penetrative intercourse ever again.

Not stuff to muck about with; there is only one set of skin to go around and only one chance to get it right.

I went to Dr. S because he guaranteed sensitivity after the surgery. I really wanted to be able to enjoy sex for the first time in my life. How he did that was more complicated, quite ingenious, and involved a much more invasive procedure with a lot more stitches and a longer recovery time, but one that is infinitely more subtle in result.

What he did was remove the hateful gonads, source of so much misery, but retain the skin of the scrotum and use that for the interior wall of the vagina as it is the most elastic. He uses the skin of the penis to create a vulva, retaining the tip of the penis (the sensitive bit) as the clitoris. I'd be fully orgasmic after six months, I just had to get through the painful bit first.

Several years later, I was invited for a vaginal swab by my doctor. I don't have ovaries, so rather a pointless procedure for me. I went along out of curiosity. I had my feet up in the stirrups when I 'fessed up. My doctor couldn't believe it. She had no idea. Nor, looking at my wee flower, could she tell. She was so fascinated, she put on her head lamp and went diving around down there to get a proper swatch.

My vagina is perfection itself.

I can assure you it all works as it should. Orgasms are toe-curlingly perfect now, as they should be. Dr S was as good as his word.

I had to be quite the warrior to get through the process.

The pain began to bite. My groin was massively swollen. My morphine drip was self-administered. Press three times and three precious drops of relief entered my bloodstream. That first day, I pressed that switch as often as I was allowed. The morphine was only part of the pharmaceutical emporium opened before me. I took basket after basket of pills: anti-inflammatories, antibiotics, more pain relief, and sleeping pills. Whatever was offered, I gladly took to make the pain go away.

Six months earlier, when my head had been reconstructed, Dr. Suporn had opened my skull like a can of tuna. He had peeled the skin of my forehead back, making an incision that would mark me from ear to ear like the seam of a tennis ball, right across my forehead. He had taken a hammer and chiselled the protruding bone mass around my eyes and nose.

A man has an excess of bone over his eyes, the better to protect them in combat, or to shade them to aid vision. A man has a characteristically protruding forehead. A woman has a flat forehead, to make her more attractive, to open the eyes. My 44-year-old skull needed a lot of work: testosterone had wreaked its worst. Dr. S needed a very big hammer.

Once the bone mass around my eyes had been pummelled, he grouted the results with surgical cement. Taking his bone hammer, he then broke my nose and carefully scraped the hook in my cartilage into a ski-slope of femininity, before straightening the entire mass. He worked from within the nostrils, which allowed him to lop off the downward-shaped tip of my nose, bobbing it, so that my nostrils were now visible.

He then cut the flesh from around my eyes, taking away all the excess skin. He took years off me with a couple of simple strokes. He then re-sowed my eyelids into two very carefully etched almonds. Sowing up the results of his work, he moved my brow line up a full inch. My eyebrows now sat carefully atop my newly created eyes: the perfect female face. As my eye sockets had been remade, I could not close my eyelids. My eyeballs were filled with a waxy solution until the skin stretched sufficiently.

Lastly, he cut away the flesh between my nose and my upper lip, shortening the distance between them. This had the effect of turning my upper lip, so that my teeth were more visible. I have always been blessed with full lips. Dr Suporn's last finishing touch gave me the Bardot pout. The man is a genius.

My body had never given up resisting the demands male hormones had placed up on it. My jawline remained soft and rounded. I do not have a square jaw. My cheekbones are as rounded as Ava Gardner's. I needed his help to remove the unwanted effects of testosterone. The rest of me had kept the female form.

When I came round from the facial surgery, I suffered from weeks of intense migraine headaches. My entire balance system was badly out of sync from the reconstruction of my nasal tubes. I walked like a drunk person for months.

Six months later, as I lay there recovering from my realisation surgery, I knew from first-hand experience how miserable those hospital beds would be.

I love Dr. S's work. All the pain was to be truly worth it and always will be. But, boy, was it a long journey.

Every few hours, somebody would come into my room to give me more drugs, or to offer me food I did not want. I lay there and remembered the past, adrift in a half-life of opiates and pain.

This was my second time around in the Suporn's care. I had known it would hurt. I hadn't realised quite how much. There was nothing to do but dream, of a better life, a better place. As I drifted back to unconsciousness, my life again floated before me....

ABERDEEN, 1976

When I came back from Belfast, my world had changed. I was sullen, withdrawn, angry and defensive. I spoke with a strong Ulster accent. The lesson I took from boarding school was to survive. I had become cunning as a rat, my first defence my fists. Belfast had made me a hard child, but not an attractive child. Whatever I may have been before was firmly put into a box and hidden on a shelf in my mind.

I am a girl, I had expressed my reality, and I had been jailed, beaten, and abused for that desire. I resolved to never again publicly let the world see the person within.

I didn't recognise my brothers. My middle brother was resentful of my returned presence. I'd been away for a year, and he had basked in the favouritism that came from being the temporary eldest.

My return marked a sea change in his place in the family. We immediately clashed - and that rivalry was to become a running sore in our relationship right through to his 20s when we parted company forever.

My youngest brother had been born during my absence. He had become quite possibly the most gorgeous young child you could ever imagine. He had long blonde curls, a beautiful smile and was generally swooned over by any female who came near him. The only expression of my hidden self I allowed was in my obvious adoration of him.

My father had been doing well in television and had been promoted. TV was a highly paid industry, a complete closed shop, run by an aggressive troika of trades unions, and able to demand quite ridiculous working conditions for its members. Television was a license to print money. The management were equally colluding in settling every ever more spurious staff dispute with wads of cash. In my absence, my father had been acquiring real wealth.

Right before my return, my mother made the decision for the family. I may be coming back in disgrace, but I certainly wasn't going back to Donald. I never saw him again. It was obvious that my departure from boarding school was an embarrassment that had forever to be kept hidden as a family secret.

She had spotted a huge granite pile in Aberdeen, fifteen miles to the north of Stonehaven. This was an enormous house. With six large bedrooms, it boasted a servant's annexe and a coach-house, with attic space large enough for an over-sized snooker room. The hall gave way to an enormous circular staircase, which rose vertically to a cupola, sixty feet in the air. She took my father's money, went into fulltime work herself, borrowed some more from her mother, and bought the place. It was completely, madly impractical, and way beyond what they could afford.

I adored living there, for all its leaky plumbing, creaks, and draughty windows.

For the first time in my life, I had a bedroom of my own. This was quite a revelation, after sharing with my brother, and then enduring the communality of boarding school. Not everything was new, though. Buying that house took all my parent's joint financial resources.

A large house needs large furniture, which was gradually acquired from junk houses and charity shops. My room may have been impressive and private, but my bed, mattress and wardrobe were cast-offs from somebody else.

Clothes, too, were second-hand. They came from charity shops, or from older cousins. I would obsessively keep returning them to the wash until they had been rinsed clean of the smell of mothballs or another human being.

My relationships with my parents had changed, too. My father became an even more imperious and remote presence in my life. His letter to me, at my time of desperation, had changed the opacity of our relationship. In any case, his work kept him away often. My mother became the dominant presence in my life. A person I quickly learned to please.

The pressure of purchasing such a large home kept the financial needle firmly in the red. My mother needed every cent she earned from her job as a teacher as well as my father's generous income to keep a roof over our heads and the kids in school. It made for the same pressured home environment I remembered from Stonehaven. I always felt she was just the right side of a breakdown, and I became very sensitive to her moods and their consequences.

There wasn't a lot of room for laughs, or days out. My mother was permanently irascible and easy to anger, which resulted in my father becoming equally irascible. He would resolve the issue with physical punishment: usually a beating with his fists. Or if he knocked me to the ground, with his boot. Boarding school had inured me to physical beatings. I took violence as being part of everyday life.

Just as headmaster had been quick with his cane, so my father's punches became part of the rhythm of existence. My reaction to violence was quite Pavlovian. I took being beaten as everyday life.

There was an awful lot of hidden violence in my family.

My mother was a gregarious soul who loved people and gossip. Living the life of a harassed and isolated housewife far from Belfast was not what she ever had in mind for herself. Quite often, she would say she wished she had never had us.

There were moments, though, when I felt close to her. On a Sunday, there was a golden oldies radio show that played songs of the 1950s, big band numbers with Al Martino, Vic Damone, and other pre-Beatle stars. We sang along together as we did the dishes and she showed me how to waltz. Like all children, I craved security, stability, and love. Somebody with interest in me and a role model to look up to.

Those were good moments. So many others were not.

Her pill addiction took her to some very unstable places. Sometimes affection, often indifference, sometimes violence and abrasive rejection. There were many times she would walk out on us all and we would wonder if she was coming back. My own behaviour was a little kooky too, hardly surprising with all the broken biscuits in my head. She'd offer me one of her pills, telling me it would make the hurt go away. I never took them, but she must surely have known I was different. How a mother could not see how much I was hurting is beyond me. I think what she did was put up her own walls, built from her father's rejection, and refused to acknowledge that the perfect image of the life she dreamed of had fallen so short of her imagining.

I've had a fair amount of therapy through the years, and every time I've gone for therapy, I've been told that I describe violence and chaos as if it was every day. To me it really was. I didn't know if I was coming home to a full-blown tantrum, a punch in the face or a meal on the table. Confronting the fact that this was not normal has cost me a lot of money through the years. Dealing with it took me decades.

Back then, I was well on the way to becoming two people. The private, hidden me, that Donald had seen, the real me. The other, the outwardly tough kid on the block. To reveal the former was lethal, so the latter became the default. I adopted violence as my defence mechanism.

School changed too.

The granite-built campus, which had originally housed the Duke of Cumberland during the Jacobite rebellion of 1745, was accessed through wrought iron gates, set in an imposing archway, with a quarter of a mile down a ramrod straight driveway to a tight, columned quadrangle.

This school was to become the seat of my secondary education, a home of sorts, where I learned my formative lessons in life.

Like Belfast, Aberdeen was streamed according to academic ability. At age eleven, the results of an entrance test dictated where in the system your future would belong. The top and bottom three in each class were promoted or demoted at the end of every year. For the vast majority, education - what you would learn and at what pace - became fixed at that early age until the time came for you to leave.

Graded A-E, the top three tiers were offered the chance to learn a foreign language. For the top two tiers, the chance to learn the classics. For the bottom two tiers, metalwork and woodwork beckoned in the place of language development. The rest of the curriculum was entirely fixed. There was no choice. You were taught what the college decided; nothing more, nothing less. The emphasis was English, mathematics, and the sciences. The remainder of my curriculum consisted of French, Latin, history, and geography. More than anything, my Aberdeen school acted as a feeder for the great Scottish universities. What I wanted to study had nothing to do with the choices I was given. I was in the sausage machine.

My own academic selection placed me in a 'B' stream. My parents were distraught. They wanted me in the top stream, which is where I had been at boarding school. I did well to make the second tier.

My date of birth saw me a year younger than the rest of my class. I skipped a grade to make senior school. My primary education had been spent in two different institutions, the latter part following an entirely different curriculum in a different country. Not to discount the stress of learning in a physically and sexually abusive regime.

I hated Aberdeen when I first started there, and my fellow students hated me right back. My fight or flight mechanism, so carefully learned in Belfast, got me straight into trouble. At boarding school, if somebody started an argument, you hit him first before he hit you. That was the system I knew, survive, or die. In Aberdeen, an argument could be sorted by words alone: not that I appreciated that. My fists soon got me into trouble, when a bigger boy, from an older year, beat the crap out of me for hitting a smaller boy. Rightly so, I deserved it.

No, this new school was going to be a whole other adventure.

My body didn't want to change. I was a late developer. I hung onto my female childhood for as long as possible. Puberty didn't hit me until I was thirteen or so. I remained thin, awkward, and gazelle-like, with no body hair or muscle development. I was attractive then.

I came to hate games afternoons. My new school played rugby, nothing else. At boarding school, I had come to quite enjoy football. I had some co-ordination between head, eye, head, and foot that had been admired. In Aberdeen, class structure got in the way. Middle-class public schools played rugby, working class boys played football. No more football for me. So that was the end of my love. In Aberdeen, choice was at a premium.

I hated rugby. I tried to play the game, and I still carry the scars from ill-advised tackles, but I have never enjoyed the shock of physical contact. In any case, I have remarkably small hands. Another genetic sign of the real me. I can barely stretch an octave on the piano. I could never catch a rugby ball. I kept fumbling the thing, which made me singularly unpopular.

Sports afternoons were a bus-ride away from school. I quickly learned that the masters never took a rollcall at the playing fields. As a new pupil, I could be invisible. I took to disappearing from sports afternoons.

Sports afternoons were when Abi would live, if only for a few precious hours. Back home, once again I took to thieving my mother's clothes. For good measure, I took to stealing my neighbour's underwear from her washing line too. The lady in question was a magnificently put together woman in the prime of her sexuality. I can still remember watching her walking with the sashay of Marilyn. One visit, she asked me if I wanted a cold drink, opening the fridge to pick a bottle from the bottom shelf. I saw straight down her cleavage. My body froze with alert anticipation. How I wanted breasts like hers. She was everything I wanted to be.

While my classmates sat on the top deck of the bus, on their way to the rugby field, I would pack all my belongings into a small duffel and head to the local park. I had already put my underwear on at home, my bra, tights, and knickers. The park had a few large overgrown woods. I found a small depression, where I was hidden from view, where I would do my make-up and put on my heels. I was careful to find outfits that looked a little androgynous, always wearing trousers and a blouse. I had a few lovely silk scarves that I learned to knot extravagantly. I grew my hair our as far as I was allowed. The short, Twiggy cut was quite fashionable. I found it easy, with a little experimentation to tease my locks into a suitable bouffant.

My skin was still soft enough that I didn't need foundation, and I loved curling my eyelashes and applying a mascara and lipstick. My favourite shoes were a pair of green stacked platforms, a Mary Jane with a wooden sole. They worked well with my flared jeans. I had to use socks to give myself a bust, but the bits down below, yet to swell, could easily be tucked away, out of sight.

The preparation was all really. The results something of anti-climax. All I did was walk about the park for an hour or two. I didn't speak to anybody, just wandered through the rose bushes. Nobody gave me a second glance. Which was all I wanted, to fit in, to be normal, to be accepted. Those afternoons were wonderful.

Nobody taught me how to work it all together. Somehow, I just knew. From one until three, once a week, I got to be me. As the clock chimed, I had to find the bushes again, and scrub off the make-up, with a damp flannel I always brought along for that very purpose. Then, back home, before my mother got home from work, to hide away my life in the rafters of the loft, concealed inside a couple of carefully secreted shoeboxes.

All I knew was that dressing that way, behaving that way, being that way, felt more normal and more calming to me than anything else in my life. I loved being a girl.

Which made the other side of my life at a boy's school, with all the rough and tumble that involved, even harder to bear. I buried myself in my studies, particularly history and English. I wrote long, expansive homework essays, always on a science fiction theme, of change on a different planet, where a race of aliens could self-express but were subjugated by an evil regime that suffocated change. My inner turmoil found a stunted self-expression in those early words.

Once a week, we had to undergo the torture of swimming class. The school had its own pool. The complex was made of grey polished granite, which dissipated any heat. No matter the season, the pool building was always freezing. The changing cubicles were open. We had to undress in front of each other. I hated the other boys seeing my naked body. I had taken to secretly painting my toenails.

How the logistics of remembering to remove the polish on swim days got complicated. On the days I forgot, I had to feign illness. My life would not have been worth living had I revealed my secret.

Before class, we had all to sit on a bench in our regulation school colour swim costumes. The other boys strutted along the line, showing off their nascent muscles. It was that time of life when boys turned into men. One week, we all looked the same, then, suddenly, each week, one by one, my friends developed hair on their legs, broader shoulders, bigger arms: and the thing between their legs grew from a small, perfectly formed package to a huge, dangling apparatus.

I would deliberately hide at the end of the class, anything to avoid the long walk of semi-naked shame.

One week, the change happened to me too. My body changed in front of me. I noticed the smell first. A man's skin is acidic, men smell acrid. Their skin is thicker too, which aids the production of sebum and sweat. I began to get BO.

My legs grew hair, all by themselves. Followed by my armpits. What had been an inoffensive lump in my groin turned into something with a life of its own. Hair sprouted all round it.

My body rebelled at the hormonal rush. My skin erupted into a wild rash of boils and eczema, particularly in my groin and in my armpits, the sources of all this home-produced testosterone. This was more than a small, localised inflammation. My entire body was covered in boils and pustules. I lived with that in an extreme form for over a decade, but it never fully left me.

Quite truthfully, the day I started on oestrogen therapy, it stopped. Literally within days. And it has never returned. Puberty provides me with more evidence that I was an extremely reluctant participant in the sham.

The physical change bemused, bewildered, frightened, and confused me. I didn't want this at all. I had always believed that I could, with enough willpower, change my body when I wanted. All I had to do was last long enough to be able to leave home, where nobody would be able to find out. All I had to do was keep my womanhood a secret and God would help me. Every week in church, we were persuaded to put our faith in his safekeeping. All I had to do was be a good person and God would save me. Why was he doing this to me now?

I went to my mother and asked her what was happening to me. She told me with a smile that I was becoming a man. I turned and walked from the room, broken and distraught. What was being a man? I didn't want that, anything but that.

Several years before, I had seen my father naked on holiday. His body fascinated and repelled me. He was so hairy, and the thing between his legs seemed enormous. I could no more imagine myself having such a device between my own legs than I could imagine playing rugby for Scotland.

My friends at school were a slightly oddball bunch of romantic creatives. We read a lot of Bryon and Shelley, obsessed over Bob Dylan lyrics, and thought Bryan Ferry the ultimate in cool. We went through a stage of doing the Ouija board. I know now that that is not a clever thing to do. Nobody can ever tell me that we moved that bottle of our own free will. Something inhabited the room, every time we did it.

I took to dressing as a girl and trying the Ouija board on my own. I have no idea what spirits I evoked, but I would pray to be allowed to be a girl. I knew no other way of self-expression. Where was I to go? I lived in Aberdeen in the 1970s. The place was Flintstone simple in its gender divide.

My mother confused me further. She had a habit of giving me her clothes. I suppose it was part of my parents' ever-running drive to economise to afford our enormous home. I ended up the proud possessor of pink Levi jeans and jacket. I loved that outfit! Here was something that I could openly wear with my mother's approval, but which fit the way I am inside. I tried it on, turning in front of the mirror, to see how my ass looked.

The day I got my new jeans and jacket, I proudly went skipping downtown, my pink outfit accessorised with a matching floral shirt, broad belt, and platform shoes. I got as far as halfway down Union Street, the centre of town, when a strapping young man walked up to me and slugged me right in the face.

'You fucking poof,' he yelled, aiming a kick at me as he walked off. I stood in the middle of the street, with blood running down my face, all over my new jacket, while everybody just filtered their way around me. Nobody asked me what had happened.

I phoned home and my father came to get me. He asked me what had happened. When I told him, he said:

'Well, what did you expect, going out dressed like that?'

That night, my mother and he had a furious fight about the way she was dressing his child. I took that denim jacket and jeans and threw them in the bin, as I plugged

Sugar and Spice

my burst lip with salve. Yet again, I had learned. What may have OK for David Bowie and his London trendy art school upbringing was never going to work in Aberdeen.

Those were the dark days of 1970s Britain. When I think back on it, I remember a dingy, dirty, unsophisticated country with shit culture, shit clothes and shit food. The real gift of the European Union was not in the vast wealth that membership gave this country, but in the cultural immersion it offered to different civilisations. From the simple things, like good wine and cheese, to the riches of European architecture, style, fashion, and design. Back then, such sophistry was regarded with suspicion and distrust.

My only exposure to the world before my late teens was an annual pilgrimage to a cheap hotel with a pool in Spain. Where the waiter would present a bottle of table wine to my father on the first day, which he would nightly mark with a pen to show how much was left. Where the odd German tourist would be subjected to the usual disgraceful comments about who really won the war. Where my mother would fill her case with tins of Spam and nightly cut us each a sliver of 'British' food to replace the ignominy of eating anything foreign.

No, that's not a country I remember with any real enthusiasm. And I won't go into the industrial and political strife of those days, of coming home from school to darkness because there was no electricity, bins overflowing in the streets, the dead going unburied.

I knew even then there was something else for me out there. I saw it in the movie theatres and in the American television shows I devoured. This was a technicolour world I longed for. I collected images, cut from newspapers and magazines, of glamorous people doing glamorous things in glamorous places. All I had to do was look out the window to imagine the contrast with dull, wet, grey, cold Aberdeen. I'd put on my Elvis tapes and dream.

Belfast had nearly destroyed who I am, but there remained a spark inside me, for that was my very soul. I resolved then that as soon as I was able, I would be gone from Aberdeen, to find joy in life that my own existence denied me. I'd endure the beatings, the scandalised looks, and the feral and cunning moments when I could dress as I wanted and be the woman I am. I'd put up with it all until the time came when I could finally take charge of my own destiny and get out of Aberdeen forever.

TWO YEARS LATER

Sports afternoons spent hiding in the park were getting harder to disguise. A new master had started taking a roll call. I started writing fake sick notes, to excuse myself from the mud of the playing field, but I knew my freedom was soon to end.

My body was rapidly changing. I could no longer ignore the way my body hair was sprouting, how my voice had deepened, how my muscles were beginning to grow.

I stopped eating, trying to hide the thickening of my torso. The experience of change completely traumatised me. I could do nothing to stop it. It wasn't just my body. My brain got foggy. I found it hard to process things. My concept of beauty was changing. I became less patient. I lost all perspective.

Running became my saviour. I saw on television how stick-thin long-distance runners were. I didn't want to grow, to get bigger. I began what would become a life-long habit. In the 1970s jogging was not the commonplace past-time it has now become.

I was the proud possessor of a pair of black plimsolls, required by school, and a pair of rugby shorts. Together with a cast-off cotton T-shirt, I cut an unlikely figure around the streets of Aberdeen's west end. Fitness is hard

Sugar and Spice

to gain, easy to lose, but it is perfectly possible to reach a plateau of fitness, particularly when you are young.

I thought if I ran, and somehow kept on running, I could stop this hateful transformation.

I was never destined to be a talented runner, but I did have the curious ability to keep on trucking long after my muscles had given up on me. I had a hidden and very secret desire to keep on running. I knew that every extra yard was a calorie lost, a calorie closer to staving off the inevitable. In time, as my stamina improved, I came to view running as meditation. I would disappear for hours, living inside myself, re-living my hopes and dreams and confusion. I ran while I asked God why he had made me this way. I never ran with others, or in a club, or in any form of organised activity.

I ran for solitude. I ran to hide. I ran for internal peace.

To this day, when life gets too much, I will pull on my running top and struggle round the streets. I am old now; the days when I could compete with other runners are gone. Less a run these days than a fast walk, interspersed with brief fits of a sputtering jog. I am not happy to be overtaken, but I have come to resign myself to the fact that my body is now slowly decaying. I do what I can to off-set the inevitable, I still appreciate the meditative reward of the experience.

The aging process is cruel indeed. Plus, and I take great delight in writing this, the size of my breasts makes running uncomfortable. I take such huge joy in this. So much so I am going to write that sentence again; 'the size of my breasts makes running uncomfortable.' How utterly, utterly fabulous....I will never, ever change that.

At school, I did not have the option of solo exercise. I hated being forced to play rugby. I hated the mud, the grinding clash of bodies, the closeness of the scrum. I hated the camaraderie of the plunge bath and the showers. I hated my body, being forced to reveal myself to the other boys, just as I found their own masculine boisterousness strange and uncomfortable. I was also absolutely terrified of finding one of them irresistibly attractive. I had no control over those parts. The thought of an erection in the shower would have been irredeemably horrid.

I could not control those thoughts. Sex swamped my consciousness. I hated waking up with an erection, I hated when it just happened spontaneously. I hated the size of it all in my pants. I took to sello-taping it down, taping it between my legs, then tying it off with string, then in those dreadful moments to cutting it with scissors. I really, really hated that part of my body. I used to wrap my shirt cuff around my hand to avoid touching it when I had to urinate. A urinal was alien territory for me. I found it impossible to stand and pee. Literally nothing worked. I would freeze internally until I could find a stall to sit down. Only then would my urethra uncoil itself. None of the equipment my body had been issued with worked.

None of it.

I was caught in the midst of a chasm divided by unsurmountable cliffs of desire and physicality.

By my teens, school had taught me about sex and the genders. The physiology was taught in biology. We watched a film of frogs having sex, spawning their eggs, and hatching. With a small cough, our master explained the function of sperm and the egg, of male and female reproductive capability. He demonstrated by filling a dropper with fluid and putting it inside a test tube, then squeezing the liquid out. Somehow, we were supposed to discern that the combination of glass interplay and two frogs mating was an allegory for the human sexual experience.

The emotional connection of lovemaking was dealt with by, of all things, religious education. We were required to spend one forty-minute period a week learning the scriptures. The subject was an obligatory part of the national curriculum. Nominally, we were supposed to learn about the other great world religions too, but the emphasis was very much on the story of Christ.

Religious education was where I found out about homosexuality. My teacher's comments were prefaced with, 'Unfortunately...'

With an apology and an expression of revulsion, he told us that some people went against the 'natural order of life' and became 'intimate' with other men. I do not recall lesbianism ever being mentioned. What was made very clear was that being together with another man was firmly against God and against the teachings of the Bible.

In 1979, homosexuality in Scotland was illegal. The law in England and Wales had been reformed a decade earlier, but Scotland, with its stubborn Calvinism, held out until 1980. My school was doing its job in enforcing the law and the Biblical teaching behind that legislation.

I have never felt gay, in the sense of being attracted to other men as a man, but by the late 1970's I understood sexuality and had several encounters with men, which I had tried to enjoy while I could present as a female in my mind, even if my body could not. I was something altogether different, even if I could not fully explain it. My latent feelings were coalescing into a real awareness of my difference.

At a time when all my classmates were finding girlfriends and obsessing over soft porn magazines, I felt strangely asexual towards the dance of mutual attraction.

All of this was very lonely and insular. Sex was an embarrassment. Nobody ever mentioned it. My kind of sexual and gender attraction was illegal, immoral, and sinful. Everything I was taught or socialised led me to the conclusion I was a perversion. My mother regularly stated, with real relish; 'there'll be no queers in this house…'

My one foray into the world of straight dating came with a 3rd party approach. My friends and I used to hang out in the local bowling club, sitting at the end of the ten-pin lanes, watching those with money to burn hit the pins. We didn't have the cash to afford to play, but we could nurse a coke for hours and be left alone by the good-natured owner.

The girls from the local schools used to congregate at one end. We would look covetously at each other. When eye contact was made, one of our number, a neutral party, would walk half-way across the lanes, while an emissary from the other side would meet in an equidistant neutral zone. Invitations would be extended - 'my mate fancies your mate' - to be accepted or declined. If one got lucky, the drill was to walk outside and share a forbidden cigarette under the fire escape.

My role in this teenage drama was quite circumspect. I was quite adept at reading the girls' subtle signals of female flirtation. My friends would ask me, 'What'cha think? You know these things. Does she fancy me?'

My guess-rate became quite good, so I was viewed as something of a guru in the dark arts of mutual attraction. Of course, I could never, ever reveal quite why I was so insightful. That way would lead to expulsion from the group, but my abilities did lead me to a quiet form of acceptance by the rest, which was blessed relief. I never quite penetrated the inner core of my peers. That would require ability with my fists that would forever be beyond me, but, within the group, I was protected from the other boys. My skill at reading the girl's minds accorded me the protection of the alpha males. Provided, of course, I obtained the goods for them: a kiss or a quick grope underneath the fire escape.

It was with some surprise that one day I got an offer from a girl. My mate told me that one of them liked me and wanted to walk outside with me. I didn't know what to do. I'd never actually, ever, spoken to a real, live girl. I was terrified that she would read me as soon as I opened my mouth.

The young lady in question was known by the horrid nickname of 'Buckets'. She had developed very large breasts, which were assumed to need milking, hence her acquired name. Gosh, kids can be cruel.

When Buckets sent her note to me, I had little choice but to take the dreaded walk. There was too much loss of face involved to do anything else. Accompanied by much backslapping and youthful calls to sexual action, I took my bright red face outside to wait for Buckets.

There were already several other couples necking away, the boys' hands moving ever south, to be firmly clamped by their erstwhile partners and returned northwards to safer territory. I found a spot and lit a cigarette.

Everybody smoked in those days. It was one of those teenage acts of rebellion. We practised throwing the nicotine stick up to our lips like Marlon did. This was something of a one-shot deal: super cool if you could do it in public, but if you missed, then your reputation was dust forever more. Much safer to just roll the fag into the corner of your mouth and speak in short, clipped words. Clint Eastwood was our mentor in learning cigarette-speak. The more laconic the speech, the better the impression. We all developed early crow's feet by squinting for hours into the middle distance.

Buckets appeared, just as shyly and awkwardly as I had. I recognised her straight off. She, like me, had spent her existence hovering on the outskirts of her group. The girls had just as active and competitive a social circle as we did. Ours was predicated on sporting and physical prowess. The girls' league table was rated on physical attractiveness and sexual sassiness. Which involved showing as much flesh as was publicly decent, never-ending hair tossing and an ability to blow sexually charged chewing-gum bubbles.

Buckets was more pear than willow, with hair that lay poker straight down to her shoulders. All the other girls spent hours achieving the Farrah Fawcett blow-dried curls of Charlie's angels. With her flat shoes and sensible skirt, Buckets was the sort of daughter to win a mother's approval and a teenage suitor's rejection.

We awkwardly said 'hello', while I squinted with determination and half-choked myself by swallowing my cigarette mid lip roll. She must have thought I was blind and dumb. Buckets made all the running. It turned out she didn't really fancy me. She told me she didn't really like boys, but she wanted me to do her a favour. Would I kiss her, so the other girls would stop teasing her? Why she had asked me, I wondered. She told me she had seen I was shy, and her friends had told her that the other boys had said I was the girl-friendly guru. She thought I would be sensitive enough to understand her need, without making any other demands on her: like wanting a grope.

Gosh, this was hardly the ringing Don Juan endorsement I could take back to the group. But if just one of the boys saw me necking Buckets, then I would have received my gold star of stud-hood without any real pain or drama. If Buckets kept her opinions to herself - and, in the circumstances, I reckoned she truly would - then we were both onto a winner.

We went for it. And I got straight into a drama. I held her round her waist and lowered my eyes. 'No,' interrupted Buckets. 'You're a boy, I hold you round the waist, and you hold me round my shoulders. And don't tilt your head back, I do that bit, you need to angle your head to mine, not the other way around.'

Here I was about to kiss a girl for the first time, and I was kissing like a girl. I apologised, we changed hand positions, held my head back, took a deep breath and went in for contact. Her lips felt so soft, kind of squidgy. Mine were forensically pursed tightly, the way I kissed my great-aunt, with her hairy chin and no teeth. 'No!'

exclaimed Buckets. 'This is not right. What is wrong with you? You look like you don't like kissing girls.'

I went bright red. I didn't know what to say.

'Oh, I see,' said Buckets. Comprehension spread across her face. 'I understand. Well, nobody needs to know, do they,' in that matter-of-fact way girls have when they talk of sexuality or emotional attraction. 'Let me show you what you have to do,' she added.

Under the fire escape, as a soft rain began to fall, Buckets showed me where to place my arms, how to hold my head, how to softly part my lips, how to nibble on her bottom lip. I got a master class in kissing from an expert who thought she was kissing a gay man. Oh, the irony. All I learned from her that day was another lesson in how to pretend.

I never went under the fire escape with Buckets again. When we went back inside, she sent a message over to our side that we weren't right together. The boys just laughed. All they wanted to know was whether I had earned her rejection by trying to feel her breasts. I would have l appreciated that, just to know what having breasts felt like. No, not a great success, by any stretch.

What challenges I faced. I was in a howl-round loop of miscomprehension. I owe my realization to one lady:

Julia Grant.

In 1979, the BBC broadcast a documentary of her journey. Julia was not always Julia. She began life presenting as a man and became a teacher as an adult. In 1979, she allowed herself to be filmed as she went through what was then known as changing gender.

TV listings in those days were noted in a weekly magazine, run by the BBC, called the 'Radio Times.' We had a weekly subscription, and I used to love to read the show-business gossip in the front pages.

Television then wasn't like it is now, with instant recording, catch-up channels, internet replays and multiple sources of information. With our three UK channels, there was only one chance to watch a program. At exactly the time the broadcaster said it would be broadcast. Home video recording had barely been invented. It certainly hadn't reached our house. Julia's film was a one-shot deal.

Julia's movie received scant media attention, barely five lines in the Radio Times. But those five lines hit me right between the eyes. The listing explained that here would be the story of a man who would become a woman, because he had always been a woman. I read that paragraph over and over, until I felt the printed words would melt before me.

Goodness me.

For the first time in my life, here was a summary of my life. By 1979, I was spending every hour I could find dressing as a girl. I'd started taking insane risks, wearing knickers and tights to school, under my trousers, keeping a bra in my schoolbag, changing into it for the bus ride home, blazer kept carefully wrapped around me. The whole experiment required such careful planning and logistics. However, for me, the pleasure of the material made feel euphorically happy. I might not be able to show the world, but that simple act made me feel complete.

One week, I forgot I had to go for swimming class, which involved the beastly communal changing. I pled illness – again – which, as an excuse, had been wearing mighty thin. Luckily, the usual master, a difficult, aggressive man, was off sick himself that day. His replacement was a more sensitive deputy, who quietly excused me when he saw the desperation in my eyes.

I just couldn't help myself. I felt happy when I dressed as a girl, content, whole and self-aware.

When I dressed as a girl my social stock rose because I changed as a person. I became communicative, outgoing, and normal. My homework improved, I did well in my studies. I gained a whole group of new friends, the art school set who read books by Camus and talked of philosophy: my kind of people.

I had originally avoided them like the plague in my Sam-obsessed miasma of hate. But this was my logical home. I adored the sensitivity of the group. How they were considerate of each other's feelings, how they even cried when they read a moving passage of poetry or grew passionate and angry when they talked of nuclear weapons and the desolation of war. I had not known that such people could exist. And, in return, they accepted me.

But, Lord, if anybody had ever found out about my choice of underwear, I would have faced such ridicule. I quietly resolved that if that ever did happen, I would have to kill myself.

One of my brother's friends had done just that. He had tried to come out as gay and had made approaches to another friend. Unfortunately, his radar was way off-kilter. The news soon spread, that he was a 'fag'. His complete ostracism was soon in place. He was sent to Coventry by all of us, including me. I should have reached out to him, I didn't, and he was dead a week later, by his own hand, from an overdose of his mother's sleeping pills.

Ashamed as I was of my own discrimination towards him, I was more overwhelmed with relief that he had not been me. Which made my guilt even harder to assuage.

I knew I wasn't standard gay in that sense, so I thought I was something much worse. I had no social references to deal with, no values and standards, literally nobody I could express my feelings to. I was desperate not to be this hairy man my body was forcing me to become. I knew being a girl made me happy, but my body would not let me grow that way. I knew from boarding school that my family would punish me if they knew I had not been cured. I knew that if society found out, I'd have to kill myself; to be that inner girl was akin to self-annihilation. My mind swirled with what I could do, trying to define what I was, why this compulsion made me so complete, but was so despised by society.

But Julia Grant. …Wow! Here was something I could relate to and understand.

We only had one television, which would be an issue. There was no way my family would ever watch such a show, and television viewing was very much a family experience. My father was a notable homophobe, so Julia would have been seen as obscene by him. I couldn't say I wanted to see it. My memory of his reaction to Donald was far too fresh.

My father was into caravanning, and one of his more recent purchases was a small portable television for those horrid rainy days when all we could do was sit in our box on wheels and look at the Scottish drizzle through misted windows. On a previous trip, pre-portable TV, the rain had lasted for days, and we had nearly self-immolated as a family in that smelly caravan. The portable, which had an extendable aerial and dial on the side to tune, was the compromise to mutual destruction through boredom.

On that Thursday evening when Julia was to grant me vision, at the appointed time I crept up to the loft and carefully switched on that portable. The analogue signal took ages to find. The picture was all snow and rolling frames, but I finally found the BBC. I hid myself under a pile of old coats to deaden the sound and listened to her story.

Everything she said made perfect sense to me. The clarity of what she said, how she felt, was an articulation of all I felt and believed in my heart: the sense of dislocation, the dread sense of discovery, the self-loathing, and the secret dressing. For the first time in my life, I knew I was not alone. Where Julia's story took over from mine was in her determination to do something about it all.

Her bravery was remarkable. The film depicted her undergoing a series of traumatic, depressing and acutely insensitive psychiatric evaluations. She faced the very real threat of incarceration in a mental institution if she failed to make her case. All through her ordeal, Julia stuck to her guns. The film did the usual things that TV companies always do when trying to illustrate this condition – the putting on of make-up, the buying of clothes and the dressing-up.

Julia's film ended with her under-going realisation surgery, leaving the hospital with a very inelegant bow-legged waddle, having just shaved her chin. It was a highly inconclusive finish to my first revelatory experience, but it was a start.

I now understood the testes on my body were the cause of what was happening to me. I knew then for the first time that I must get rid of them. I was on a drug regime that was causing me incalculable harm. This would be more than just ending unwanted erections. Here was the root of it all. I knew those bits were not female, and this was a means to rectify the error, end the sense of sin. If I followed Julia, I could be me.

The end credits included a referral to the Beaumont Society, which caters mostly to the transvestite community. Delivered in a very portentous BBC RP-accent message. I saw a way that I could self-identify. Here was a channel to reach out to.

I snuck back down the stairs, processing the information that I had seen in that one broadcast. To this day, I can still tell you about the sequences in the film. It burned into my skull. For the first time in my life, I knew what I had to do. I had to follow Julia. How I would do that, I had no idea, but she gifted me the power of intelligent reasoning by her shared experience.

I owe Julia Grant.

I got the address of the Beaumont Society from the telephone directory service, which caused an intake of breath from the human operator when I explained what it did. I wrote to them, one of the first letters I had written since boarding school. For weeks afterwards, I would run downstairs to catch the morning post. Children did not get letters sent to them. A letter from the Beaumont Society would have caused instant suspicion. Indeed, I strongly suspect my parents would have opened it themselves. But there was no other way then than snail mail. I couldn't phone them. A call to London would have shown up in our telephone bill (in those days, long distance calls were such a rarity, they were individually listed) and questions would have been asked. A letter, even with the risk of discovery, was the only way. I was fast becoming a risk calculator of the odds of disaster vs. my desire for life.

The Beaumont Society did write back. I intercepted the letter. They told me that, occasionally, they got letters from young people such as myself. They pointed out that they offered counselling for people who wished to dress as women on a part-time basis, not for children who were women. However, should I be available, they would be happy to meet with me at their London office.

What use was that to me? I was just into my teens, with no money of my own, living 550 miles away from London. They might as well have asked me to meet them on the moon. I had no means to get there, nor no reasonable excuse to go in the first place. I ripped their letter up, in despair and fear at it ever being found, and went back to my secret calculations of risk.

Which were about to take a massive turn for the worse.

As often as I could, I would take off for the park, for an afternoon of happiness as Abi. Not just on sports afternoons, when the place was quiet, but at weekends too, when the risk was really off the wall. Such was the level of my desperation. Being Abi encompassed everything I did. When I was her, I was infinitely happy, excepting that lump in my trousers. When I had to be that other person, I was truculent and silent.

My unhappiness at life had reached a nadir that Christmas. My aunt and her family came to visit. I spent the entire festive period alone in our lounge, listening to Pink Floyd's 'The Wall' repeatedly. That record, with its sense of oppressive conformity, the stifling of the human spirit, the nihilism of the system destroying personal freedoms and aspiration struck such a deep chord within me. I did nothing but lie there and play those tracks repeatedly. Every now and again, one of the adults would try to reach me, but I rebuffed them all. They must have thought I was being all moody teenaged difficult. I was, but for reasons that they could never, ever understand.

I was always careful walking around the park. I'd carefully map out where I was going to walk, where I would sit. I had grown my hair out as acceptably long as I possibly could. My mother would take me to the barber's and insist on a short back and sides. Purgatory for me. I'd deliberately turn my head away from the scissors so my locks would be reprieved. I took to sweeping my hair back to hide its true length. When I went to the park, I would set my hair forward, changing the style. I have no idea where I acquired this knowledge, nor the ability to do my make-up, nor find a dress sense that worked for me. All those feminine skills just came to me naturally and I enjoyed the experimentation.

One Saturday, I made a horrendous mistake. I walked around a corner and literally came face to face with an older boy from school. I knew him as a terrible bully, somebody I avoided at all costs. I tried desperately to hide my face, to brush past him, but the moment of mutual recognition was written all over his face. I had been outed, good and proper, no excuses, no escape.

His reaction at first was the usual one of revulsion, followed by anger, followed by harsh disdain. 'You fucking poof,' he hissed. I tried to walk away, but he grabbed my arm and ordered me to walk with him. I didn't resist, even as my mind was churning. My life was literally in his hands now. He took me down a quiet path, into the undergrowth, where he presented me with a proposition.

'You faggot, you have a choice,' he told me. 'I will beat the living crap out of you. Or you can suck this,' as he pulled out his penis.

I had no choice. I did as I was bid. What followed was eighteen months of the same meeting, the same result, in the same bushes, in the same roles. I did as I was told because I knew I had no option. Of course, I could have tried to out him too, but the fear of discovery, and the fear of physical violence was too much.

In truth, our relationship changed gradually too. On occasion, he would speak to me. Once he brought me a gift of a few flowers he had pulled from one of the seedbeds in the park. But the baseline was always the same, of cruel sexual dominance and abuse set against the fear of discovery and the desperate desire for acceptance as a female.

What ended the charade was my delayed puberty. Eighteen months later, I could no longer even remotely hide the changes to my body. I believe my physiology fought the change right up to the last minute, but the twisted plan for me eventually came to pass. My voice deepened, my arms thickened, and hair grew on my chin. I couldn't publicly be Abi anymore without obviously being something else, nor could my tormentor pretend I was anything other.

Which was at the root of his abuse. If he could convince himself what he forced me to do was not gay sex, then he could persuade himself that he was not gay. His public behaviour towards anything he saw as effeminate was obvious. In my life, I have often found that those who protest the most have the most to hide themselves. Just look at J Edgar Hoover.

Our relationship, if you want to call it that, ended as quickly as it had begun. The legacy remains with me to this day. The two formative sexual experiences of my youth were both abusive ones by older men while I was dressed as a woman because I am one.

You try coming back from that.

I had a secret and private domain in the big house. I adored living there. It was a big, cold, and draughty place, with a ghost that mysteriously moved things about the place. You'd come down in the morning and a glass would be broken, or an ornament moved, but I always felt the spirit was a good presence. I never felt anything but love in that house. That home was my refuge.

I hid in the loft. It was floored with pine, the walls oak panels. The space was unheated, in winter my breath spiralled around me in pale wisps, but up there in the eaves, I could live undisturbed. Nobody ever went up there but me. There were two annexes off the main space. In both rooms, I had a shoebox of stolen women's clothes, trinkets, and newspaper clippings, hidden under the floorboards. I collected fashion articles make-up tips and pictures of glamorous women I wanted to emulate. The loft was my private home, where I could lock the door and soar. The stairs to the top were ridiculously steep and winding. My parents never ventured there. I knew I was safe. I would only be disturbed by the door opening and a shouted hail to come down for dinner. I would have time to hide, time to cover up, time to revert to my disguise for the other world I lived in.

I would secretly put on a couple of easily disguised items of girl's clothing, to make myself feel happier, and sit and read. I loved books, for they took me away to another place. There was no internet, no google, no means of reaching out to the wider world without books. Each week, I would go to the large and forbidding public library on my way home from school and borrow a huge pile of heavy hardbacks. That was how I learned about the world. When I found an author I liked, I would obsessively mine everything they had written.

While I was fascinated by history, my interest was more in the people who inhabit the subject. Even at that early age, I wanted to know what motivated them, their strengths and weaknesses, the lucky confluences of fate that brought their disparate characters together. That study of social history was not what I was taught at school – which was all didactic learning of dates, places, and great events – but was, I think, an early indication of the person I might have been had I not been hide-bound by the conventions of gender. As much as was interested in human beings, the more I withdrew from human beings and human life.

While my classmates were out playing football and trying to get off with girls, I found a new hobby to indulge my fantasies: Dungeons and Dragons. In that imagined world of goblins and heroes, I could create my own Tolkien-inspired fantasy of beautiful princesses and handsome princes. The published books were woefully thin on female characters to inhabit, so I devised my own. My favourite was a character of a houri, which was later to become part of the established folklore of the hobby. I imagined myself in the role of a scantily clad Amazon, who could equally dispatch an enemy with her bare hands, or entrance with her beauty and dancing skills. And the best part? None of my fellow dungeoneers thought any the worse of me for my created fantasy figure. That was, indeed, the entire point of Dungeons and Dragons: to become somebody else entirely in a world that could never exist. And in any case, those of us who did play were the odd-ones-out of our peer group. The ones who didn't fit in anywhere else, the be-spectacled and diffident ones for whom winning a sporting colour at school rugby was not just a distant dream, but anathema itself. Nobody was gonna judge me in my lovely group of nerds for my imagined fantasy character.

Paradoxically, the more I secretly indulged my inner self, and the happier it made me, the more liked and popular I became at school. At the start of the second year, you could have blown me over with a feather when I was unanimously voted as class captain. Hardly taking the White House, I hear you say, but at the start of my

second year, I suddenly found myself being accepted by my peers in a way
I would never have thought possible. The job didn't mean much in reality: all I had to do was keep a tab on the daily and weekly attendance register, and occasionally represent the class for master-inspired pep talks, but I was very flattered.

Unfortunately, my new-found confidence at school, even if enhanced by my afternoons off from sports, was rapidly undermined by a worsening situation at home. My parents had seriously overextended themselves financially, and it was causing a huge amount of strain on the family relationships.

BANGKOK, 2007

Dr. Suporn sat me up in bed. The pain was almost too intense to bear. My head was bound in swathes of thick bandages, gauze, and padding. My head looked like an ice-cream cone, heavy with dressings on top, tapering down to my chin below. Around my chest, I had been wrapped so tightly in gauze and bandages that I could hardly breathe. Alongside his work to change my facial appearance, sawing into my skull, he had implanted 270cc breast augmentations.

Four days earlier, he had explained to me that, once only, he could make an incision under my armpit, from where he would place the implants. They would sit under my chest muscles, so the implant itself would be near impossible to spot. In time, my natural breast tissue growth, enhanced by the flow of the hormone patches I will wear for the rest of my natural life, would fill around the implants.

This day was the day of days when I would get to see the results of his handwork for the first time. I had been lying down, unable to move, for the previous four days. Dr Suporn and a nurse gently elevated me into an upright position. I groaned with the effort and the pain. For the first time ever, I felt the weight of my new chest. For years, I had stuffed old socks down my brassiere and dreamed of this moment. Now, I felt my new body change and move beneath my touch. For the first time, I couldn't easily cross my arms over my chest. There was something else there now. My, it was odd: but incredibly moving. Oh, my….to feel the curve of my body, the roundness, and the weight. I burst into tears. With this one, simple moment of joy, the dam broke all over again. I grasped Dr S's hand. He was my saviour, this kind, gentle man, who I had come to visit with as a penitent pilgrim. That morning was the first of many transformative stages where my chrysalis came to slowly peel away.

I had breasts of my own.

What wonderful happiness.

ABERDEEN 1978

The big house was when my daddy started to go out of control. It wasn't until decades later that I learned he had fallen in love with somebody else. I was told he had met the love of his life, a PA in the same television company. He made the decision to stay with his wife and family. Which must have cut to the core: but whatever the pain, he bore it alone, as he did with all his emotions. He chose what he saw as his duty over his personal happiness. He never permitted himself the reasoning that he may have made a mistake.

My father was an only child, the same as he was deliberately alone as a man, husband, and father. He made his decisions alone and he lived with the consequences alone too.

Whatever the reason, he began to drink – a lot. And he wasn't around much either, forever working for more overtime. The pressure of paying for the massive pile of a house must have been intense. The dam broke when Independent Television went on strike for more money. The money tree stopped shaking.

Not helped by having two of us at public school. One day, the headmaster came by our class and asked me to step outside to talk to him. Now that set the cat amongst the pigeons. Stifled giggles and nudges filled the room.

In those days, teachers were limited in the number of strokes of the tawse they could administer, but the head had unlimited corporal punishment rights. A call to visit with him invariably meant very bruised hands.

We didn't go to his office. The head merely informed me he was very unhappy to ask me to do this, handing me a brown envelope to deliver to my father. I did as I was told. I gave it to him at the dinner table: and watched as he opened it and put his head in his hands. He never showed it to me, but it must have been the final demand for the fees.

My father went back after nine weeks out, but the ship was holed below the waterline. Besides his job at Grampian, he started doing extra work in the evenings, which meant I saw even less of him. My private domain was invaded to further lessen the financial burden. My wonderful refuge suddenly filled with boarders. My brother and I bunked together again as a succession of strange men filled all the spare rooms. Which must have been something of a déjà vu moment for my mother, as she recollected her own Belfast boarding house childhood. No matter that I lived in the grand house, I stopped bringing school chums over after we met a rather drunk oil rig worker on the stairs one day. I made up a story that he was a long-lost cousin, but my shame was apparent. All for the great God of money and an over-extended lifestyle.

My father worked every weekend on outside broadcasts. The gig came with a very healthy expenses allowance, which must have helped, but it meant he was never around when we were off school, leaving my mother to pick up the pieces. As I was going through my own personal hell with my park abuser and the usual sullenness of teenage years, I couldn't have been a lot of fun to be around either.

When my father came home, he'd be regaled with tales of how I had been argumentative, difficult, or sullen. Invariably his weekend away had involved a fair amount of alcohol, and some hidden guilt about proximity to his PA. His return invariably resulted in a beating for me. As the oldest, no matter what the issue was between the three brothers, I was somehow held accountable as the oldest 'man' in the household.

My nadir came when he went away to America for a business trip. By the time he got back, the atmosphere between my mother and I was truly toxic. She was in the middle of one of her pill-enhanced mood swings, and I was completely riven internally about my identity. We'd argued pretty much every day he had been away. When he got back, I went to bed early, and my father cracked open the whisky bottle.

I'd taken to wearing one of my mother's nightdresses, but, for whatever reason, that night, I'd taken it off early, in my usual desire/disgust cycle of despair at myself. Which was timely.

Just as I'd put head to pillow, my father burst into the room and dragged me out of bed by the hair. He pulled a good handful out by the roots. He dragged me across the landing and kicked me down the flights of stairs of our soaring foyer, rolling downstairs all the way. At the bottom, he pulled me to my feet, put me against the wall and punched me in the face, before dragging me into the study, where my mother sat with a face like thunder, nursing a martini. My father forced me to my knees, as I spat blood onto the carpet, and forced me to lick my mother's shoes and beg her forgiveness. He then threw me into the hall and slammed the door behind him.

I sat in that hall for a long time. Then I went to the bathroom and washed the blood off my face.

That, dear reader, was only one beating. They lasted right up until I was big enough to hit him back. Then we went through a period of slugging it out, including one epic in the back garden that went several rounds, before I got strong enough to best him. Strangely enough, the beatings stopped then, even if his drinking didn't. Once my father started on the whisky, you could judge his mood swings on the spin of a penny. He just got that look in his eye, and out came the usual; 'so you think so, do you???'

And then we'd be off, duelling windmills.

I stopped loving him a long time ago, even when he got older and less dogmatic and goddam aggressive. Even now I can't help but swear when I think of him. I owe him the work sacrifice he made to provide for my education, but I can't ever say I ever loved him. I feared him, sure, but that is a different thing. And not a very healthy one for a father/ son dynamic.

Right before I became Abi, my mother despaired of my very infrequent visits. I'd hug her briefly, but I only ever shook my father's hand. The memories were too strong. She asked me to hold my father, she said he'd appreciate it. I did what she asked, but only as quickly and as perfunctorily as I could get away with. Even when he was shrunken with age, and half-deaf, I just couldn't forget. Maybe if he'd written me a different letter when I was in boarding school…then again, maybe not.

Not that it makes any difference now. They are dead now, and they took their hatred of me to the grave. But I'm ahead of myself again.

Back then, I was in a fair old pickle. I found my saving grace in a uniform.

DREAMING OF SOLDIERS

My school was a recruitment ground for the army to find its next generation officers. A roving recruitment team visited the public schools to deliver a lecture that was purely designed to offer us young ones a sugar rush of glamour of slides of foreign travel and good-looking folks in uniform having the time of their lives.

I hadn't yet twigged to the class apartheid of the army, but the officer recruiting team only went to the posh schools – and then only the schools with boys. If you went to a state school, you'd have to go find them. Girls weren't recruited at all. It was the sort of glass ceiling stuff that kept the 7% in the officer's mess. I was in that 7% of privately educated folks.

The announcement was made at assembly by the headmaster. Leave was given to attend a lecture by the army recruiting team in the main hall at 1100. I wasn't that excited. Except that at 1100 that day, I had physics, which I detested with every fibre of my being. Science and mathematics were my mortal enemies. A chance to bunk off physics? I was in.

We duly assembled, to find the stage draped with a large camouflage net set behind a projector screen. Signs either side of the stage displayed huge posters of a man on a surfboard and on the other side the same handsome man laughing in a bar with a gaggle of beautiful women huddled around him. Both posters had the strap line, 'life in the army'.

There was a soldier fussing by a projector, resplendent in his green trousers and jumper, all business and efficiency. The sounds of a brass band echoed from the PA, playing the theme from 'Lawrence of Arabia'. My sense memories were already twitching.

And then, without a word, we fell into silence, as the most incredibly handsome man strode from the back of the hall. It was the man in the posters. Black boots, green trousers, camouflage smock, with a belt casually slung low, his thumbs insouciantly looped within. A shock of long-ish blonde hair, drooping sideburns, moustache, full lips, a broad smile. And on his head, a maroon beret. Within it, a silver badge, of outstretched wings. He was as glamorous as Elvis in 'GI Blues'.

The music faded and he introduced himself as a captain in The Parachute Regiment. He was going to tell us about his 6 years in the army and his tour of Northern Ireland. And then he was going to tell us how we could join him in his Regiment as an officer.

Oh, my.

All my memories: of Belfast, of the paratrooper in my gran's front garden, of watching 'Lawrence', of Elvis in 'GI Blues', my dreams of being in another place and space.

They all coalesced in that one young officer.

My dreams were no longer dreams. They were reality. This man wasn't in a film, he didn't live in another fantasy world. He was right there in front of me, promising me I could join him one day....

I fell instantly in love. With him, with The Regiment, with the world it offered. That was the day my life changed forever.

After his talk ended, I waited as everybody left. He was confidently talking to the headmaster. Everything he said had been presented with such assurance. He stood with such poise, forward on his toes, using his hands to point with a karate chop, his smile always following. Oh, to be so self-assured!

There was a map of Belfast on display, where he had been stationed. He saw me waiting and came over. I had so many questions. All I could think of was to point to my old school and say 'the road on this map is in the wrong place...'

He just laughed while I squirmed. And then he said,

'Well, the next time I am there, maybe you'll be there too, to help me find the right road....'

I have never blushed so vividly or so profoundly in my life. If he'd asked me to marry him, I'd have been all in, no quibbles.

Then and there, I knew The Regiment was my destiny. I was going to get there, one way or the other. And everything they stood for was instantly deified in my eyes. I was obsessed. The Regiment was how I was going to get out of Aberdeen. The Regiment was what would save me.

There was one fatal flaw in my new obsession. Women weren't allowed in The Parachute Regiment, indeed in the late 1970s barely allowed in the army at all. But I also knew I could fix that. Had I not been living a double life for years already? Could I not continue to act that part? And once in my dream, like Lawrence, I would be free to be me.

There's a scene in the film where O'Toole abandons his male western uniform and adopts Arab dish-dash, a stunning cream garment, edged in gold, that looks remarkably like an evening dress on a woman. O'Toole was so pretty it could easily have been just that – Florence of Arabia. His delight in the film at dressing that way had struck a hugely deep chord in me.

I could do that. All I had to do was get in and then my dreams could be my life.

I had found a role model. Until that moment, movies had been my closest companion. A fantasy. Yet, here he was, flesh, and blood, right in front of me. This was reality – achievable reality.

Then 16th August 1977 rolled by.

It might not mean much to you, but to me it was calamitous. That was the day Elvis died. He'd been there all my life, smiling down at me. He hadn't released any more movies for a few years, but I had been to see his two concert films, when he was deep into his jumpsuit pomp. I was as riveted by Elvis the live performer as I had been by Elvis the screen actor. In his later period, he'd started doing show tunes, songs about longing, loss, change and regret. I deeply related to all of that.

I was eating my lunch at home when the news came through on the radio that he had died. I stood up and left the room. I found my tape recorder, went up to the loft and refused to leave. I didn't go back to school for the rest of the week. Even my parents understood something deep within me had broken and I was wrestling with something very profound indeed. It was the first time in my life I had to deal with death and existential grief.

Elvis' death became the day I grew up.

I knew I was on my own then. My protector had left me. I could still revel in his music, my imagined perception of who he had been. But he wasn't going to arrive from Hawaii and rescue me. Not ever. I was so isolated from the world, so wrapped around my own private existence that his loss was very, very real to me. When the beatings got too bad, I'd always drifted off to be with him.

I resolved to find my own reality.

It took a couple of years to put it all together, and it came in the form of yet more films, but put it together I truly did:

The first film was 'A Bridge Too Far'. This was one of those starry 1970s compendium of all the matinee idols of the day fulfilling small cameos in service to a broader narrative. In this case, the true story of the Allied Airborne efforts to secure a lightning strike against the Germans at the tail end of 1944. Central to the entire story is The Parachute Regiment. The Arnhem adventure was an epic failure, fatally undermined by dreadful planning and over confidence. But the actual fight was a testament to the endurance of the individual and the cohesiveness of the team. They belonged together, fought, and died for each other, and did so in the kind of censored 1970s gallant way where gunshot wounds were marked by a splash of ketchup and soldiers died gracefully in a kind of 'kiss me Hardy' homo-erotic embrace. This wasn't combat as I would later find it, but it was the kind of 'losing with grit' existence I readily understood then. To be the underdog, to be badly beaten, but to find a way through, to carry on, to survive, to never give up.

Here was my newfound role model, real life paratrooper captain being portrayed on the screen in my fantasy world. The two dimensions collided violently.

I adored it.

Sean Connery played the British paratrooper general. Again, a chime in my head. Here was a paratrooper with a Scottish accent and a moustache, looking the same as the paratrooper I remembered from my grandmother's front garden. I could relate directly to that. What struck me was Connery's power. He was 47 when he made Bridge, still in his matinee idol days. He ran like a lion,

Sugar and Spice

all shoulder roll, straight, direct. That was hugely impressive to me. I immediately changed my own solitary running gait to emulate his.

What manner of people were these? Even the Nazi's tanks couldn't defeat them. They just laughed and drove on…I was completely hooked…

I loved co-stars Robert Redford, James Caan and Ryan O'Neal, but they were the American paratroopers. That was fantasy. Here was Connery being what I'd just seen in my school hall.

This was all achievable. I'd seen it with my own eyes. I'd been invited to join them.

I still had to overcome my fear of men, of being around male society, of not being afraid to play rugby with them, or share a communal shower. How was a girl like me going to overcome all of that?

The answer came in another film, of a very different variety.

That film was 'Yentl'. Directed by and starring Barbra Streisand, it tells the story of a young Jewish woman denied the right to study in a male-only Yeshiva by virtue of her gender. So, she disguises herself as a man and enters the world of men.

Yentl was delicious to me.

She learns to be with men by adopting their mannerisms, their speech, their walk, and to out-think them with her intellect. She hides within them by becoming them. She also finds a protector, a man as handsome as my paratrooper captain, and the two have a very carefully expressed obsession for each other. The film ends with Yentl having discovered what she was looking for and setting out on a boat for a new horizon - America.

There was my solution - what I had to do to make my own dream come true.

I took Yentl's example to heart and learned to be Sean Connery without changing who I am inside. I would use The Parachute Regiment to get me out of Aberdeen. I would find my protector and have adventures together, just as Lawrence had done. In the end, I would leave it all behind, reveal who I really am, and set sail to find America, exactly as Yentl had done. Off to the land where Elvis had lived.

I figured all that out myself. I didn't have a role model to rely on, or anybody to discuss any this with, but I knew then what I had to do. And if you look over the trajectory of the next fifty years of my life, that's exactly what I did do.

My first hurdle was to get manly.

I needed help for this bit. There was one teacher I looked up to.

Most of them were the usual sausage-machine delivery agents for getting you through exams. I don't remember many of them, they were inter-changeable. Several merely walked into the classroom, turned their back on us, then wrote on a chalkboard without a sound as we sat there copying what was written.

Doug Stewart was different. He's dead now, and I mourn his passing, for he was a true inspiration to me. He taught history, which was right down my lane, but he brought it to life by talking to us about the human beings behind the big moments in our world's narrative. He'd strike up a discussion and a conversation. I vividly remember him asking me what I thought Kerensky should have done once he knew Lenin had arrived in St Petersburg. Should he have arrested him? Should he have him assassinated? We went through truth and consequence. I took my first lesson in the demands of leadership and how history can turn on a pin.

This was radical for 1970s Scotland. We pupils weren't expected to speak. We spent forty minutes in a classroom, then a bell would ring, and we'd shuffle off like penitents to another classroom for another forty minutes of turgidity. Doug tried to change that – and he didn't use the tawse to exert his authority.

We had one teacher who, on the first day of every term, would single out a child and whip him at random, just to set the scene for what he expected for the rest of the term. All of this was not only tolerated it was encouraged.

Doug didn't need to do that. He had this natural authority and charisma that enchanted me.

He had been an officer during the war, and after had been in Palestine, witnessing the King David Hotel bombing. He told me of his deep sympathy for the Jewish cause and how, at the end of the mandate, he had deliberately and conveniently allowed British tanks to be left behind so the Israeli state should have a chance in the war to come. That moral decision, to do the thing you believed in, spoke deeply to me.

I was all in, 2 for 0. First my Parachute Regiment lecturer, now Doug. Two men I admired, both products of the army.

He'd been where I wanted to go, and I quizzed him on my route to market. I was very earnest, stood by to make notes. He asked me what part of the army I wanted to join, and I told him The Parachute Regiment. He didn't laugh at all, which, given I was reed thin and barely ten stone, was remarkably sympathetic of him. My notes from his advice that day?

1. Get fit, get really fit.
2. Get determined to succeed, get really determined.
3. Get used to ignoring 'no', get really used to that.

I obviously didn't tell him about the other part, about the Yentl story. That was too personal by far. Half my story would stay hidden for decades to come.

He asked me to keep him up to date on progress. He stayed really interested in my development right up to when I left school and went off to the army for real. I've always sought out father figures because I didn't have one of my own. Doug was the first. And the one that gave me the confidence to find my road.

In my quest to get fit, I'd heard from somewhere that an ability to climb ropes was a vital skill for paratroopers. No idea where I'd picked that up, but off to the gym department I went and secured permission to climb the 20 metre ropes in the gym during my lunchbreak. Which is exactly what I did, every day for a year. Much to the bemusement of the gym staff, who barely knew who I was, I progressed from ropes to the horse to the rings. All the tropes of gymnastics, and I got to be pretty good.

Kung Fu and Bruce Lee were very much in vogue. We all went around karate chopping each other. I knew Elvis had done karate, and I'd been spellbound at his stage performances on film, where he bounded across the stage in a stylised demonstration of kicks and flurries. I took up Tae Kwon Do. I had the gymnastic part already sorted, and in short order I was doing the splits and high kicking ceiling lamps.

I volunteered for the rugby squad. I didn't do it for the playing part, I did it because they trained in the gym three times a week. It was my only way to get into circuits, to build up my cardio fitness. The price the staff exacted was that I'd also turn out for the squad. I'd have to play rugby. Turn out, I did. I discovered very quickly that I had no desire to put my head in between the ass cheeks of two other men, so the scrum was out. I also rediscovered my small hands and lack of ability to throw and catch put the back line out of contention too. However, I did discover that I had an ability to run very fast when chased, so off to the wing I went, where essentially all I had to do was catch the ball once, run faster than everybody else and fling myself and the ball over the line. I got to be quite good at that and turned out for the 1st XV a couple of times. I was a rather one trick pony, though. I was execrably useless at kicking a ball and tactically rather hopeless. I fundamentally wasn't interested in the game. But – critically – it was another part of my Yentl strategy complete.

What made my joy complete was that dear old Doug Stewart, my history teacher, turned out on game day to watch and cheer me on from the touchlines. Somebody was interested in me…Of my own father, he didn't even know I played rugby. We rarely conversed. He never once turned out for anything I did. Ever. But I was already disassociated from him. I just took that as the natural order of things.

I got to be very athletic. I was careful not to get big, I was after that long, lean bodycon look, with slim hips. Those were the days when you can make your body do anything, and I revelled in it. All the usual tropes of handstands and cartwheels.

My rugby career came to a sudden and deserved end. A mis-timed tackle saw my eye socket badly gouged by a stud and I received a dozen stitches. The scar still visible to this day. I decided there and then that I wanted to stay as pretty as possible and ended the madness forthwith.

I found another sport, that of orienteering, and revelled in it. It suited my solitary nature and my running ability. At one time, I came 3rd in the Scottish championships. I discovered I had an innate ability to read ground and orient myself that was to prove rather useful much later in combat. Once again, Doug Stewart supported me. Orienteering was a niche activity, off the curriculum. I organised my own participation, but Doug took to meeting and running me to the events, waiting patiently for me to finish.

Before you say it, there was no exploitation in this. This wasn't boarding school. He just believed in me. Maybe it was him fulfilling a military bond, I don't know. He certainly recognised my sensitivity and how hard I was trying to be something other than my natural self. Maybe he saw something of that rebellious nature in his own history of giving tanks to Jews. He's gone now and I never asked him. But I do know I wouldn't have made The Regiment had he not been there for me. Nobody else was.

For all this temporary success at school, at home things remained as ludicrously fragile as ever. My mother's mental health was not in a good place, and we lived in fear of the consequences. She had gone back to work teaching typing and shorthand, but that only reminded her of the iniquity of her existence next to my father. He had been promoted again and was now the head of outside broadcasts. His weeks and weekends were spent as a road manager, producing the big showbiz spectacles of the time. A life of locations, parties and mingling with the stars. I rarely saw him, and if he was around, it was generally in the evenings. All three of us would go to bed not knowing if the volcanic temper would appear, the bedroom door would be flung open, and we'd receive another battering for something unknown and unexplained.

It happened less to me, though. One time he tried dragging me out of bed, but I was now fit and strong, and held his grasp. I wasn't yet at the stage where I'd hit him back, but he realised I wasn't the easily vanquished anymore.

I found myself trying to be the conciliator in the family. Making sure my brothers were protected, taking the blame on my shoulders. Finding the right thing to say in the middle of a brewing argument, trying to keep my mother calm and prevent another melodramatic scene. Reading the room became a critical skill.

It got very Norma Desmond.

A successful band at the time was called 'Boney M'. Three ultra-glam women and a mad-cap dancing male in skin-tight leggings. I loved their flamboyant costumes, uber-camp styling, and ear worm songs. In the 1970's 'Top of the Pops' was a Thursday evening family viewing ritual. They had a hit with a protest song about my birthplace – a song called 'Belfast'. We all watched it together. Mid-song, my mother stood up and walked out of room. My 6th sense twitched. Minutes later, I heard the front door open. We all went after her. She was stood in the doorway, with tears in her eyes, and announced,

'I am going home....'

She was off to Belfast, the city she'd never wanted to leave. My father went to grab her. I grabbed him and told him, 'I'll do it.'

She was on the drive by the time I reached her. I got down on my knees in front of her and begged her to stay with us because we needed her. I didn't mean my father; I meant my brothers and me.

It paused on a knife-edge. Behind me, the traffic buzzed past. The rest of the family stood in the porch watching. My mother stood there a long time. And then she stared at me with such violence in her eyes. She knew she had been emotionally bested. She turned and came back.

As with everything in that house, it was never spoken of again. Nothing was ever resolved. Except that my mother and I parted that day. She never forgave me for reminding her of her fate and her responsibilities as a mother. We never recovered from that. And when it came time for her to get rid of me, she did so with no regret.

At the root of my parent's issue was their basic incompatibility as human beings. My mother needed calm love to restrain her melodrama. My father was incapable of expression of love. He was an introvert and a loner. He'd persuaded her to leave the love of her family behind to pursue his dream of riches, and they had done a devil's deal for the money. It ended up with my mother tied to three children she didn't want and my father leaving her behind for a life of glamour he almost stumbled into by accident. They transferred all their own unhappiness onto us.

They were fervent in their desire for us to pursue their version of a life dream. Which failed to take account of the fatal flaw in all of this; we were our own human beings, with our own dreams.

The realities of life brought the family down each week. They could have lived a middle-class life of some comfort had they been willing to compromise. Yes, the house was big, but they could have afforded it without the long line of boarders and absent parenting had they not also decided to send all three of us to a private school. My father earned big, but not that big. They had a choice to make; the big house and the respected and free Grammar School for us, or a smaller house and private schooling. For my parents, though, that compromise would have been a rebuttal of their own working-class aspiration and the jealousies inspired at Cambridge. In consequence, they pushed on with a life that was beyond their means and a marriage that was equally unhappy. My brothers and I more than paid the price for their obstinacy.

Of my secret me, I had changed so much physically that I could no longer venture outside. However, I did still have my shoe boxes hidden all over the house. My life continued to be split between the public me and the private person. It made getting up in the morning a difficult moment. Not like now. I woke to a body that didn't belong to me. Wore clothes I didn't want to wear. And was forced to behave in ways I didn't want to behave. I got to be quite good at mimicking men in their mannerisms, but I could never truly wipe out who I am. When I look at pictures of then, you can see my feet instinctively in a ballet pose, or a hand on a hip, or a fringe carefully placed.

What you'll also see is a wariness in my eyes that increased as the years progressed. I was a wounded bird, alright. In time, that made me quite attractive to women. I could never shed my innate sensitivity, and the softness of my features never really left me, for all the effects that testosterone wreaked. But I was so, so careful then, and would continue to be for many decades to come. It wasn't schizophrenia, nor any mental illness. I am an intelligent person. I just devoted all my waking consciousness to divining the moment when I could manage the risk, revel in who I am, and to getting though those terrible days when it was impossible.

There was no question of talking to somebody about any of this. I would have been seen as homosexual. Homosexuality was illegal. The church, which was very powerful then, had condemned homosexuality as mortal sin. When 'The Omen' came out, it was a movie sensation. In the film, the boy Damien is marked as the son of the Devil. He finds this out by discovering the number of the Devil – 666 – on the back of his neck. I was so convinced of my existence as a sinner and criminal, I remember spending hours looking in the mirror, examining my scalp for the same numbers. As horrific as that may sound, I wanted answers.

Children don't know they are different until adults tell them.

I applied to the school amateur dramatics club. I had an audition and was offered the lead in a Tennessee Williams production. I was awfully excited. I have always been in love with acting and the dramatic arts. I rushed home to tell my mother. Who balefully looked at me and said, 'There will be no homosexuals in this house.' Now that's a confluence of a lot of misconceptions, but that's what she told me. I was terrified my double life would be under the family microscope again. I turned the drama folks down and put that dream on ice.

I developed a desire to dance. I was fit and lithe then. I was quite entranced by Gene Kelly, even more so by Cyd Charisse. Such an exquisite dancer. My interest went off the scale when I saw Lisa Minelli in Fosse's 'Cabaret'. Oh, the delicious and exquisite joy of bohemian Weimer Germany. This desire was harder to navigate, as society was against male dancing, which was again somehow seen as homosexual. A confluence of prejudice. I found a jazz and tap class and secretly went off to dance once a week with a bunch of middle-aged housewives who gently indulged and fussed over me. I soon gave up in frustration. For them, it was an evening distraction. For me, it was too intense a desire to dance to be just fun. Not to mention confusing. I loved the whole spandex and leg warmer Olivia Newton John vibe of it, but that was far too risky to be seen doing.

Dance was a mask for my inner desire and belief. I wasn't Gene Kelly, I was Cyd Charisse. I couldn't take the risk of any of that being exposed again.

I never had the necessary confidence to follow through on being an actor or a dancer. I would have loved to have been either or both. Neither was permitted.

It was the army that came to the rescue. I was desperate to find a way to self-express, to dress up, to be somebody more flamboyant than my circumstance dictated. I found the Combined Cadet Force.

We weren't a 'force' of any kind, merely a bunch of kids. My school had a branch of this military supported organisation. Kind of Boy Scouts with added marching and limited exposure to guns. Most critically for me, it came with a uniform. This was dress-up! And it looked exactly like the clothes Sean Connery had taken Arnhem Bridge in. They had me at hello. That uniform was my equivalent of Elvis' jumpsuit.

Of course, the whole thing was a feeder for the military, but that was exactly what I was after. I had my mission, to join my gorgeous blonde Parachute Regiment captain and examine that map of Belfast together. If this was the apprenticeship, lead me to it.

As soon as I was old enough, I was down there in cadet corps HQ, listening to the welcome brief. I learned that we could stay until the end of our school days, and that one of us would be made the Sergeant Major. From the beginning it was a pyramid, competitive environment. But I also learned we would be taught to live outdoors, to fire a rifle and to work as a team. We would learn self-confidence.

My, the army hit all my buttons in all the right order. Self-confidence? I was desperately short of the stuff.

I looked around the room at all the usual rugby jocks and the popular kids and wondered which one of them would be the Sergeant Major? It was idle speculation. I was in this for me. This was another step up in my escape ladder.

I joined up that very day. The tailor took my waist measurement – 24 inches. My uniform arrived the next week. A huge bundle of clothes, still in their plastic wrappers. I'd never had new clothes before. Everything I had outside of my school uniform were cast offs from my cousins or mother. I remember peeling off the plastic and inhaling the smell of them. They were new and they were mine, unworn by anybody before me. The army was bounteous indeed.

We changed there and then, and my gawky, awkward body disappeared before my eyes. Black boots, brown putties – long lengths of cloth wrapped around the ankles - camouflage trousers with hip pockets, khaki woollen shirt with breast pockets, and over it all a green jumper with cloth elbow and shoulder pads. On our right arm, we had a brassard with an embroidered 'Combined Cadet Force' in gold lettering over a blue backcloth.

I was most taken with the shirt and jumper combo. The breast pockets gave me a faint, but discernible bust. Oh, my.

And to top it all off, we put on our hats. Being Scottish, we were issued a traditional Glengarry, a black side cap with red and white dicing down both sides, a red bobble on top, and two long black ribbons that hung down the back to our shoulders. I loved that I had ribbons in my hair. All emblazoned with a silver badge of a stag's head and antlers, the symbol of the Gordon Highlanders, our local Regiment.

I had never felt so glamorous in my entire life.

I refused to change, bagged up my school uniform and proudly took the bus home in my army greens. From being a nonentity, people now looked at me differently. Women smiled at me, men nodded and acknowledged me. I had acquired a superpower.

I walked in the back door, late for dinner, and stood there in my uniform. The family was sat around the table. Normally, this would have kicked off another towering rage. That night, for the first time in a long time, my father sat in silence, just looking at me, as I stood there, trembling under his gaze, hesitatingly proud of what I had done. He stood up, walked over to me, and put his arm on my shoulder. I took my Glengarry off, and he tousled my hair. 'Come have some dinner, soldier,' he told me.

That is the one and only time I ever remember receiving his praise. But it wasn't really me that he was praising. It was a suit of clothes. I had fooled them all. My Yentl disguise was in place. Now, I had to prove to myself I was worthy. Like Lawrence, I had to not care that it hurt when I burned myself with a lit match. My challenge would be as much mental as physical, but I would persevere.

I was twelve. I had started to live my military dream. The first escape plan from the pain of how I had been forced to live had begun.

A COMBINED CADET

I spent five years as a cadet. I loved it. Cadet Day was Tuesday, and we were allowed to wear our uniform to school that day as rollcall was immediately after lessons. That was the day I got to show off. It was also the day I got to wear tights to school. I deemed hose too much risk in normal trousers in case my ankles showed. But with putties, my trousers were tucked in. That was acceptable risk. I was a very happy cadet.

We were a remarkably belligerent lot. The school had its own armoury, which held a hundred Lee Enfield rifles, a handful of light machine guns, and a mortar. We also had our own indoor shooting range, with converted .22 rifles to use. The older pupils were allowed to supervise the younger ones on the range. 16-year-olds supervised 12-year-olds firing bolt action rifles, discharging a bullet that could kill you. Remarkable.

Twice a year, we traipsed out to the army barracks at Bridge of Don and fired full bore .303 rifles and light machine guns on 300 metre ranges. I first did this at fourteen. I could barely lift the rifle into the shoulder. Firing my first round in a standing position, the recoil knocked me over. Everybody merely laughed.

On those Tuesday evenings, we learned small unit tactics, practising in the playground how to flank enemy machine gun posts, using whistle blasts to guide us. We learned target recognition, and how to build camouflaged positions. We learned battlefield first aid – how to treat a gunshot wound. We learned how to sleep out in the woods under a poncho. We learned how to use a bayonet. And we did an awful lot of marching. And then did some more marching.

Three times a year, we went on camps.

Two of those were camping expeditions into the Cairngorms, in October and March. Neither were pleasant months to be camped in the heather. Our commander was one of the gym staff, his deputy the religious affairs teacher. Both had been at D-Day. They were ridiculously competent, but I am convinced neither would be let near children today. Instead of tents, we slept in bin bags, wading rainwater swollen streams during snowstorms, camping up remote valleys, in an age before mobiles had been invented, hours away from any rescue. I remember going swimming in a lochan in the middle of winter sleet, shivering and laughing at the same time at the insanity of it.

The third camp was in the summer, for a week, in a place called Cultybraggan, near Stirling. This had been an Italian POW camp during the war, and we slept in the same Nissen huts they had. During the day, we fired our rifles again, and happily ran about the hills practising our pretend attacks.

I adored every second of it. Steadily, I rose the ranks, gained all those little achievement badges for tactics and shooting that mean so much when you are young.

And then, finally, when it came my year's turn, it was me who became the Sergeant Major. I beat all the jocks and the popular kids. I got picked, and I couldn't have been prouder. The day I got my sergeant major's badge of a crown to wear on my sleeve, I marched up to accept the applause from the school, and equally proudly felt the silky sheen of my tights under my trousers.

I'd proven I could be tough enough for the army. But equally, I had proven to myself I could do it on my own terms. That was my Yentl high-water mark at school.

Intellectually, I'd been doing alright. I have literally zero interest or aptitude for mathematics or the sciences. I'd got around the Scottish exam sausage machine by realising the didactic nature of it all. If you could regurgitate facts, you could manage a pass. With maths, you were required to deliver four proofs randomly selected from a portfolio of ten. I literally learned every single one as hieroglyphics. I had absolutely zero idea what any of them meant. Nor am I interested to find out. But come exam day, out I trotted the selected four formulas: letter and number perfect. That got me close enough to the wire to cuff a 'B'. As much a surprise to my teacher as me.

It was the same with the classics. I memorised 400 lines of the Aeneid, word perfect. To get me over the top, I knew I had to answer two essay questions, which were of the nature of 'evaluate Octavian's victory at Actium in establishing the system of Emperor'. Not overly exciting. But I noticed down at the bottom of the lengthy potential list; 'describe the dress, jewellery and make-up of Roman women'. I reckoned that the sole female question would come up, just to fill the quota. Plus, I was genuinely fascinated by the subject. I was particularly taken by the fact that Caesar divorced Pompeia, his second wife, because he caught her in a clincher with another man - who was dressed as a woman. Sauce indeed for my confused ears. And the question on jewellery did indeed turn up. Aced that exam. But I never told a soul that the question I'd answered was on using soot as eye shadow and mascara made from crushed ants.

My conflicted and torn life was beginning to work. Like so many persecuted generations before me, I'd found a way to live with risk. I couldn't deny who I am. I worked a compromise that was painful, but which did let me exist. It wasn't joyous in the slightest. A never-ending howl round loop fraught with consequence without conclusion. Running madly to go nowhere.

My stock amongst my peers went up. All that army cadet stuff did wonders for my acceptability. After being knocked down with a feather to be elected class captain in my second year, I was re-elected for the third, the fourth, and then the fifth. And I didn't even campaign.

The cadets, being the feeder organisation that it was for the Regular Army, had this retired Scottish Brigadier fella that was the regional inspector dude. He came round a couple times, watched my progress through the years, and made his canny pitch. He told me he thought I'd make a fine officer, and would I like his help to find a suitable regiment? Wow...outside of Doug, my history teacher, nobody had paid me any attention at all. Now here was the army again picking up my chit.

I didn't understand then that the army is a collection of gangs and tribes. I wanted to be a paratrooper.

To get inside the mentality of the army hierarchy for a second, there's a lot of jealousy about The Parachute Regiment. The Scots Regiments regard themselves as just as tough as the Airborne (largely true) and just as glamorous (IMHO, nothing beats the maroon beret, but I have no objection to a skirt on a man). I do remember mentioning the Airborne but getting that standard Scottish officer response that I'd find just as many challenges and adventures in the Scots Division. Every recruiting officer does this. Doug Stewart knew this. It's why he counselled me not to take 'no' for an answer. I didn't grip this then, so I went along with the proposed solution to make the recruiter happy. I would be sponsored by the Gordon Highlanders, my local, and very undermanned, Regiment.

A very formal envelope marked 'On Her Britannic Majesty's Service' arrived with my name on it.

Inside was a train ticket and joining instructions to go to a place called Westbury, down in England. This is where army officer selection is done.

My mother was very inquisitive as to why I'd had mail, and equally dismissive as to why a letter with such formal marking had been sent to a child. I told her it was from the cadets, and I'd be going away for a couple of days to camp. She had always been very ambivalent about my engagement with the cadets. She was filled with sense memories of her father beating her when he was in uniform and of the army's draconian approach to security in Belfast.

To me, though, this was wonderful. Somebody cared enough to invite me to leave home, if only for a couple of days. This was what had happened to Lawrence.

I'd never been on a train on my own before. It was thrilling. The slam of the carriage doors, the shunting, the shrill of the guard's whistle. Opening the window as we crossed the border, seeing poplar trees for the first time in my life, watching the starkness of the Scottish scenery turn to the fat, pleasant lands of the south of England. What a thrill.

I had a brief on what to expect from the old brigadier before I left. He told me that I'd be carefully watched and that I was very young. He didn't expect me to pass, but it would be good familiarisation for later when I could go back again with a bit more maturity.

I knew I had to dress smart. I wore my one and only jacket, a cast off like all the rest, over my school uniform. I didn't have anything else that was posh enough for officer school.

That was my first exposure to lugubrious, sleek, confident, English public-school boys. Not only my fellow candidates, the examining officers too, all from the same background. Everybody sounded like Prince Charles and had brilliantine in their hair. They all wore pinstripe suits with fancy buttons and red silk linings that I was told were double-breasted. I'd read Evelyn Waugh, but I'd never seen anything like it.

I wasn't intimidated, though. In fact, they annoyed me. When I listened to them, to the drawl and extended vowel sounds, I thought they sounded ridiculous. When I analysed what they said, I thought it the most utter twaddle. This was posturing and posing. I knew I could do better.

As unfamiliar as they were, the tests were catnip. I loved them. They were basically a variation on a theme of getting a burden like an empty barrel from one side of an obstacle to another using a selection of bits of rope and planks of wood. The physical bit I loved, and the intellectual bit was little more than an understanding of pivots and levers. What we were marked on was our ability to command or follow in a variety of situations. Sometimes as leader, sometimes as idea floater, sometimes as teammate. Always with an emphasis on contribution and compatibility.

All my experiences thus far came out. I'd learned to lead in the cadets. I'd learned to cope with my difference. I'd learned to be sensitive to others and a team player. No, scratch that. I was sensitive to others and a team player. Women always are. That part I'd learned to hide physically, but it has always been there. I was by far and away the youngest there. Most of them were at university. I didn't give that a thought. It was all very natural to me.

The only time I felt inferior was when we had to give a five-minute presentation on something we'd done. All these posh Eton types stood up and talked about yak farming in Australia, or an expedition down the Amazon. I'd never been further than a package holiday to Magaluf.

I did my talk on what I knew - orienteering in the Cairngorms. How the posh boys rolled their eyes in boredom. My one flash of inspiration was entirely accidental, but it brought down the house. This is entirely true, but a moment purely of fate. My brother kept stealing my Silva compass, the essential orienteering tool. I'd taken to hiding it in my jacket pocket, my only jacket, the one I was wearing that day. I hadn't planned to do a talk on orienteering, it was an impulse solution to the question given. But when I came to mentioning how you got about while orienteering, I fished my compass out of my inside pocket. Cue gales of laughter from the directing staff. The army likes a bit of dramatic licence. I scored big. Was it meant to be? I think so, now I look back on it.

My other heaven-sent charm came in the form of an examining officer like me. This was a time when to be gay was a court martial offence and instant dismissal, but people like me have been around since the dawn of time, and we all know each other. It's a kind of radar, often unspoken, but I know we recognised each other.

He was particularly taken with me during one command task where I had hung upside down from a bar, feeding a scaffolding pole with my hands, then artfully spinning myself off the pole with a backwards somersault. That got a round of applause from the staff. I'd defeated the set solution with my amateur gymnastics.

There was one formal dinner at night, and he contrived to sit next to me. We spent the entire evening doing the dance of attraction. Of course, nothing was said, and to have expressed anything was not only inappropriate, it would also have been complete suicide for us both. At that time, homosexuality was a court martial and instant dismissal offence for him, and a jail sentence for me. Being gay in
Scotland was still illegal. Let alone the social shame it would have brought. Then again, as I've repeatedly said, I wasn't gay. But he was extremely attractive.

Now, it would be a very different story. I'd be all over that like butter on hot toast. But he wouldn't be interested in me now. I'm not a man, never was, even if he saw one then. See how the wheel keeps on spinning for folks like me? It's a never-ending maze with no exit.

A week or so later, an equally impressive 'On Her Britannic Majesty's Service' envelope arrived. Inside was a single piece of paper. I had passed officer selection. The army wanted me. More than that, should I pass my exams, they were willing to offer me a temporary officer's commission and pay my way through university as well.

I was sixteen.

I called my brigadier chap to tell him (he'd asked for an instant update) and he was mightily impressed. He told me it was unheard of for somebody so young and from my background (non-posh Etonian type) to be awarded this accolade. To this day, I think passing Westbury at sixteen must stand as some sort of record. I may have had a favourable grade from my officer chum, but I earned that pass. All by myself.

I was walking on air.

By my own efforts, building an identity in my mind, bringing it to life, I had achieved something very mighty indeed. I'd laid out the plan, followed through, and achieved it all by myself, against all the odds.

I went to proudly tell my mother that I had been on a bit more than a cadet camp. I'd been on selection and would be joining the army as an officer.

She slapped me in the face.

She told me there was no way the sacrifice she had made for me was going to be rewarded by my joining the army and risking my life in foreign wars. And off she went on one of her more hysterical rants and screaming sessions, all directed at me. I just stood there, absorbing it, going back to my inner voices.

Even by my family's fucked up standards, this was a new level.

Looking back on it now with the perspective of decades passed, I can't excuse her reaction, but I can see her logic.

First off, her reaction was premised on her own childhood. Of her soldier father beating her and then abandoning the family. Then of the British Army patrolling the streets of Belfast. There is a lot of unexplored traumata in all of that. She didn't see the military as anything honourable.

Secondly, she would have been hurt by the fact I hadn't told her the real nature of why I went away for the weekend. That was couched in my essential lack of self-confidence. Nobody had given me a chance in succeeding at Westbury. I had fully expected to fall

Sugar and Spice

short, and I couldn't bear the thought of bringing another perceived failure home. I'd had quite enough of that.

Thirdly, my life decisions were in clear opposition to her own dreams for me. Our neighbour to the big house was a lawyer. While we had a succession of boarders traipsing up our driveway, he arrived at night in a chauffeur driven Jaguar. This spoke too deeply to her unresolved issues of envy of Cambridge and her upbringing in her mother's boarding house. For some years, she had obsessed over the idea that I would be a lawyer. Not an army officer. Not in a month of Sundays.

The limits of her horizons were that I would emulate our neighbour and enter the law. That, to her, was ultimate success.

I hadn't grown up in her environment.

I had been to a minor public school, and I had been taught of history, geography, and the classics. I'd seen 'Lawrence of Arabia' and I understood where Damascus was. I'd seen 'Blue Hawaii' and I understood where Hawaii was. I was resolved to go there: because I believed when I got there, I could finally be me. Yentl was my compass. My Parachute Regiment captain would save me, I'd wear a dress like Lawrence, I'd fall in love with my man and openly become the woman I am.

That might sound fanciful, but that was my internal bargain. I'd hide who I was until the day came when I didn't have to.

The key to my journey was the army. The Parachute Regiment captain had shown me the way was possible. He'd told me I'd be in Belfast with him one day. I'd trained hard, set aside my childhood dreams of girlhood, and now I had succeeded on the first step.

At no time was my future ever being a lawyer. As much as she wanted it, my mother's dream for me was her dream. Not mine.

When she slapped me, my mother and I parted ways again. I'd always tried to please her. But after that day, I never again did.

My father tried to find a compromise. He was quietly pleased I was engaging in masculine pursuits. But the demands of marriage meant he had to side with my mother. He directed that I should do a law degree and enter the army as a lawyer.

That turned me against him, once and for all. I'd had enough of compromises. I didn't say anything at the time, but what remaining respect I had for him disappeared. He was a weak man and I despised him for it.

But I still needed them. I wasn't an adult and I had to find room under their roof. I kept my own counsel and used the house for board and lodging and took charge of my own life. So far, so teenage, perhaps. But I had a dream. It was nothing to do with professional success.

I am a woman. I was going to get there. The army would be my passport.

I was decades ahead of my time. Nowadays, this generation are all about personal fulfilment. Then, I was a criminal revolutionary. I could tell nobody. That way led to a jail cell for perversion. I wouldn't have been able to articulate my resolve in this way, but that's what happened.

I achieved all of it.

OFF COURSE

I had my plan and my future. All I had to do was pass my exams and take up the army's offer of paid university. History was my passion, I resolved to study that. I was never going to do the legal thing, but I had to keep the peace. I told my parents I would apply for a law degree, without telling them I also made other choices. My mother then insisted I stay in Aberdeen, go to the local university. There was no way I was going to do that either, but, again, I kept the peace, and ostentatiously filled in the necessary forms.

Quite secretly, I enquired via Doug how I could go to Oxford or Cambridge. I'd read Waugh's 'Brideshead Revisited' and had been really taken with the whole homoerotic narrative of Flyte and Ryder. Easy for them, not so easy for me. Oxbridge is incredibly hard for a Scot to enter. The education systems are very, very different. Scottish exams are done a year early and not rated as highly by the English system. My school was very much Scots parochial. I was also a year younger than my peers, having skipped a year. I was therefore two years younger than the equivalent English candidates. Doug did some digging and told me if I did my history Scottish higher qualification in my 5th year and successfully got an 'A' in an advanced qualification in my final year, called 6th Year Studies, then I'd have proved myself beyond the

English entry level and I'd be eligible to enter the Oxbridge exam system. He told me it was hard, nigh impossible, but there was a route if I chose it. All I had to do was get an 'A' in history in my 6th year. That was my route to victory.

I didn't tell anybody, least of all my parents, but I assiduously went for it. I passed my higher history with flying colours and enrolled for the 6th Year Study. Doug would be my teacher. It was on the cards. I could taste success.

One last obstacle, then I'd have my chance. One of the all-time great universities, and a long way away from Aberdeen, as part of the army, being paid to study.

That was when it went all wrong again.

My mother had become beyond unsettled. She had tired mightily of her life as a teacher and managing a home. At the weekend, my father and her had taken to visiting a small hotel/bar across the street, where they had fallen in with the lugubrious owner, a kind of Aberdonian Peter Stringfellow. My mother became convinced that if she too owned a hotel, she could mimic his success and become independently wealthy and a person of importance in her own right.

Despite having literally no experience of the hospitality business, they sold our big house in Aberdeen for a song and bought a small hotel back in Stonehaven, backed by a massive loan from the brewers.

At a time when my life needed an element of stability, everything was thrown up in the air again, right at the moment when I needed to concentrate on that vital exam.

The movers came. I frantically disposed of all my shoeboxes of clothes and jewellery. Time for Stonehaven, redux. Shorn of my secret identity. I hadn't forgotten how it had ended the last time. Donald was long gone, moved away. None of it would be easy.

I didn't have a space of my own in the hotel, which was a small affair of twelve rooms and two bars. I had an ever-changing succession of vacant rooms decided daily by the nightly trade. What possessions I had, I kept in a suitcase, with my school stuff in a rucksack. I did my homework on the bed of whatever room was free that night. In the mornings, I'd pack it all again and leave my stuff by the back door. When the hotel was full, I slept in the kitchen. As did my brothers.

Every night, we went to bed with the smell of booze in our nostrils and the laughter of the crowd in the bar ringing in our ears. Through the wall, I'd hear violent sex in the room next door. In the mornings, I'd walk past a succession of travelling salesmen and other oddities.

I lost all my friends. I now lived fifteen miles south of Aberdeen. School was a 2-hour commute via train. I'd gather up my two younger brothers, one of whom was eight, and we three would walk to the railway station and get on board by ourselves, both ways, no matter the weather. Three children, left to fend for ourselves.

On nights when my father finished early, we'd leave school at four, walk to his television station, wait for him to finish the evening news at half past six, and then drive an hour back to the hotel after two hours waiting on a sofa. I'd do my homework in Grampian Television reception and go straight to bed when I got in.

It wasn't a life for any of us.

The business was a failure.

Peter Stringfellow dude was a canny businessman, he made his money on location. His hotel was right in the heart of oil country. Aberdeen was a wealthy market. Stonehaven was a backwater. Nobody but locals and impoverished travellers would stop over. The hotel itself was falling apart, with leaking roofs and ancient plumbing. It was a money pit.

The violence came back then.

First, in just being in Stonehaven. My brothers and I went to an Aberdonian private school with its own distinctive uniform; we lived in a small town where being different was not approved. We took the train every day. My brothers and I had to walk the gauntlet in our uniforms, past the social housing estate. At the very least, it would be name calling. At the worst, and it got worst most days, it'd be a running skirmish just to get to the railway station. The same in reverse.

At home, my mother's dreams of being sat by a bar with a cocktail while her staff attended to her 'A' list clientele soon degenerated into a life in the kitchen, serving quick meals of chips with everything to the public bar. She became even more irascible and impossible to speak to. My grandmother came over to help, but she was getting aged. My brothers and I were soon brought into the staff.

I spent my 17th birthday tending bar and washing glasses. It was a rude awakening to the ways of men and drunkenness. I was attractive then. I hadn't learned to give back the same level of abuse I received. I was an easy target for every homophobic slur going.

My father's money was going to subsidise the hotel, and that made him angrier. He took to sitting in the bar all night, drinking the remaining profit away. The issue was unsolvable. No matter how hard and how long my mother worked, there were only so many rooms and so many bar customers.

Between the loan repayments to the brewer and the defined income ceiling, the figures didn't match. The whole venture was slowly sinking into a valiant but incremental failure.

I needed to concentrate on my studies. Moving from room to room, spending hours travelling, trying to do my work on trains, in the back seat of cars, balanced on the edge of a bed, wasn't cutting it. I redoubled my efforts to block the chaos out.

Sugar and Spice

I'd hit on a hot topic for my history dissertation. I did 15,000 words on Hitler's invasion of Russia, why it failed and the repercussions for the world we lived in. Not too shabby a result for a lonely kid just turned seventeen. Doug told me it was a very impressive piece of work. All I had to do was ace the exam itself with a couple of essays on topics I'd written about before and I could try out for Oxbridge. I'd told nobody, but it was still possible. I just needed to do the work.

In the move to Stonehaven, I'd put aside all my boxes of clothes. I had no way of getting them to Stonehaven unseen. I'd been fighting an acute mental battle to keep it all together, staying on track to get the exam done. My ticket to getting out of there. The woman in me was dying, but it wouldn't be forever. Just one more push…
On the big day of my final history exam, the make-or-break moment, I came down to the kitchen for breakfast. My mother was at the stove. She turned away from me as I walked in, awkwardly turning to offer me a plate, hiding her face. I asked her what was wrong. She said nothing, her face turned to the wall. I walked to her and turned her round. She had a black eye and a cut on her cheek, half her head badly swollen. The tears were running down her face.

I knew who had done this.

I took the stairs two at a time. He was in the bathroom.

I kicked in the door. He was shaving.

'If you ever touch my mother again, I'll kill you,' I told him.

I could see the anger begin behind his eyes. I went into a fighting stance. He started towards me, then thought better of it. In my eyes, he could see if he had pushed me further, I would have killed him, there and then, that very day.

His frame collapsed, like crystal shattering. He mumbled 'OK' and closed the broken door.

I stood there in the hall for a long time, frozen in that Tae Kwon Do stance. Whatever string attached me to my father was well and truly broken.

My mother was in the hall below, waiting and listening. I went to her and told her it would be alright. She was upset. Not at the beating, but at me. Not in the angry way she usually was, this time with resignation and finality.

'You'll have to leave now,' she told me. 'This is his house.'

She was right. There was no roof big enough for both my father and me to live under.

I went to school, sat there as the exam papers were handed out. Two hours later, I was still sat there, looking at a blank piece of paper in front of me.

I wrote nothing.

My dissertation was good enough to get me a 'B'. I got a school prize for giving it a go. It wasn't good enough for Oxbridge. I had needed an 'A'. That chance was gone. I'd blown it. I couldn't get past that brick wall of family drama. It was too late for Oxbridge.

My other option was the compromise application I'd filled in to please my parents. I'd done enough to get accepted for law at Aberdeen University. Precisely what I had never wanted. They were happy, I was cut to the core. My fate was sealed. My plans were shattered.

That's when my opposition to my parents became unstoppable. All I knew was I wasn't going to go do law at Aberdeen University. I was outta there.

A wife beating father had changed my life. My resolve that day was he'd never have that power again.
I still feel that white-hot anger.

Never. Again.

TRYING TO FIX THE ENGINE

The hotel was an utter disaster. Yet again, we'd been thrust into another degenerative crisis by appallingly poor decision-making.

Sugar and Spice

To turn it around, my mother decided she wanted to have a disco in the bar on a Saturday night to bring the punters in. It was kind of clutching at straws, but by this point anything was worth a go. And in crisis, opportunity…I jumped at the chance to be Noel Edmonds. There was a performance part to this I found very attractive. I welcomed the opportunity to do something creative. Like any teen, I fervently followed the charts. 'Top of the Pops' was a weekly appointment to view.

Most importantly, this was the era of disco. Subversively gay, the movement cemented my community in the mainstream for the first time. I adored it. Nothing finer than the 'Village People'. There still isn't. Disco would be a moment to legitimise who I am.

A seed fund investment from my mother got me a very second-hand mobile disco from a very dodgy bloke. Two battered speakers, a two-turntable deck, a single lighting unit and a box of non-entity 7inch singles. Not much to work with, but a basis for making it into more than the sum of its parts.

I did a bit of home construction and built a couple more lighting units, acquired a smoke machine and a strobe, a few Top 10 records, and I was off. I built a wee business off the back of that, renting my rig out to the local community centre and other hotels.

My weekly community session was a roaring success with the girls. I made a bit of money and got seriously into the disco/ early New Romantics dress-up thing. I'd pitch up in three-inch platform boots, harem pants, a silk blouse and cummerbund and a velvet turban, titling myself the 'Queen of the Scene'. Very 1970's fantastic. I discovered the British truth of the panto costume. Dressing-up camp could be a camouflage. It may have been that folks were laughing at me rather than with, but it was a wonderful release. My dance training came into its own. I'd stick on a 12-inch platter of 'Chic' or 'Sister Sledge', while the girls and I would do a line dance as the smoke machine made us all look utterly glam. Then the girls started putting make-up on me, which, of course, I adored. It was the first time in my life I'd socialised with women, and I just loved it.

I didn't do any of this for my mother's hotel events. That was strictly Status Quo and bar room rock. No, sir, no disco fever there. My gigs there paid back her investment, then I'd be off doing my own thing.

At the community centre, I'd bring along a black bin bag of fabulous clothes, get changed to go on stage, then hide it all away again afterwards. I'd been doing that all my life. It wasn't a big deal.

I was revelling in the usual teenage female thing of gossip, friends, music, dress, and make-up. It was the first time I'd felt accepted by women. This wasn't a sexual attractiveness thing. The girls told me they trusted me. In those moments, I put aside my hatred of my body and dived deep into the female sisterhood.

Sugar and Spice

The boys hated me for it. Stonehaven men all had one social identity – a love of heavy metal. They wore greasy denim and ripped T-shirts. They'd ask me for Black Sabbath or Led Zeppelin and then stand in a circle playing air guitar, while the girls drifted away. It was blatant patriarchal control stuff. I refused to play metal. They'd stand and hurl homophobic insults, but the girls stood round me, doing that sisterhood thing of strength in numbers that I adore.

The women loved me even more for taking their side. The camper I got, the more of me I revealed, the better the disco party got. I was making playing records entertainment. The big hotel in town picked up on my act and I was soon playing there on a Sunday night. In 1979, while still at school, I was pulling in an easy 150 a week. That was double the average salary. This thing was going like a rocket.

I bought every import US disco record going, ordering them direct from the big store in Aberdeen. I owned pretty much everything Philly came out with. I had money beyond my dreams then – I bought my first wardrobe of lovely clothes. I discovered Matinique silk blouses, Gaultier belts, Halston pants. I had a purse from Gucci. Aberdeen was a wealthy, oil-rich town. The stores were there. I was probably the youngest and the most unusual client the ladies' up-scale fashion stores had. I'd found an identity and a purpose. I wasn't quite me, but it was as close an approximation as I was going to get.

Then, in true Stonehaven style, it was stolen from me. I was unloading my gear after a Sunday gig, leaving the boxes in the car park, going back in rotation for the rest. I came out as a gang of the metal boys were kicking my rig over the car park. The girls were screaming, trying to stop them. It was a scene. I went for the metal heads, knocked over a few, but they were a pack, and I was in two-and-a-half-inch kitten heels. They'd deliberately targeted me. I got a bit of a pasting, my speakers were smashed, the records either stolen or broken. The police came, took one look at my make-up and blood smeared face, my ripped blouse, and lost interest. The cops weren't going to help what they saw as a gay man. I could dress up as a soldier, but I couldn't dress as me. That much was made very clear.

Very end of Weimar, 'Cabaret', 'Tomorrow Belongs to Me', kind of moment. I'd truly almost been me, barring the physical tragedy of my body, and yet again, I'd tasted blood in reward. I had the money to replace the gear, but my spirit was broken again. I abandoned the disco, got rid of all the clothes.

That was when I started to get angry. It's a negative emotion, but when you fill yourself with it, you can move mountains. It comes at enormous personal internal cost, but it does mask the pain. I poured petrol over my collective trauma and lit the taper. For a few years, I was going to become quite an ugly person to be around.

Sugar and Spice

BANGKOK, 2008

It was big reveal day. Eight days earlier, I'd had everything below remodelled. I'd lain in bed with 50 feet of wadding inside me and 300 stitches holding it all in place, a catheter doing the necessary, my arms wired to morphine and plasma drips. The bed was excruciatingly uncomfortable. Thai people are small framed. Not only was the bed too short, but the mattress was also paper thin. I'd been lying on my back on little more than a board for over a week, unable to move.

I was desperate to get out of there.

Dr Suporn told me he'd remove the dressings, check the integrity of the stitches, and I'd then have to pee to prove the plumbing was connected and pointing the right way. If that all worked, I could leave.

In he came, with his usual polite diffidence and hand-steepled bow. He asked me to bend and open my legs, while he pulled back the sheets. He put on a head torch, bent over, and grabbed the end of a piece of cotton protruding from my vagina. He looked up and told me:

'This is going to hurt…'

First up was the catheter. This has barbs to keep it in place. Pulling it out goes against the barbs. It was like being stabbed. 'Motherfucker!' Like a magician pulling a rabbit from a hat, he tugged on the cotton wadding. 'Motherfucker!' The dressing had absorbed the blood, but it had dried inside me. He was ripping the scab away as he pulled the wadding out. 'Motherfucker!' I yelled that many times over. There were yards of the stuff. Holy Gods, that hurt.

Then it was done. For the first time in my life, he invited me to look at my vagina. Everything was swollen, but I revelled in the flatness of my body. For the first time in my life, I could squeeze my legs together and not feel the insistent bulk of flesh I hated. This was quite wonderful.

I chugged a ton of water and waited while Dr S congratulated me. First part done, pain down to a dull roar, I had to pee before I could get out of there. They helped me to my very unsteady feet, and I walked like John Wayne over to the toilet bowl. For the first time in my life, I was going to pee sitting down as a woman.

I can't overstate how profound all of that felt. There had been so much to fuss over before, penis, balls, all that skin. I'd been taping it up for years, disabused of owning any of it. Now all I had to do was sit down. I was delighted when I urinated. It was so much quicker – the plumbing was shorter now. And the urine came out the right way. Sometimes, the urethra doesn't point the right way and patients are a bit surprised to get pee in their eye. That was another operation to fix. I was done with

Sugar and Spice

hospitals that day. No more for me. I'd have done pretty much anything to get out of there.

Relief. I was good to go.

The morphine buzz carried me to the car, and I took my first hundred yards from the car to my hotel room. I stopped a lot, had to be helped by two nurses, but I was just about upright, walking, living, breathing, smiling. The sensation of nothing being there…of space between my legs. My, it was wonderful.

By the next day, the morphine had worn off. Down below seriously hurt. I couldn't get out of the hotel bed. They brought me breakfast, carried in by Ai, my personal nurse.

'Today is the day we teach you to dilate,' she told me.

She gave me a silk box containing three glass rods, shaped like dildos, each one bigger than the other. The biggest was truly fearsome. She told me in a very matter of fact way that while I healed, I needed to keep my vagina open by keeping one of these inserted inside me for 6 hours a day. If I did this, I'd be able to have penetrative sex within 3 months. Today was the day I would start.

I waddled through to the bathroom, and I sat on the loo as she showed me how to lubricate myself and then insert the smallest glass rod. I'd never had anything rigid like this inside my body. If I'd been correctly female, I'd have been doing this since my periods had begun. Here I was, at 44, doing this for the first time ever, sat in a Thai bathroom, being coached by an impeccably dressed and uber-polite Thai nurse, using a glass rod and what seemed like gallons of KY. I'd love to say I cried, but I burst into uncontrolled laughter at the ridiculousness of the situation.

Ai wasn't convinced I was taking this entirely seriously. She got quite stern and invited me to touch my new body. I found my labia and my clitoris, using a hand mirror as a guide. Wow. Now that really was special. I was still a mess of stitches and dried blood, but I could see what I would be in time.

That was enough for one day. I was exhausted. I went back to bed and tried to sleep, not easy with a glass rod embedded in me.

But I loved it. I understood then how profound the act of penetration is for women. Such a different sexual experience. I was beginning to understand my body, experiencing virginal sensations.

I revelled in that knowledge. My body was finally, finally, finally, after so much hurt and pain, finally female. I cried then. Deep pillars of pain being released, trauma expelled. Too intense a lifetime of rejection to be expunged in one, but the depths were lessened.

To be replaced with a glowing ember of joy.

I am woman. Internal, external, forever.

HOME NO MORE

The hotel went bust. My parents got out with their shirts, but not much else. After two years of wasted effort, we packed up again and headed back to Aberdeen. My father's union protected job kept a roof over our heads, but it was a much smaller house that we returned to.

It was the year I left school. I'd failed my history thing and my only option was to take up law at
Aberdeen. My parents seemed happy with that, even if not happy at all with me. Nor I with them.

At the top of the house was a converted loft room. I got that. Up in the eaves like Cinderella.

The disco was gone. I was done with any sense of order in my life. I needed to find a purpose. I was angry.

I found a twisted redemption by feeding the two halves of my life.

None of that was healthy.

I joined the Territorial Army as a private soldier. I was underage but they let me in with a wink. I went every weekend. I learned about the big army and its weapons. I mingled in the world of men and came home smelling of gun-oil. I became callous, in language and tone and presence. I wasn't remotely tough, but I acquired a swagger and a sneer. I also found alcohol. The Army revolved around the stuff. We drank often and deeply. I got into all the stupid scrapes you do when you're drunk and young and in the company of agitated men showing off. Once the booze wore off, I would punch my groin for having led me there.

None of that was healthy.

I got a job during the week at our local Wimpy bar. I flipped hamburgers in my brown smock and side cap. I was pretty good at it and got promoted to shift manager. The restaurant was right in the middle of town, with a downstairs seating area and toilets. It became an unofficial meeting place for the gay community, who could meet up in the basement toilet for casual sex. As the manager, I had to floor walk. I hated my body and hated myself too. I gave a load of blowjobs in that toilet. They didn't get to touch me. That was off-limits. I had literally no self-respect left. So, I debased myself and then punched my groin for leading me there.

None of that was healthy.

I met another soldier in the TA who liked me as I liked him. I took him back to my garret room one Sunday night. We were having vigorous sex when my father burst into the room. He'd heard two sets of footsteps and had come to investigate. I was in full receiver mode. As you might imagine, he went utterly berserk. My soldier chum told him to calm down and it got a bit heated. I was riven with a lifetime of shame and disgust at myself, at him, at my father, at my body, at my life. I walked my friend to the door as he dressed. He kissed me goodbye and left. I went to sit in the downstairs room while my mother and father laid into me about perversion and evil and criminality. I went up to my garret room and punched my groin again.

None of that was healthy.

Everything boiled over the next night. My TA unit was about to go to summer camp for a fortnight and I'd been down getting a briefing on my minor role in it all. I had a couple drinks in me as I came home. My father was waiting on me coming in and wanted to pick up again on my depravity from the night before. I'd just been snogging my soldier friend and wasn't in the mood. I was tired and angry of it all by then. I'd had a lifetime of sanctimony on what I couldn't do and shouldn't be, which was everything I wanted.

He came at me that night for not listening to him with respect. I told him if he really wanted to go for it, then let's go outside and do it properly. He paused then, but the dam broke in me. I grabbed him by the jacket and dragged him out to the back garden and we went at it. It was a shock to hit him the first time, but after that, the blinders came down and I wind-milled him into the ground. It was payback for a lifetime of beatings.

I distantly heard my mother yelling to leave him. I pulled back when I heard her voice, then her words, 'Stop it! I've called the police!'

That paused me. I had an army camp to get to. I went upstairs, grabbed my gear, and made for the door. I went down to the territorial hall, let myself in and camped the night outside the armoury. We were leaving the next day. The police must have figured out where I was because they came down to the TA the next day and asked to see me. They told me my father was a bit beaten up but didn't want to press charges. They told me I needed to get out of town. My sergeant major only wanted to know if I had been arrested. When I told him I wasn't, he shrugged it off as one of those things young soldiers do and told me to get on the truck. I punched my groin for leading me there.

None of that was healthy.

I spent the next two weeks in Belgium, mock defending a big ammunition dump. I disappeared into guns, explosions, mock attacks and all the braggadocio of young soldiers. It was a very effective anaesthetic.

My soldier chum and I had some great sex. I still didn't let him touch me there, though. I may have slunk down to the basement level of self-regard, but I hadn't forgotten who I am. I took the pill of oblivion, but my spirit still flickered. I punched my groin for leading me there.

None of that was healthy.

I came back a fortnight later, full of the booze from a last night session. I was a soldier, with all the privilege but none of the sense of responsibility. My father was waiting for me in the hallway. He was obviously boozed up himself and accused me of stealing his whisky. I pointed out how ludicrous this sounded as I had been away on Queen's business for the past fortnight. He had none of it and off we went again, spinning windmills. Again, my mother intervened and said she would call the police. We were in the front room, with its big bay window. I said, 'Let's get the police, then,' and did a side kick karate move with my boot that shattered the window. There was glass everywhere.

My mother was screaming. My father stood rooted with shock – he realised I genuinely could and would kill him if he pressed me any further. I knew I'd gone too far. I'd lost any remaining shred of self-control. I picked up my gear again and headed for the door. I spent the night sleeping it off under my poncho in the park. I punched my groin for leading me there.

None of that was healthy.

I phoned my mother and agreed to meet her separately. We sat on a park bench and looked at each other. She told me I had to leave now. I couldn't go back home. Being me had broken her rules and she wouldn't live with the shame. I asked her why she put up with him – why didn't she leave, too? She was honest with me for the first time in her life:

'If I came with you, it wouldn't last. You'll grow up and meet somebody and I'll be left on my own. I am staying with your father. That is my choice. I can't keep you as well. You cannot come back.'

She pressed 50 pounds into my hand, with a phone number of a local boarding house, and walked away without looking back. I took a rented room that night. I had my Wimpy job. I could make a living of sorts. I was still in Aberdeen, but I was out of that house. Bar an odd Christmas visit for a day, I never did go back. Ever. Not for the rest of my life. Or theirs. I was on my own. I was 17. I punched my groin for leading me there.

None of that was healthy.

That was the moment when I really did need to see a psychotherapist. It wasn't just a horrendous series of personal traumata and circumstances that had driven me to this point. It was what testosterone was making me do. I was literally a drug addict on entirely the wrong drug. Anger was so easy to reach, then. What my body was producing drove me there. My mind was in complete torment. I hated the urges that testosterone drove within me. I hated how it made me feel. My sweet, kind womanhood was being roasted on a rack of self-hatred. Once more, my body collapsed in on itself. I came out in huge, pustulous boils, all over my body. They just kept on erupting, in never-ceasing waves. They stayed with me for years. I punched my groin for leading me there.

None of that was healthy.

That was when Freemans' catalogue came into my life. The saviour of many tormented souls. Freemans was a mail order company that offered two hundred pounds worth of clothing on credit. In those days, there were no credit checks. All you needed was a mail address.

I stabilised myself by buying two hundred pounds worth of lingerie, dresses, heels, and jewellery on tick. They came in an anonymous brown paper bag delivered to my anonymous boarding room. At night, I'd lock the door and become me again. No mirrors, I couldn't bear to see what I looked like. I wanted the memories of when I'd been young and pretty before testosterone had ruined me. But I was calmer again. I had a moment where I could be me, a kinder, gentler me.

It didn't work with my soldier friend. He wanted a man. When I told him of me, he was repulsed. But we had a confidentiality agreement. Tell on me, I'll tell on you. That would have meant a jail cell. So, we parted without a grand reveal.

I wasn't going to Aberdeen University to do the law in the autumn. No chance. I wrote to the army to tell them I wanted to start straight away. They were surprised, but agreed, providing I could get a reference from my school headmaster to be sure all was fine.

I asked to go see him in his grand office. He'd been surprised by my request and had phoned my parents to find out why I needed a reference. I don't know what they told him, but it was obvious it wasn't good news.

He told me he'd write me a supportive note because I'd done well at school, even if I was a profound disappointment in everything after. He advised me not to let down my parents again.

I sat there looking at him with disgust and unabashed fury.

I took his reference and booked my slot for Sandhurst. I wasn't yet old enough. I had to wait a few months until I turned 18.

I didn't bother telling my family. I went to see Doug one last time in my TA uniform. We drank beer and he cried a bit about his time in the army. He wished me well and told me to never accept 'no' as an answer. We embraced as he left. I think he knew…

That was it. I'd short circuited it all. Too many obstacles, too many hurdles to jump. I needed to get out of Aberdeen. I needed to go, to keep moving, to keep my mind away from the despair of where I found myself. I wasn't remotely winning, in any way. Geographising. That's when it began.

The day before I went south to the Royal Military Academy, I took all my Freemans ladies' clothes to the park and set fire to them.

I turned 18 a couple weeks before going the Academy. Just old enough to join the army. I headed to England on my second train journey south. It was a very cold January day. I punched my groin for leading me there.

None of that was healthy.

SANDHURST

The Academy does what every basic training outfit around the world does. It breaks you down and rebuilds you into the image it wants. As an officer, you get to keep a bit of your brain, but you're a junior officer, so independent thinking isn't required. You are not ready for that then. First, you must learn to obey. What they do is a system reboot, reloading the ROM into what they need. It's the army, it's all about rules. Particularly at the beginning.

My first time at the Academy was over forty years ago. It was a different military world from now.

For a start, Sandhurst was exclusively male. There were literally no women. What female officers existed (and there were very few) went to a different Academy. My Sandhurst time really was my Yentl Yeshiva. A forbidden domain.

I should add being the first female to attend Sandhurst to my list.

What that absence bred was a kind of machismo that would today be regarded as toxic. Back then, they said 'jump!' and you jumped. No room for questions. Basic training is always full of bone stuff, that's part of the process, but none of it was explained or justified. If you did ask a query, you got an extra parade for your troubles. It was very rigid then, very dogmatic.

The army was also an organisation that hadn't fought a war for a long time. It wasn't nearly as good as it thought it was. A life of service was either swanning about Germany during Cold War exercises, a spot of Northern Ireland doing patrols, or a long, dreary posting in what was left of the Empire. A lack of war meant an organisation that hadn't fired a shot in anger for a long time. We were still trained in tactics and doctrine that had been developed in the early 1950s. Extended time stuck in military barracks breeds a reinforcement of orthodoxy. Of process and procedure and of waiting your time. No army does well in peacetime. It's a football team without a ball to kick. Sandhurst was like that. Big on spit and polish; not so good on actual soldiering. The Academy training was half what it is now; seven months. Far too short when more than half of that time was spent marching up and down and polishing things.

My motives for going were a mash-up of longing from the movies. I wasn't in it for life, I was in it for the adventure of becoming Lawrence and becoming me. I wanted away from the life I had. I was, as I think I've now established, different. I wasn't in it for a career. Nor did I particularly want to fit in. The army had very different ambitions. It's a big organisation, with a big system and big rules. I never reconciled that, and the army wasn't going to bend. Why would it?

That made my military career something of a day-to-day arrangement.

I was to find the army didn't have its Lawrence bit, not then. Nor was I to find The Parachute Regiment - not for another 15 years.

Of course, I didn't know any of that. I had to find it out and live it for myself.

I arrived on the train in Camberley in my one jacket and leftover school uniform, with a single suitcase and the ironing board I'd been told to bring. I walked to the front gate of the Academy, following the map I'd been given.

At the gate, I could see lines of cars filled with versions of the posh kids I remembered from Westbury selection, being driven by fathers with the same brilliantine in their hair and the same pinstripe suits and double-breasted jackets. Nervous looking mothers sat in the rear seat, all pearl necklace and tweed skirt suits.

It's over a mile from the gate to Old College reception. I tramped all of that in the gutter as a succession of expensive motors rolled on by with the chosen ones. In the car park, there were lots of hugs, tears and firm handshakes exchanged. I walked past all of that on my own. I hadn't bothered to tell my family I was there.

I discovered the army tribe system. The sergeant instructors at Sandhurst came pretty much exclusively from the Guards Division. The crew that wears red jackets and tall furry hats and stands around outside royal palaces. Lots of razor-sharp trouser creases, pointy sticks and speaking out of the corner of their mouths. Lots of shouting as well. I got put in my class of 30-plus pink cheeked folks. I was at least two years younger than any of them. I was also the only one with an accent. The rest of them all sounded like Prince Charles. Dressed like him, too. The sergeant instructors took one look at my cast-off jacket, my New Romantic extra-long haircut, my black suede winkle pickers with the tartan elastic, my drainpipe trousers, heard my Scottish accent, acknowledged my youth, and put me right down at the bottom of the unspoken caste system. I wasn't going to be a general. Not in that system. I knew it, and so did they.

Which was pretty much how it rolled out for me at Sandhurst. I'd earned my right to be there, same as the rest, but I always felt the instructors would have been much happier had I stayed a private. That's without considering my other difference, which I could never erase, no matter how hard I tried. The toxic masculinity came in there. I was obviously too camp for them. That marked me from the get-go. I remember being shouted at a lot to 'stop running like a girl.' I smiled when they told me that.

As Guards were in charge, we spent inordinate amounts of time polishing things. Shoes, floors, uniforms, beds, cupboards, walls, toilets. Endless hours, long into the night. Which left us exhausted for the actual learning bit. We'd struggle not to fall asleep in the classes that did matter. The stuff on tactics, leadership, and weapons. In between this were endless hours of running around in ridiculous red cotton tracksuits and endless hours of marching up and down in hob-nailed boots.

Some of this was relevant. Much of it was tangential. No army has ever won a war by being able to see a face reflected in a toe cap. Too little was spent on the ground, doing the bread-and-butter stuff of commanding troops, learning the down and dirty business of closing with and killing the enemy.

This was the time before The Falklands War. It was very gentlemanly, very polite, but not exactly an act of war. More like boarding school in green suits.

We were occasionally released at weekends from running around, marching very fast and being generally abused. To get out into the world, rules said we must wear a jacket, tie, and collared shirt. I had my one outfit, so it wasn't exactly a big fashion choice for me. A bit different from the posh boys.

Cadets were expected to have a rolled-up umbrella and wear a bowler hat if going to 'town', by which they meant London. They also had a rule that cadets couldn't take the Underground, because officers always travelled by taxi or private limousine. I'm not exaggerating. Those rules genuinely existed.

I didn't have a rolled-up umbrella, or a bowler hat, or a limousine. I was keener on accessorising. I had style. I am me.

Coming back into the Academy one Sunday, I had my jacket over my shoulder, my shirt sleeves rolled right up bicep high, with a packet of cigarettes tucked under my right sleeve, my tie tucked inside my shirt. I'd stolen the look from James Dean, who'd stolen it from wartime American GIs. I was, even as I look back at it now, damned sharp looking, fully on point. I was handsome, fit, and fashionable. If I saw me then with my female eyes, I'd applaud me.

The Academy sergeant major didn't agree. He saw me striding across the parade square, itself a hanging offence, jiving like Jimmy D, with my left hand turned out. I heard him before I saw him, but it was hard to miss his spit-flecked diatribe on 'mincing'. Lots of yelling later, I found myself on a company report for conduct unbecoming. More high-speed marching and lots more yelling later, I found myself standing to attention in front of a pink-faced and brilliantine haired company commander. It would have been a bit fierce, even for then, to have gone at me for my walk, so they chose to concentrate on my sartorial brilliance. The officer reminded me of his dress expectations for a cadet, told me I had unacceptably presented as a common labourer, charged me under the 1955 Army Act, and asked if I cared to accept his award or go to trial for court martial?

I told him I much preferred a court martial.

The sergeant major behind me, who had been doing all the 'left, right, left, right' yelling to get me there, couldn't help himself:

'Accept the officer's award! Who do you think you are?'

I knew very well who I was, and I'd read the rules. As far as I was concerned, I'd followed them. I pointed out I was required to have a jacket, tie, and collared shirt. I pointed out I had had all those in my possession and on my body. I pointed out what they were judging was how I chose to wear them. Where, with all due respect, was the rule governing that?

I didn't see this as brave or insulting. Merely intelligent. The attribute to this day I am told is 'intimidating in a team setting'.

The company commander glowered at me and asked, 'Why are you being difficult?'

I thought for a moment. Lawrence came to mind. The scene in the movie where he goes to see Jack Hawkins, as General Allenby, and he is asked the same question, 'Why are you being difficult?'

I used O'Toole's very response, 'I'm not difficult, sir, I'm different...'

I thought they'd get the movie reference, you see. I thought that was helpful. What I got was a week standing in front of the guard house at 6 PM sharp in my best uniform. I never did get my court martial. I did ask.

My accent didn't help.

There's a point in the course where every student must deliver orders. This is core to being an officer. It's essentially telling your team what needs to be done, why, when, with which tools, and how it will be done. A cadet spends a lot of time learning the format. From an army perspective, the same system means everybody gets the same information in the same way; the uniformity is important. The stage debut, done stood behind a handmade model of the ground to be fought over, is a big proving test for a cadet officer.

There's a lot of kudos to be gained and lost on this. While the format is the same each time, cadets are marked on performance, content, and concept. That's the individual bit, the bit officer school tries to bring out. It's the difference between a leader and a manager.

For my turn, I remembered Edward Fox' performance as General Horrocks in 'A Bridge Too Far' where he talks about cowboy and Indian films as a metaphor for his mission. I loved that and tried to repeat it. Might have worked for a 4-star general in a movie, probably not the wisest moment for a cadet first time out of the traps. All I had to do was stick to the script. I couldn't resist the moment on stage.

Sugar and Spice

My pastiche fell flat with the instructors. Like the major, I suppose they didn't get that movie reference either. I was rather good, though. Just the wrong audience, wrong time.

What really hurt, though, was my review from my fellow cadets in the audience. They told me they couldn't understand me. They said I spoke too fast and rolled my R's like a farm worker. My accent was too thick for the posh boys to follow. A well-meaning colour sergeant took me to one side and told me in his estuary English accent that the soldiers would understand me, but when I spoke to officers, I should remember they weren't like us and to speak slowly and simply. Which missed the point; I was training to be one of them, not one of him.

Still, I did everything they asked me to do. I wasn't first in anything, but I did take part to the best of my ability. In the actual running around, getting mucky, shooting guns bit, I was good. I enjoyed it. We didn't do nearly enough of that.

In those days, being a combat soldier was only a part of the required output. What they were aspiring to do was build gentlemen as well as officers. I wasn't the gentlemen part, particularly the 'men' part. I came from a hard knock Belfast and Aberdeen background. I'd dragged myself there. Then, I lacked the polish and the poker face I needed to display to satisfy them.

Later, I was to prove myself in the real officer bit when the bullets were flying. My soldiers understood my accent easily enough then. I have also mastered the art of posh boy diplomacy. I now represent countries in ambassadorial roles. Blend that together and know that I can shoot you in the chest from 400 metres away and toast your corpse in French with a crystal flute of lightly chilled Bollinger.

Huzzah!

Now wasn't then.

I let the posh boys intimidate me. I didn't yet know that in battle, the other ephemera are not important. What I did in reaction was to go with the flow and disappear into the grey blob. I was too Yentl.

It wasn't what The Parachute Regiment was looking for, not in the slightest. I could have got past the class thing with them, but I was too diffident, too immature, and too average. That bit of the dream, which was why I'd got into this in the first place, wasn't going to happen for me. Not then.

Still, it was a process, and it had an end.

There comes a point in Sandhurst where the teachers put all the effort into the star pupils and everybody else becomes a non-speaking cast member to fill out the narrative.

I was one of the extras. It wasn't a bad place to be. I'd had enough of constantly being harassed and rejected for being me. Nonetheless, I'd sold myself short. I have much more talent than I let them see. Then again, the class-based system being what it was, I remain unconvinced I'd have got any more recognition. But I might have been left with less of a sense of incomplete business.

There were nights, though, when the romance of it all became overwhelming. They call them 'mess nights', when all the instructor officers got gussied up in their splendid red jackets and tight trousers, and we cadets sat by candlelight in our dress blues offset by the green tiled dining room of New College. When the port was passed, and we looked deep into each other's eyes and measured the person within. I felt it then. The affinity and bond. The Academy band would play rousing tunes of glory, and we would thump the tables in appreciation. I hadn't been to war yet, but I could feel the gossamer threads that tied me to the past. The army has a fine sense of theatre and tradition. When my time for war came and I had been blooded, and I wore my own red jacket with maroon facings, on those nights I walked 15 feet tall. Those were moments when I understood the camaraderie of fighting soldiers. I was seen as one of them then. Such memories I treasure, for they will never come again for me.

On the big day of the pass-off parade, the Queen came to set us on our new careers. The spectator stands were filled full of uber-proud, brilliantine hair, pinstripe suit wearing fathers and hat wearing, sensibly shod mothers. Nobody came to see me. I'd written to my parents to tell them what I'd done. My father had written back to tell me it was my choice alone and not to expect them to pick up the pieces of my failure. That was the only time we had contact.

The Queen was cool, though. She looked us all in the eye as she walked past. Tiny woman, huge presence. Didn't talk to me - why would she? But I genuinely thought she cared about us all. I was later presented with a scroll signed by her, confirming me as an officer. The first in my family to be commissioned. To me, that's a thing.

It should have been a thing to my mother. Her obsession with socio-economic class had been achieved. I had made the 'A' stream. An army officer is up there, top drawer. I sent her my commissioning scroll to prove it.

She sent it back.

Still, somebody had shown they cared. In my day-to-day bargain with the military, I'll always be proud of the faith they showed in me. The army is the only organisation that ever invested in me.

Usual type won the top prize, the Sword of Honour. Destined for the Guards. The sergeants were happy. He got issued with brilliantine on his way out of the gates.

It's different at Sandhurst now. A bit more inclusive, less posh boy. More focused on military business. There are female cadets. They march about a lot and polish things, but they have a year to do it. More getting muddy. There are huge issues of male toxicity. There are issues of class. There are ridiculous levels of sexual harassment and assault. But it's not what it was 40 years ago. Wars have made it more professional. It's not an elite country gentleman's club anymore. This is mostly good.

I know this because I count an Academy Commandant General as a friend. We've talked about Sandhurst. Over dinner at his place.

Yentl made it, she showed her talent.

It took another 4 decades, but I did get there. I paid my debt to the army.

Eventually.

US EMBASSY, SKOPJE, 40 YEARS LATER

I stood in my best frock outside the gates of the Embassy of the United States of America. I acknowledged the salute of the sergeant in charge of my ceremonial guard of seven splendidly attired US Marines. They escorted me in as the guest of honour.

Ms. Abi Austen, late The Parachute Regiment, now UK Strategic Defence Advisor to the Republic of North Macedonia, was going to the ball.

I had just finished two years posted to North Macedonia, a land-locked country in the Western Balkans. I'd been competitively selected by the UK Ministry of Defence and Foreign Office to represent the UK in advising and assisting the Macedonian government on achieving their national ambition of membership of the North Atlantic Treaty Organisation.

I'd spent two years sat between the Chief of the Defence Staff and the Minister of Defence, laying out my plan to reform their security forces to achieve NATO membership goals. I'd learned what the NATO standard was after seven years in Afghanistan working as political advisor to the US 4 star general in charge of the war, doing the same NATO Partnership drill for that country. I know my business.

Macedonia had overthrown its nationalist government in a velvet coup, formed a centre left coalition and gone for the Euro-Atlantic Alliance. For a small country that had come very close to civil war a mere twenty years earlier, this was heady stuff indeed. They urgently asked the UK for help.

The UK sent me.

I was very open about my gender identity. At interview, I had argued that just having me in the room spoke volumes about the standard of human rights, inclusion, diversity, and democratic principles North Macedonia needed to fulfil.

It has taken me a lifetime to reconcile it all, but that's where I am now. I won't be denied any of my life. Nor will I let you deny me.

The Minister of Defence was, most unusually, female. We bonded immediately. She is a remarkably talented lady who had had her own mountain of misogyny to climb. I had to put up with a huge amount of trans and homophobic abuse uttered behind my back, but HE Radmila Sekerinska was my champion. She saw my talent. She listened to my advice, initiated my plan, and kept me in the room when the key decisions needed to be made.

I worked extremely closely with the United States Embassy. It helped I'd served several years on combat tours with the US Army. It helped I was a paratrooper with US jump wings. It helped I had US decorations, as well as several from other allied countries.

There was a moment when it was all going very wrong, Macedonia wasn't going to make it. I walked into their Ministry of Defence alongside the US Defence Attaché to call them all to order. The night before, he and I had dinner and I'd sketched out on the tablecloth what Macedonia needed to do to make urgent repairs. Complete with Edward Fox 'Bridge Too Far' cowboy and Indian analogy.

Right time, right place.

The Attaché and I sat down in the walnut panelled diplomatic conference room, resplendent with the US and UK flags behind our respective chairs. Flunkies brought us all refreshments and we shuffled paper as the room stilled.

The US Defence Attaché spoke first. He told the Chief of the Macedonian Defence Staff and his assembled generals,

'The United States of America endorses whatever Miss Abi is about to tell you…'

That was a moment.

It quite took my breath away. US Green Beret Colonel Tim Buchen didn't know it, but the ghost of Elvis reached out and touched my shoulder. America trusted me as one of their own. Wow.

All my childhood dreams come true.

The grown woman Abi Austen led that day. No cadet criticised my accent. Nobody charged me for how I wore my clothes. I was my own Lawrence.

My plan worked.

In March 2020, North Macedonia became the 30th member of NATO. As President Stevo Penderovsky signed the accession document, the National Security Advisor sent me a photo of the moment with a one-word message,

'Thank-you.'

That was why I stood outside the gates of the United States Embassy. At a very posh celebration dinner, I sat with the Minister of Defence, the US Ambassador, and the Chief of the Defence Staff. NATO's Supreme Allied Commander for Europe shook my hand and nodded approval.

I made small talk, drank champagne and represented the United Kingdom.

I was gentle, diplomatic, and respected. I danced with all the men.

I had to find myself first. I've done that now. I have paid my debt to the army. I have more than lived up to the standards of a Parachute Regiment officer.

Airborne. Utrinque Paratus. Ready for Anything.

BERLIN, 40 YEARS EARLIER

The army found a job for me in Berlin.

These were the days of The Wall, when the city was stuck with a World War hangover and city governance divided by the victorious Allied Powers - the British, French, American and Russian zones. We all had a military presence to represent our interests. In the case of the British, a couple of battalions of infantry and an assortment of other services and combat arms.

In the event of an actual war, we'd have lasted a matter of minutes. What was more important was in the being there. The Cold War was all about tripwires. The doctrine that backed up our security was the concept of Mutually Assured Destruction – MAD. Attack our thin line of troops and we'll fire nuclear weapons at you, which will end the world. You'll have just enough time before you die in a fireball to fire your nuclear weapons back at us to ensure we also die in another fireball. Therefore, let's not attack each other. That really was a thing then. Mad to even contemplate.

Our job in Berlin was to be the British tripwire.

Twenty years earlier, the Russians and East Germans had wielded a concrete razor blade and constructed this phenomenal and frightening wall right across the city. The idea was to keep us out.

The reality was to keep them in. It wasn't just a wall, it was a football field width of obstacles, mines, swept sand, barbed wire, watch towers, machine guns and guard dogs. An entire branch of the East German security apparatus guaranteed its integrity, backed up by Russian military folks mandated to watch over their sector.

They were the Russian tripwire.

I took my tiny part in it all very seriously. My job was to take pictures of it all, log the stuff I saw, build a picture of the daily rhythm of life along the border. I was an observer of people and things. I sketched charcoal drawings of checkpoints, watchtowers, uniforms – all the stuff that added detail to our intelligence picture. I was creative, engaged, interested. I was a living, breathing, human realisation of the UK's tripwire resolve.

That meant fun could be had. We knew the East Germans took pictures of us and recorded our conversations with parabolic microphones. We had a huge dress-up box of different Regimental hats and berets. We'd change regularly, to confuse them who was in Berlin. The same with rank slides.

When we went round the wall, some days, I'd be a colonel, other days a sergeant. Some days a Scot, other days in an English Regiment. We knew what was being recorded would be transcribed by female clerks, so we'd tell the filthiest and bluest jokes we could think of. All very junior amusement, but a mission we took with the seriousness young people do over these things.

It was Berlin that kicked off my passion in photography. The army had very expensive Leica cameras, with super long lenses and very fast wet film. I learned how to use them and to develop film in the dark room. Very simplistic Harry Palmer type stuff, but I loved the creative possibility and was soon taking art shots as well as the bread and butter of trucks and guns and people.

Going through Checkpoint Charlie was one of those historic moments I feel awed to have witnessed. There was a deadening hand over the atmosphere. The American side had a big tank and MPs in white helmets and M-16s pointing right at the East German side, which had an equally foreboding concrete tower and machine guns pointed straight back at us.

Going through to the Wall to the East was passing from light to darkness. The buildings got shittier, the people drabber, the electricity dimmer. Communism literally sucked the joy out of life. We drove around in a black Range Rover, with a Union Jack on the front. Quite often, women would offer us their babies to take across to the West. At night, our side of the city would be ablaze with light and activity. On theirs, nothing but silence and darkness.

At the Brandenburg Gate, we had a viewing platform, restricted to the military, where we could stand and look over at The Reichstag and the massive Soviet war memorial and its equally massive red flag. In between, The Wall. From their side, they could only see the tops of our heads. At Potsdamer Platz, The Wall widened to a vast open field. This was where Hitler's bunker had been. All that remained was a small knoll. Everything else had been razed to the ground.

We lived out at Spandau, in an old SS barracks, next to the prison where Rudolf Hess was the only inmate. I worked out of the former Reich People's Court, where the 1944 July plot conspirators had been tried and hanged. The city was still in the depths of post-war occupation.

West Berlin at that time offered exemption from the military draft for its residents. As a result, the city was stuffed with the artists, the non-conformists, the oddballs and the different. It was a creative vortex. The party never stopped in West Berlin.

The Wall was set back fifty or so metres from the actual border. There was a thin strip of land on the Western side that was technically East Germany, but which, because of The Wall, the Communists let go fallow. The West German authorities also left it alone, as it didn't belong to them. There, nobody governed.

In this neutral zone on the Western side, a row of decaying tenements and apartments ran through the city centre, untouched since The Wall had gone up, which housed all the funky people, who lived rent free and away from the gaze of the authorities. Anything went there.

This was the Berlin that Bowie had found. He wrote three ground-breaking albums in West Berlin with Brian Eno that stand as a record to what an intellectual and creative hotbed it was. We were right on the frontline of the Cold War. Berlin lived with armed soldiers, watchtowers, and the scar of The Wall. West Berlin was an enclave of exuberant hedonism, for we were never sure if there would be a tomorrow.
That's where I found my Cabaret.

At night, I'd go out and ogle the beautiful people. West Berlin was stuffed with outrageous extroverts. The district of Charlottenburg, which we called 'Grotty Challotty', was a favourite with the soldiers. Stuffed full of bars and sex clubs, it reeked of vice and passion.

I was infinitely aware of my secret popping out. Anything sexual set off huge, screeching internal klaxons of impending shame. But I did revel in street walking, examining the detritus of life, the exuberance of the party.

I stopped one night outside a darkened doorway, from which hidden speakers pumped out Bowie's 'Aladdin Sane'. I stopped because in that place the song reminded me of dancing with Donald, my childhood sweetheart. I was intrigued by the fact that alongside the row of brightly lit taverns, filled with drunken Berliners waving tankards of beer, this doorway had no light, no sign – no evidence of any activity at all. Why then, the music of Bowie?

The door was heavy wood, with a barred window and a heavy iron door knocker. A small brass plate proclaimed in German:

'Dreimal Klopfen.'

Knock three times.

Everybody from my community knows 'The Wizard of Oz' inside out. Dorothy clicks the heels of her ruby slippers three times and says 'there's no place like home...'

We have our code, the same as everybody else. What's different about us is we know it instinctively. It's there, in the air, like heady perfume. Bowie, Dorothy, knock three times. Inside was wizardry. I understood this was my Oz.

I knocked thrice and waited. The window spyhole shot back to be filled with the face of a bearded man with crimson painted lips, rouged cheeks, and the longest eyelashes I'd ever seen. He didn't say anything, he just looked at me, examining me, my stance, my demeanour. The grate whooshed closed. I heard iron bars being pulled back and locks being turned. Somebody was being very careful about who got admittance.

Sugar and Spice

The door opened, and there he was. Completely naked, very hairy, except for a full flowing negligee and enormously high heels. 'Willcommen, Englisch,' he announced and beckoned me in.

Oh, my.

One thing at a time. How did he know I was a foreigner? I was deep into the orthodoxy; my job made me do it. I had short hair and the obligatory polo shirt/ chino outfit that every off-duty British officer sports. It didn't make me happy, but it did make for a quiet life. Yet he had opened the door. Why? Well, you can take the girl out of Aberdeen, but you can't take the girl out of me. My people always knew.

For my part, I experienced the first rush of self-discovery. I'd never been in a pan sexual club before. I was utterly thrilled. My senses went into instant overdrive. Which is the test of heterodoxy. I've told this story many times over the years, and I pose the question: would you go through a darkened Berlin door at the behest of a naked man dressed in women's lingerie? Every one of my hetero male acquaintances' recoils at the thought. If you are intrigued, I posit you are a little bit gay...if, like me, you are in like Flynn, you are female or full on gay. The former of which I am and the latter I used to suffer on grounds of medical impediment. The prosecution rests, m'lud.

Bowie gave way to Cole Porter played on a piano. Inside, round a short wood panelled chicane, then through an artfully draped velvet curtain, opened a vista worthy of Christopher Isherwood. This was Lisa Minelli's 'Cabaret' on steroids. A fine deco inspired bar, with eglomise mirrors and raised rows of exotic spirit bottles on one side, a row of booths on the other, a baby grand being extravagantly played by a woman dressed as Marlene Dietrich in top hat, cigarette holder, monocle, tails, spats and…nothing else.

Oh, my.

Through the cigar smoke, I saw booths filled with men kissing women, women kissing women, men kissing men, men kissing men dressed as women, women kissing women dressed as men, and a variant I struggled to divine as it involved a group of people of whom all I could see were a variety of arms, legs, and other body parts.

Oh, my.

I sat at the bar on a stool. The barman approached me in very brief black and white maid's costume and fishnet tights. In a very deep voice, I heard 'champagne?'

I was about to say something when I realised this wasn't a question, but a prescription.

Oh, my.

I felt better than I had ever felt. I loved it. I was home.

The stage show started then. The first number featured two naked men tap dancing in flippers and snorkels. The comedy came when they jumped up and down, their penises flopping in turn, as they outdid each other's dance in envy of the size of the other's willy movement. I thought it hilarious and infinitely inventive.

Then came the fan dancer. A beautiful woman, provocatively swishing two enormous ostrich feather fans over her obviously naked body. Oh, the shapes she snapped. Utterly elegant, purely sexual, completely feminine. Quite exquisite. Revealing her hips, her midriff, her long legs, then a naked breast and perfect nipple. As the music swelled, she shimmied forward and outstretched her fan filled arms in a complete body reveal. Utterly naked, utterly beautiful.

With a small and perfect penis.

I was transfixed. Time stood still for me. This was me then, reflected in human form. For the first time in my life.

She saw me, rigid with shock. She elegantly folded her fans and swayed over to my bar stool. She beckoned me with bended finger, pouted her lips and head towards me. I awkwardly leaned forward to kiss her, as she gently placed her other hand over my lips to stop me. I was close enough to smell her scent, admire the delicacy of her skin, see her perspiration, drink deeply from her gaze. She withdrew her hand and stroked the back of an outstretched finger, as if to caress an erect penis. She waved me off with a languid pose, walking backwards with sashay before blowing me a kiss as a last insult. She threw the stage curtain over her naked form and disappeared off stage.

That was my first real seduction.

Such sexual control. Utterly in charge of her body, her performance, her womanhood.

Oh, my.

The whole bar knew then. I was well and truly outed. And I was overwhelmed by the realisation. This bar was me; her dance was me; her body was me; this was me. I wasn't alone. I was home. I had the most enormous erection. For the first time, I wasn't afraid or ashamed of it either.

The barmaid leaned over and whispered, 'Eloise will be finishing soon; she'll be at the bar. She likes you.'

Eloise – that was her name. To this day, I think that was her stage name. The band The Damned had had a recent hit with a song of the same name. We all had quite nihilist humour in those days. It was deserved. I faced military prison for being me. Eloise faced jail. We had reason for dark humour.

We met that night. I was impossibly embarrassed. She was divine. I was in love, quite possibly with my own reflection. In time, we became physical lovers. She lived in that grey, ungoverned space along the wall. From the front window of her squat, we could see West Berlin, from the back, the searchlights and concrete of the wall. I became entwined in her life, dressed as she did when I was with her. For the first time in my life, I felt empowered to explore my form, my desires, my sexuality, and my womanhood. That bit was physically difficult, but she showed me how to not be embarrassed by my body. We talked about how to get rid of that part that disgusted me, for me to be whole. It was the first time in my life I came to terms with the process. I understood why Eloise was happy with her sexuality. That was who she was. It wasn't me. She understood that and tutored me in finding an equilibrium until I could find my way. She loved me for me. I'd never known that before.

Oh, my.

My military superior then was an intellectual man. He was kind to me, encouraged me in my enthusiastic military endeavours, and was always careful to credit my pictures and summaries. He was good at his job and respected by me.

On Mondays, he would point to my face and suggest I wipe away the lipstick. He knew. He told me to be careful, but then smiled. I knew too…friends of Dorothy together.

We were having coffee in the mess when the MPs came for him. They brought a dog. The adjutant ordered him to stand up and he was handcuffed. They took his badges of rank off and led him away. The word came back that the cleaner had found homosexual magazines on top of his bedroom wardrobe. In the eyes of the army, this made him a pervert and a criminal. In his job, he was deemed acutely vulnerable to Russian blackmail and may very well already be a spy. Those were the rules then.

It could be me next. I resolved to finish with Eloise and stayed in barracks until it came time to return to the UK. I never went to see her again. It was like that, then. We all lived by subterfuge, lived with fear. We all understood the transient nature of our lives. We had to. The state and the church gave us no other option. Geographising again.

I ended up in Dover, training to go to Northern Ireland. I was back in the orthodoxy. Northern Ireland was seen as a big deal. Service there came with a medal, the only one going at that time. Northern Ireland was a rite of passage. I wasn't interested anymore. I was back doing infantry stuff, no longer taking pictures, no more charcoal drawings.

We went on exercise to Salisbury Plain, lots of firing guns and running and crawling around. I'd enjoyed that before, but this was in winter; cold, wet, grey, and miserable. It was Stonehaven again, only in a uniform. I couldn't forget Eloise.

A television crew came to film us one day. That bit I enjoyed. The 'action' part, as we extravagantly rolled and ran about for them made me excited about life again. I spent a lot of time talking with the cameraman about lenses and photography. He let me look through the viewfinder, showed me how the system worked.

It grew dark and very, very cold. We were in trenches. It was going to be miserable. I offered the crew my sleeping bag to make them more comfortable. They laughed. They told me they were done and were off to the Holiday Inn for the night, but they'd see us again in the morning. That night, I sat shivering in my hole in the ground, feet in a pool of freezing water, looking through the mist at the lights of Salisbury in the distance - and asked myself if I'd rather be sat in the bar with the television crew, or here in the sub-zero pretending to fight a war.

As our deployment orders were being cut, I was asked to go and see the adjutant. He told me my family had called to tell me my grandmother in Belfast had died. I was told that as grandparents were one family stage removed, this wasn't a priority case. We were imminently going on operations. Her death wasn't deemed sufficiently grave for me to be granted leave to attend the funeral.

I remembered her kitchen, her smell, and the picture of Elvis. I remembered her warning to me after she caught me wearing my mother's bra that men didn't do that and I'd have a long and difficult life if I did. I was angry:

'Sir, I am going to the funeral.'

Again, I was told I wasn't granted permission. Again, I said I was going, and I didn't care what he thought. They relented. I flew to Belfast on a Hercules transport aircraft. I took a taxi to her terraced home, just off the Shankhill Road.

She was lying in her open coffin, in the front room. She was smaller than I remembered. Her eyes closed, dressed in black, hands crossed over her chest, holding a posy of snowdrops. I touched her, the first time I'd ever touched death. Her skin was dry and fragile and alabaster. The senior men came and replaced the lid. They carried her out into the street and paraded her coffin on their shoulders down the road. Every neighbour came to their front step and stood in silence as the man in the black top hat with the veil blowing behind him in the wind led the way in a slow march.

She was cremated.

I sat with my mother for the first time in a long time. We didn't say much. My father had left her and moved to England. She didn't explain the reasons, she didn't have to. She had moved to an even smaller house. She was back teaching. That was about it.

I walked through Belfast and looked at all the bored soldiers leaning against their armoured cars, rifles wedged on hips, bodies made big by their body armour.

That would be me soon. I'd be on the other side, another soldier in a front garden for a small child to find.

I resolved that wouldn't be me. I was done with the army.

Instead of getting back on the Hercules to England, I wrote to my Commanding Officer and told him I resigned. I'd read David Niven's 'The Moon's a Balloon' and I knew he'd done just that when he went to Hollywood, leaving the army in Malta behind. I thought I could do that too. The army didn't see it that way and I was ordered to present myself to the General in Belfast.

I went out and bought myself a camera. I had found something creative in Berlin that I had loved. I couldn't be me, that was forbidden, but I could legitimately be a little bit of me in the taking of pictures. That was artistic. I found a calling in my military rebellion.

It was the beginning of marching season, when the Protestant and Catholic communities parade through the streets in aggressive affirmation of their identities. I took pictures of it all. The marches, the army, the crowds, the emotion of it all. I wrote a thousand words on how it felt to be back in Belfast, about my gran's old home and finding a paratrooper in her garden. I sent it all to The Belfast Telegraph.

They published it. My first ever paid gig as a journalist.

I was neck deep in a new obsession. The editor had given me scant self-worth by reproducing my work. The army telescoped to a distant past. I went to see the General. He didn't try to persuade me to stay. I thought the less of him for not bothering. He reminded me that the army could be a family but only if you followed the rules. I told him I was different.

And that was that. I was released from service.

I had nothing more than a suitcase and a camera. Yet I had travelled and in the doing so, found a little of myself.

I was independent. Free to make my own choices.

My mother taught at Aberdeen's College of Commerce. Often called the 'school of last chances', I knew it had a photography course. She was on her own in Aberdeen, estranged from my father. It was safe enough for me to return. I called her up and she worked a favour and I got accepted at short notice for a year's course in photography. She helped me. I am grateful to her for that. There were other photography courses in other cities, but I needed to ground one leg of my life in the familiar while I found the new. I went back to Aberdeen.

I stopped being horrid and slowly went back to a much nicer version of me. The army and I were too much oil and water then. I used my last pay cheque to get the boat train from Belfast and booked my old room in the boarding house again. I was going to be a student of the creative arts.

I loved it.

What really blew my mind was the exploration into art, of composition, texture, style, and emotional connection. I learned the golden section, how ancient Greek and

Roman concepts of proportion and framing echoed our human eye and sense of symmetry. I revelled in the history of painting and sculpture. I learned the development of architecture and design. I fell in love all over again with old Deco Hollywood, the great photographic studios such as Harcourt and the pioneers like Sid Avery and Slim Aarons. I fell in love with the great female war photographers such as Lee Miller and Catherine Leroy, found empathy with the great designers like Billy Baldwin and Romaine De Tirtoff.

For the first time in my life, I could self-express in a creative and artistic way. Nobody cared if I wore a knotted silk scarf or yellow socks. It was part of the scene. Photography gave me an avenue. Photography school was my big bang moment.

Film cost money, and I was using a lot of it. I took extra gigs to buy my emulsions.

The first was selling magazine subscriptions door-to-door. I was slim and handsome then. I knew if the lady of the household came to the door, I could flim-flam my way to making money. I got pretty good at the elevator pitch. I learned to hustle. Charisma is a mix of sexuality and danger. I was enough of a performer then.

I took a job working bar in a local gay haunt. I turned it into performance art. Eloise had taught me well. I knew how to seduce. The bar had an American pastiche to it, so I got gussied up in my uber-tight Wrangler jeans, Cuban heels, darted cowboy shirt with a fringe, matched with an electric blue crocodile skin belt and enormous turquoise and gilt buckle. John Travolta had just had a big hit with 'Urban Cowboy', and I aced the style. I had gone back to karate school and was pretty good at all the showy stuff. I'd pull full on Elvis kick displays as I shimmied round my workstation, making all the old queens happy. It was a lot of fun.

I caught the eye of an older man one night, who kept tipping me. So far, so gay. He heard me singing along to The Eagles 'Take It Easy' and joined with me on the line about a girl in a flat-bedded Ford rolling on by. I hadn't forgotten who I am, I was just a different Yentl. He intrigued me and I him.

He asked me what I did outside of side rising kicks carrying glasses of prosecco. I told him I was at photography school. He told me he was a television director. We got talking about movies. We shared a love of the classics, all the old-time stars. We talked a lot about scenes and motivation and the ingredients that make a movie great. He was in town directing a theatre production of a television serial. He stayed in Aberdeen for a week, and we had a great time. He had money and I wanted to be loved. He gave me confidence. I had my own room then. Nobody was going to burst in and shame me for being me. At the end, he told me I should try television. I knew that this was a union-protected profession, with all the issues of getting in, past the golden door. He told me to never take 'no' for an answer.

After Doug, the second person to tell me that. Another pivotal mentor.

His affection for me changed my life.

I'd gone back to Freemans again and had a trunk full of dresses, heels, lingerie, all the same old tropes. I'd go out very late at night, just round the block. It made me happy and was quite erotic to be me. That part became self-destructive again. I'd found a purpose, but I couldn't get rid of the culturally embedded notion that I was evil and wrong. I was roasting myself on the spit again about my body and all its imperfections. I was still living a lie. Time to geographise again.

I did a bit of digging and found that the national consortium of Independent Television companies had just set up a brand-new college outside London. I could go there and enter my union ticket training with two years at their television school, then another two years professional training. After four years, I'd be in the business, fully qualified and union approved. They were taking applications on a first come, first-served competitive basis.

I was on the first train out of Aberdeen.

I took my portfolio and made my elevator presentation. I wore my high heel winkle-pickers, black drainpipes, cummerbund, a ruffled evening shirt and a green velvet jacket with a contrasting silk scarf in teal. My inspiration that season was Ricardo Montalban in 'Sweet Charity'.

I was having a Fosse summer; with a gold bangle I nicked off my mother as a good luck charm. They wanted technical qualifications I didn't have, but they gave me a bye based on my style and creative pitch. I was in. The last student to make the first intake. It was the first time I earned something by being as authentically me as I could be in that body.

That school was part of what is now Ravensbourne University. David Bowie studied there. I graduated from his alma mater. Fate wound its coils around me.

I learned my trade. I went from stills photography to the moving image and got a professional grounding in directing, camera, editing, stage design, sound, lighting, and production. I worked really, really hard at all of it. I'd be studying at 3 in the morning and be waiting for the lecturers to come in at 8 to ask more questions.

By the time I finished both schools, I'd had years of intensive training in becoming a visual artiste. All of it was foundational to who I am now. I got a job in Soho editing commercials and pop promos, spent a lot of time at Raymond's drag bar, diving into the usual Soho experiences, before Scotland called again.

I won a job at Scottish Television as a camera operator. I was off and running in show business. Wouldn't have happened without dressing up as a cowboy in a gay bar, though. Life then wasn't just slowly acquiring professional achievement; it was learning about who I really am.

New me, new job, new life; an independent life. I could write my own script now.

THAILAND, 2008

I'd been in Chonburi for five weeks. Slowly healing, ever so slowly. Daily dilation, daily painting my groin with iodine. Daily taking handfuls of pills; antibiotics, painkillers, goodness knows what. The first two weeks were utterly grim. Hormone treatments can thin the blood, making it harder to clot. I'd had to come off my oestrogen patch a few weeks before the surgery and was still off them. My body went into crash depression. Between the pain and the nihilistic life in a hotel room surrounded by medical swatches and pills, I couldn't cope.

One night, I took too many pills.

I fell unconscious. The hotel staff got worried I hadn't called for room service and used their master key to open my door. I had my stomach pumped.

I went back onto my patches the next day. Within 12 hours, I was demonstrably more mentally stable. It was a close call. Right on the threshold of happiness, my body and mind ran out of road.

Coming just three months after invasive surgery to fix my face and breasts, the rest of it nearly broke me.

That last week, Dr S took out the external stitches, did a little bit of cosmetic tidy up under local anaesthetic.

I could walk a hundred yards or so. It was an achievement. Outside Dr S clinic, there was a bridge over the main trunk road. On the other side were several junk food restaurants. Each day, I tried to climb another step over the bridge. That last week, I could just about make it. I earned that milkshake.

One last examination, feet up in the stirrups, Dr S pronounced himself happy. I still had hundreds of internal, dissolvable stitches, but his work had enough integrity. I was out of danger.

I could fly home.

I got a special chit from Dr S. At the airport, the airline quizzed me deeply. I was their liability. I'd stupidly tried to save money and had gone for a multiple leg return with a long layover in Qatar. I'd be in the air and travelling for 26 hours.

I couldn't rest comfortably. I had an inflatable rubber ring to sit on, much as a child would use in a swimming pool. Dosed up on painkillers, I waddled onto the first flight and suffered. By the time I made Doha, I thought I was going to faint. I just made it to McDonalds. The sugar, salt and meat protein helped.

By the time I reached Manchester, I was completely done in. I still had two trains to get back to Lytham St

Sugar and Spice

Annes, South of Blackpool, where I had a small apartment over a chip shop. Trailing a large suitcase, I made it to Preston Station. I had to change trains there. It was late at night; I'd been on the go for over a day.

To go between platforms, Preston Station has an underpass. I lugged that suitcase down the first flight, dropping it a stair at a time in front of me. Going back up the other side, each step was a weightlifting feat of excess. I was in excruciating pain. Halfway up, I felt something rip. I could feel dampness in my knickers. I put my hand down there. My fingers came back smeared in blood. I'd ripped my stitches.

I sat for a long time on those stairs in an empty station, freezing cold, completely on my own. I had nobody to call, nobody to help me. I was alone.

I pushed a bunch of tissues into my knickers and took those steps one at a time. Step up, pull up my case, step up, pull up my case. One little victory at a time. I did it on my own. I never gave up. I made it happen.

Airborne. Utrinque Paratus. Ready for Anything.

SCOTTISH TELEVISION, 1986

I stood outside a pair of massive metal doors, thirty feet in height, with an arm sized lever arch handle. On the wall beside me, a red light blazed inside a message box; 'STUDIO A – RECORDING'. On either side of me, cage boxes on wheels filled with props, behind me painted scene drops.

The light went out, a bell rang. My escort pulled the handle and struggled to push open the enormous sprung doors. I walked inside to the darkened space within.

The studio was the size of half a football pitch, sixty feet high, with a gantry seating area at one end. A white cyclorama stretched right round three sides of the interior, the walls behind covered in electrical breakout boxes. The floors were meshed in snaking cables, half hidden in the gloom, all leading to an impossibly brightly lit stage set.

I walked past a thirty-foot counter-balanced crane, on the end of which sat a man with an enormous camera. On cue, the men at the other end lifted him high into the air, elegantly elevating as a bird takes flight. Other cameras on gas-operated pedestals sat around the studio, manned by serious-looking men in headphones. On a dolly, an operator wound out a twenty-foot boom with a microphone. An electrician used an impossibly long pole

Sugar and Spice

to bang in a barn door on the huge assortment of massive lights hung above our heads by an endless series of adjustable bars.

Under the lights, nestled between an enormous U-shaped staircase and ornamental candelabra, forty musicians in evening dress tuned their instruments. On top of the stairs, four lithe chorus girls in satin dresses and ornate hair stood draped around a dapper man in tails and top hat. The star. Around them, a small team of hair and make-up people fussed and fretted. The star smiled a hundred-watt smile and practised his time step.

This was my Hollywood. My first day in television. My glam period was beginning.

The star was Stanley Baxter.

Mr. Baxter is a legend. He starred with Bing Crosby and Bob Hope. He worked with Hollywood greatness. For thirty years, he had his own series on BBC and ITV. His musical ability, dexterity of impressions, and sublime comic timing put him at the very top of the hallowed tradition of British music hall and television stars.

My first day in television. My Busby Berkeley moment. I was absolutely, completely, utterly, irredeemably entranced.

Stanley is gay. I knew that, instinctively and intrinsically, just by looking at him. I also instinctively knew in the entertainment world, it doesn't matter. Just beyond the studio doors, the hateful world of the 1980s had only just made gay sex legal in Scotland. To be open, let alone be me, would have meant dismissal in any other profession other than this one. But in that place of magic and theatre and lights and tinsel, to dream of fairies and unicorns, to be one yourself, was not only acceptable, it was downright encouraged. The creative business of show is the realisation of dreams. An act of imagination. I'd spent my life dreaming of being somebody else. Working on a soundstage gave my dreams temporary reality.

I thought I should make an impression on that first day. I'd worn my velvet jacket with a Nehru collar chemise, micro-cord trousers and my old army George boots, polished to a deep patina. All the other camera people were in jeans and T-shirt. I hadn't quite read the job description. I got put straight to work in the corner with a huge pile of figure 8'd camera cables. This might be showbiz, but I was in the technical apprentice basement. My job was simple enough. When the cameras moved away, I uncoiled the cable, when they moved closer, I coiled the cable. That was about it. It gave me time to watch the rhythm of the whole production.

Up above me, a director sat in the gallery with a team of folks cutting the different camera images into a montage. I could see the result in a monitor and watched the red lights blink on and off the various cameras as the vision mixer cut it all together. I'd learned the basics of this at college but seeing it all on a real soundstage with the

Sugar and Spice

pressure of creative endeavour set against budget and time was crack cocaine to me.

One figure ran the whole floor. A beautifully dressed, impeccably attractive lady who called us all to silence, cued Stanley and controlled the orchestra. She was the floor manager. A lady very obviously in charge.

I'd not exactly had a lot of positive female role models in my life up to this point. My mother? Nope. Nothing at school or the army. At art school, all the teachers were male too. This was the first time I'd ever seen a fabulously female leader in action. The crew were pretty much exclusively male. The star was male. The orchestra was male. The only other women on the soundstage were the dancers. I found her fascinating. Elegant and charismatic. She was sexual and dangerous. Catnip to my tortured soul.

The show was under pressure. The orchestra was running into overtime. Forty musicians on union rates would be a budget buster.

Stanley had one big entrance to make, side kicking his way down the big staircase, dancers in each arm, while the orchestra sawed away at Lerner and Loewe, before he ended up centre stage. This was a live recording. It was the big entrance scene, the show setter. The crane had to swing around the studio, marks had to be met, a complex choreography of artiste and technology.

There was time for two takes.

Everybody readied themselves. A hundred people all concentrating on the big moment. I readied my cable coils and stood by. On the floor manager's cue, the orchestra swelled, Stanley set off, shimmying down the staircase. It was magic…

As Stanley reached the bottom of the stairs, one of the dancers caught her foot on something. It was a technical cable somehow draped over the bottom step.

'CUT!!!'

The bell rang.

'RESET!' shouted the elegant lady, who then talked to the camera supervisor with concern. Time was running out. Budgets were on the line. Huddled heads discussed; faces were turned in my direction.

'Where is the new camera trainee?' the floor manager asked loudly. That would be me. I swallowed deeply and walked into the light.

The floor manager pointed to the offending cable, and asked, 'What is this?' The studio fell into silence. Star, musicians, crew, all looked directly at the cable, then at me. Ooops…

I walked over to the staircase and looked at the wire. I turned to her and pronounced, 'This is a sound cable, I am with cameras.'

Which was, I think, bold indeed on my first day. Silence turned to a deathly hush.

The elegant floor manager looked into my eyes and replied:

'Irrelevant. Trainees should be always aware of all cables. At all times.'

A hundred studio folks burst into laughter. I turned as deep a shade of scarlet as is humanly possible. I removed the offending wire and scarpered back to my corner.

'STANDBY!' shouted the floor manager, before asking, 'everybody set?'

The whole studio was on a hair trigger. There was time for one more take. Only one. She looked theatrically looking around the studio, and added,

'Including the trainee?'

A hundred stifled giggles gently drifted across the studio. When they stilled, the orchestra was cued, and Stanley impeccably sauntered into another classic.

Last take, last chance. Showbiz calamity averted in a very showbiz way. It was brilliant leadership, using humour to settle the team before the big moment. Sure, I was the butt of it all, but I knew genius when I saw it. And I was the trainee. You gotta start somewhere.

'THAT'S A WRAP!'

Sugar and Spice

As the crew and musicians began to pack up, the floor manager walked over to my corner. Yellow knee length pencil skirt suit, cerise blouse with a hint of exuberant embonpoint, nude tights and heels, blonde hair carefully back combed, pale pink lipstick. Quite exquisite. Quite impractical for a studio (how did she stand in those heels all day?) but utterly glam.

I watched her walk. So confident, she owned her femininity, her sexuality. Different from Eloise. Not so overtly sexual, more sophisticated. All the men acknowledged her passing and she smiled or waved in reply, as if it was her due.

She stopped before me and asked, 'What's your name?'

I told her and waited for her to reply with hers. She didn't; she just stood there, shrewdly eyeing me from top to bottom. Her eyes stopped at my George boots.

'Why are they so shiny?' She asked.

'I was in the army, I polish them, that's why they are shiny,' I replied.

She took a step forward, and quite deliberately ground one heel into my toecap. She looked up at me and said,

'Not so shiny now, are they?'

She turned and walked away, the air redolent of her scent and her perfect wiggle filling my gaze. She stopped, half turned, pointed to herself, and added,

Sugar and Spice

'I run the studio. Don't forget it.'

As if I could. Half turning away, she paused and turned back, pointing at herself again,

'Mary.'

And with that she was gone, embracing Stanley, telling him how amazing he had been and offering all the other praise an artist needs.

I was entranced. I'd never seen such a naked display of female sexual power and prowess. Ever. Not ever. Mary was her name. Goodness me…. I've met a lot of female movie stars, many powerful female politicians. I've never met anybody quite like her that day; before or since. In her pomp, she was unstoppable.

Eight years later, as the African sun dipped over the bush and the crickets chirruped, Mary and I were married in Kenya.

Something of a surprise to everybody. Including me.

MAKING MOVIE MAGIC

Being in Glasgow in that decade was the most fortunate decision I ever made.

Glasgow was still a dirty, grimy city, struggling with the end of the industrial revolution and the end of the industry that had made it. Shipbuilding, steel, coal; they'd all gone. The docks by the river Clyde were rusted and abandoned. The housing schemes on the outskirts were global bywords for socioeconomic poverty.

But the people; they hadn't changed. They were itching for renewal.

Glasgow has a word for it:

'Gallus.'

Gallus is a state of mind. An unambiguous belief that every Glaswegian is the match of any other woman, man, or child. No matter you are King, Queen, Duke, Duchess, poet, or painter. Glaswegians carry that self-identity, self-purpose and self-pride in themselves, their city, and their class. They will never be put down. Be their friend and you will find an irreverent, street smart jester of life, love, and happiness. Be their enemy and you will find

William Wallace beats strong in their hearts. A Glasgow Kiss about sums up that duality.

Glasgow made my personality whole. The city gave me a confidence of self-expression. After my years in Glasgow, no posh boy has ever made me feel inadequate again.

As a child, I'd driven through its soot-stained streets on my way to see my grandmother. It was scary and forbidding to my young eyes. It was equally forbidding as I arrived on the overnight bus from London.

The terminus was literally an abandoned bombsite from the war. I took my first step off the bus into a crater filled with dirty rainwater. The only buildings standing were a pub and The Blue Lagoon chip shop, each marooned by acres of weeds and piles of discarded masonry. It was just the way Hitler had left it.

I timed my arrival with Glasgow's great creative renaissance. The city had just been awarded the title of European City of Culture. Millions in inward investment were about to change the city skyline.

Artistically, I couldn't have started my career in television at a more propitious time. From that
Glasgow post-war poverty came an understanding and compassion for the human spirit that was to deliver remarkable working-class creative expression. All Glasgow needed was money. The European festival of

culture kicked it off. The city never stopped thriving after that.

'80s Glasgow was home to musicians like Texas, Wet Wet Wet, Orange Juice, Altered Images, Horse, Eddy Reader, Belle and Sebastian, Deacon Blue and Franz Ferdinand. Personalities like Muriel Grey, Carol Smillie, Kirsty Young, Kirsty Wark, Kaye Adams and Billy Connolly. Largely self-taught painters like Jack Vettriano, McAlpine Miller and Peter Howson. Politicians like Margo McDonald, Jim Sillars, John Smith and Donald Dewar. Footballers from the two great teams of Celtic and Rangers like Davie Cooper, Charlie Nicholas, Mo Johnson and Ally McCoist. Actors like James MacAvoy, David Tennant, Alan Cumming, John Hannah, Lynn Ferguson, Craig Ferguson, Tom Conti, David Hayman, Robbie Coltrane and Bobby Carlyle.
Glasgow School of Art and the Royal Academy of Dramatic Arts and Music sat a hundred yards apart in a city centre ripe with the architecture of Charles Rennie Mackintosh and Greek Thompson.

Scottish Television was at the epicentre of that artistic intersection. The '80s was the decade that Glasgow roared.

My only regret is I didn't realise just what a significant cultural and artistic moment Glasgow was having. I should have paused more to take it all in. The city drove Scottish national innovation and a renewed sense of its own identity. I took it for granted that being part of the extraordinary was every day. It wasn't. Glasgow was having an international moment as significant as the London swinging scene had been. From those times, Labour politician Donald Dewar rode the crest of a creative wave that would give Scotland its own devolved governing Parliament before the century was out.

Donald lived just down the road. I'd nod to him at parties. It was that kind of a time.

It all coalesced in Glasgow.

Scottish Television led the popular cultural charge. I understand that now. I am very proud to have been part of that television renaissance and that artistic movement.

The Stanley Baxter special was merely Day 1 of that odyssey. The sheer variety of programs the station made then was extraordinary. The studio complex hummed with creativity. I was part of a camera crew of eight. We were one of three teams that worked in rotation through the various productions. One week, it'd be drama serials, another light entertainment, another politics, another children's programming. I spent that first year learning my trade, understanding the complexity of multi-camera operations, developing my hand and eye co-ordination to move the huge pedestal and camera technology of the time.

The union was everywhere. I'd been met on day 1 by the shop steward and instructed where to sign the various forms and membership affiliations. Every week we'd sit in the canteen and the camera supervisor would dictate to us all what hours we had collectively worked and what overtime to claim for. They were the years before Thatcher broke the unions and the multi-channel universe broke the advertising monopoly. There were very strict rules on multiples of salary for overage. Equally strict rules on who did what and when. The union controlled everything and made its members a lot of money.

Working in television was a very lucrative business.

By the time I was 26, I was earning four times the national average salary. By the time I was 28, I was having meetings with management to try to compromise on the money I was entitled to claim through the union agreement. The financial exposure was too much for any business model. I caught the tail end of the champagne years.

We all took it for granted. Just as we took the endless party atmosphere of the life as our due. We worked together, socialised together, loved, laughed, and cried together. The station and the work were everything.

Alcohol fuelled a lot of the merriment. It was nothing to us to start the day in the pub, equally nothing to end it in the same place. I made an awful lot of shows half cut. We all did. There were four pubs within a hundred yards of Scottish. If you couldn't find somebody, it was a safe bet to go on a trawl. They'd be in one of those hostelries.

In the building, there was a lady whose job it was to walk the corridors of the creatives pushing a drinks trolley, from which she would refill the office cocktail cabinets. We even had our own brand of whisky, named after the long running station soap 'Take the High Road'. After big shows, we'd all get gifted a bottle of the stuff. Annual wage negotiations consisted of management and union reps hiring a suite at the Holiday Inn and drinking their way through the day.

That was very much the Glasgow culture. Folks were judged on their ability to hold drink and still function, and in their willingness to get the rounds in. It was just the time and the society. I had the money and very happily joined in with it all.

I had an absolute party for years.

Mary was my agent in this. She was the one who opened my eyes to the good life.

That first year, we worked together on the big network Hogmanay show that went live to the whole UK. Barbra Dickson and Lulu were the stars. I was a bit part player, hauling my cables about. Mary was the floor manager. As glamorous as ever in her style. She had a habit of painting her nails during production meetings that I thought was the most outrageously sexual and provocative 'fuck you' to management I could imagine. She'd just haul out this big bag of cosmetics and go for it, as if she'd seen it all too many times before. I was quite mesmerised. I followed her around like a Collie dog.

After the show finished, there was a full buffet in the studio where we all mingled (impossibly glam) and then the director, a charming man, invited us back to his place. He was the kind of showbiz personality who always wore a fur coat, smoked cheroots endlessly and called everybody 'darling'.

He lived in this massive pile in the West End, with an actual bar (and house barman) and an actual white grand piano in his drawing room. The production musical director tinkled the ivories, and Lulu and Barbra asked if we had any requests. Folks waltzed on the deep shag pile carpet and lounged on the futons.

As the sun rose, I followed Mary out the door and asked if I could walk her home. She asked me in for breakfast. As we sat there, she asked me if I would comb her hair. I was delighted and put it up into a chignon. She smelled extra-ordinary. She looked at my chewed nails and gave me a manicure with polish.

It started then. We didn't leave her flat for three days. Mary was twenty years older than me but had never married or lived with anybody other than her mother. There were reasons for that. She told me her story and I told her mine. We found an affinity in each other's broken wing. From that evolved an agreement that we had our private, personal moments when the doors were closed, and then we had a carefully controlled public relationship. In work we never acknowledged affection for each other. In every other way, we became inseparable.

There's a famous seafood bar in Glasgow called Rogano. That's where Mary introduced me to champagne and oysters. We had dinner with Rod Stewart. And with Chris Rea. She took me into another world of art deco, showbiz glam. She would do this thing of offhandedly dropping a story about working with Sean Connery in Switzerland or picking up Sophia Loren in her car from Munich airport. She really had done all that. As a kid who'd lived in the movies as an escape from reality, Mary was a very heady intoxicant indeed.

A female floor manager was such a rarity, and Mary so empathetic to the stars, she was forever dining at the best with the best. I got to tag along. Before Mary, I couldn't read a menu. Before Mary, wine was booze in a bottle. After Mary, I was bon viveur of the year.

I had the clothes thing down, I knew about art and architecture from school, but I couldn't bring it together in that smooth Cole Porter way I'd seen the posh brilliantine boys in the army ooze. Mary gifted me that social smoothness. I gifted her unthreatening companionship that the world saw as her handsome young man. We were very, very good together.

The real me was still there if you looked hard enough. My first car wasn't a Ferrari. It was a Fiat Panda, limited edition, emblazoned with stencils of ballet dancers and fluorescent seat covers. I adored it. Even Mary thought that was too much gayness. Some of my clothes had too much colour, too smooth a silky sheen. I had to tone down the tinted moisturiser. She'd moderate it all for me. In return, I made her happy.

Who are you to judge? I think we both deserved a bit of happiness.

What changed the orbit was my ambition. And my need for control. I'd made senior cameraperson three years ahead of the curve, but I was still part of a team with a load of folks ahead of me in the promotion queue. The glamour crews weren't the studio crews, they were the film cameramen, who had their own units, who travelled on location, who walked through the station like they owned the place. Who earned twice as much as me.

As well as I was doing, I was spending it just as fast. Mary and I had started going to the States three times a year, renting villas in Tuscany, cruising down the Nile. I loved it, adored it; revelled in it. But as much as we both earned (and Mary was on a lot more than me), I needed that single camera gig to keep the show on the road.

Saddam Hussein changed my life for me by invading Kuwait in 1990.

In response, the UK sent 33,000 troops to Saudi Arabia as part of the half million strong force assembled under United States' leadership to take it back. Around half of

Sugar and Spice

the UK contingent were Scots. I knew many of the mid-level leadership from my time in uniform.

I took my chance and made one of my elevator pitches to the Head of News and Current Affairs. He wanted to cover the war, but the existing single camera guys (they were all men) were making life impossible by wanting the full union deal. That was far too expensive. I impressed him with my skills and background. I made a money deal on the side. That turned into my union blackball moment. The management backed me all the way, but a lot of my former colleagues would refuse to speak to me for a long time to come.

I didn't care. I was on the make. Just as I had done selling magazine subscriptions door-to-door. I was young, convinced of my own talent, and utterly determined to find the war I hadn't seen first time around in uniform. My first Lawrence moment came by covering a conflict in the desert for television.

Just in the being there, I captured images that the world wanted to see. I learned my job on the job. The mistakes were less important than the actuality I captured. I saw it all, right down to filming the burning debris of an Iraqi division being bombed into oblivion North of Kuwait City.

The folks in Scottish started calling me a hybrid of my dead name and 'Rambo', the movie character. Later, when I did finally appear, many of them expressed surprise because they had always seen me as this person desperate to go to war. To me, that's gender pejorative. I don't see why the martial art of war should be a male activity. I was interested in the human experience. I found it in war. I also got to forget my own inner turmoil when I was at war. Through television, I got to find both: war and erasure.

Mary encouraged me in all of this. I still had my bags of Freemans' ladies' clothes, my happy go to. Each time I went away, I'd drop them off at Mary's and she'd look after it all for me. Saved the expense of burning and re-buying them every time.

After Desert Storm, I took her to Las Vegas. I booked a suite above the showroom where Elvis played. First day there, we went to see Liberace's Museum. That night, we sat front row for Tom Jones and screamed with all the other women as he wiggled. Tom kissed Mary and ignored me. Bless him. Not his natural demographic.

After my time helping liberate Kuwait, the station offered me a position as a camera/director, the first in the company. This was unheard of as the role cut across three union agreements. With the company's connivance, I broke the monopoly on working arrangements. I'd not only be shooting my own stuff; I'd also be making my own films for the network. I got there after less than five years in the business. I earned my first British Academy Award nomination the year after. A lot of people were very jealous of me.

Sugar and Spice

In late 1991, Mary and I finally went public. We had been an open secret for some time. There were lots of looks and chatter, but nobody questioned her. I didn't question her thinking either. We bought an enormous flat in Glasgow's West End with the cash I had made in Desert Storm and openly proclaimed our love for each other. Together, we stuffed the place with antiques and art. Together, we went to Rogano every Friday and shared oysters and magnums of Bollinger with any showbiz folks passing. Together, we shopped for dresses and shoes. Together, we stood at the top of the Empire State in New York and told each other this should last forever. It was all fabulous. The day John Smith died, a man well known to us both, we were walking out of the Uffizi Gallery in Florence. It was that kind of a life.

Then, Bosnia happened. I went back to war. Another conflict to cover. I pulled off another multi-documentary deal there by a bit of sleight of hand, offering to film with the UN in return for access. I was super stoked to go. I thought it would be like the adventure Desert Storm had been.

Mary was less convinced. She was right. Life was never the same for us after that.

Sugar and Spice

TRAVNIK. BOSNIA, 1992

Bosnia: the war where it all came home to me. I had believed in all that John Wayne mumbo about service and sacrifice. Yet there is a point where war becomes mangled bodies, blood, and ripped flesh. Real war can never be forgotten. I'd gone to war to forget myself. I replaced that with another awful chimera just as overpowering.

I became very good at war: both in covering it for television and, later, as a soldier and diplomat. I have paid a price for that. I live alone. I have too many compound interest traumas from it all. But I chose it because the yin and yang of war came to create me and sustain me. I'm not sure I totally understand my desire myself, but wars have been the greatest days of my life.

Bosnia was my first big multi-year conflict, and it was to prove my near un-doing. Bosnia was a horrible conflict. There were no good guys in Bosnia, nothing noble about it, in any way shape or form. It was fought for no other reasons than hatred and greed.

The Bosnian War began because a monster died. When Tito passed, the cork he had carefully tapped into the bottle of Yugoslav resentment blew right off. Within two years, the entire region was aflame. Bosnia lay on the fault line of it all, where Christians had stopped Muslim

Sugar and Spice

invaders in centuries passed. Tito had applied a poultice of communism to stay a weeping wound of sectarianism and hatred. When his secret police lost their master, the evil surrogates – Milosevic, Karadzic, Mladic - came out to play. By 1992, the body bags were piled high in an epic spree of murder and destruction, while the rich Europeans wrung their hands in futile do-nothing horror and the Americans looked the other way.

In central Bosnia, there is a T-junction entering Travnik. Coming from the South in '92, a traveller had two choices. Go west - to the front-line of the vicious civil war. Or east - to the United Nations base at Vitez, where the British army sat in sullen stubbornness. Contributors to a farcical international effort to stop the violence, the UN-mandated 'protection force' had little more influence than the ability to wag a finger. For all practical purposes unable to decisively change events, the British army had shackled itself to ridiculous rules of engagement that stated the UN was only there to provide 'aid' to the population, not stop a war. The British army's job was merely to make sure the calves were flattened for slaughter: the soldiers knew it and suffered for it. The Serb commander, the infamous war criminal, General Mladic, knew it too. He accurately denigrated the UN and, at the same instant, slaughtered thousands of innocents under the gaze of those international soldiers sent to prevent it.

I had first covered the Balkan wars as a journalist at the merciless siege of Vukovar, during the initial invasion of

Croatia by Serbia. Initially, I viewed the Croats as heroes, standing against aggression. I had cried for a city surrounded and systematically destroyed building by building, in fighting not seen since Stalingrad.

By the time Bosnia blew up, I knew better. That civil war had no heroes: it was a nasty and vicious degradation. Life in Bosnia in the '90s was a series of gradations of grey, coalescing and shimmering in nuances of religious and ethnic strife and division. There were no good guys in that war.

I got into Bosnia as part of the UN mission. Of all things, to help with their press coverage. My first days there were spent on loan as a public affairs officer making informative and optimistic videos about how effective we all were. In return, I got to file stuff for Scottish in my newly minted camera/director job. In Vitez, I learned to lie. The UN was not effective. It was useless.

Ahnici was a Muslim village within a Croat enclave, besieged by Serbs. A rather unlucky set of circumstances for Ahnici. Bosnia was a war where nobody had any friends. Croat hated Serb, both hated Muslims. Frontlines, such as they were, changed from house to house and individual street to street. Each coveted the other's possessions, for this was a war of greed and material possession as much as nationalist perception, one hating the other with a terrifying and incomprehensible passion.

The Croat army came to call on the Muslims of Ahnici one summer's morn in 1992. They took a family - a mother, father and three children - tied them up and put them in their basement. Then they put a gas canister in the cellar with them, opened the nozzle, lit a candle, and left. The family witnessed their own destruction approaching. They were burned alive in the explosion. It was a warning for all Muslims to leave. Ahnici was ethnic cleansing in action.

We got the word in Vitez later that day. The local British UN commander, Lieutenant Colonel Bob Stewart, led the way to Ahnici in a small convoy of white painted UN armour and scurrying press vehicles. The Croats tried to stop us. We pushed past. Bodies that have been burned smell like barbequed duck. Their odour hung in the air before we even saw the house. The local mosque had been dynamited. Nothing moved except the shimmer of summer heat. The family lay where they had been hog-tied. Their body fat had exploded with the heat of the blast which had eviscerated them, stripping flesh from bone. Father, mother, children, laid together in a grotesque tableau of family, united in agonising death.

I wondered what their last words had been. Was it surprise, fear, or anger at their captors? Or had it been a simple expression of love for each other as they had listened to the hiss of escaping gas, watching, and waiting, as their inevitable fate had unfolded?

We reckoned ourselves to be hardened in the ways of war. Yet this was not war. It wasn't even murder. It was genocide being played out with our unwilling connivance.

Bob went outside and stood, leaning against a fence, like an old, broken man. It was the only time I heard him lost for words.

The Croats came and told us to leave. Bob turned on them:

'The Croat army don't tell me where to go. I'm the United Nations,' he bellowed in righteous indignation.

At once, he expressed both our disgust and utter helplessness. We all knew what we did was hollow. Our soldiers were the expression of the will of the United Nations. It had bigger guns, professional soldiers and the weight of law and international opinion behind it. The UN weren't allowed to use them. Those people had died a horrible and excruciating death. The UN had done nothing - and the rules of engagement prevented anybody from finding those who had done it.

Western spectators and participators alike were powerless. Bosnia had no moral compass. It haunts my dreams to this day. Yet war was where I came home: war was where I could forget the gender demons in my head.

Enter new demons.

Sugar and Spice

The killing had been swift and prodigious. Each offensive in the hills above Travnik had left bodies lying in the fields. Nobody knew which side they belonged to. In a war where armies had no uniform, it was impossible to know which body part went with which cadaver. The fields were full of mounds of decaying flesh, each of unknown origin. This had been rich farming country. Not anymore.
Slaughtered livestock lay next to dead human, bloated animal carcasses side by side with cadavers.

When the cease-fire came, Bosnia Bob led us on a clean-up. The mighty UN, unable to stop the fighting, became undertakers for a day, removing the spoils of war while all sides looked on and laughed at us as we stumbled around the minefields. The bodies had lain for a while. When the young soldiers picked them up, they split, like a macabre Marx brother movie. One squaddie took the arms, another scooped up the legs. The Serbs had given the UN an hour's grace, so they put the pieces in the back of their truck as fast as they could move them. They had no way of knowing which part belonged to which. In the camp, the soldiers laid them all out in a giant jigsaw puzzle. The officers directed a torso to lie with that forearm, the soldiers infuriated when – try as they might – not every corpse could be re-united with all their parts. Off to one side, a dump of spare flesh that could neither be joined with its constituent body, or, in some cases, even identified as to which body part they were. Hand, foot, leg, arm? Nobody knew.

Bob had invited us to cover it. Having the Press there generally gave us an extra half hour of respite before the killing began again. The Serbs might not have had any respect for the UN, but they did respect world opinion – and they wanted as little attention on what was really going on as was possible.

The longer the world's indifference lasted, the more killing they could do.

Afterwards, the BBC team invited us to their house for beers and a burger. They travelled in style, with food being shipped in overland from Marks and Spencer. They had better armoured vehicles than anybody else, better sat phones, better sleeping bags. Better everything, really. War reporting for the BBC was combat by Coxes and Kings. We hungrily ate their food, drank their beer, and watched their satellite TV.

That was when the tracers started. The Muslims had the low ground, the Croats the high. We were in the fold in-between. The rounds passed over our heads, so low we could see them whizz by like phosphorescent glow-worms, slow in the distance, then speeding by, faster and faster until they whipped over our heads to explode behind us with a *'Crump'*. The military boss, a newly arrived major, said in his peremptory, pompous Sandhurst way,

'Right, everybody to the shelter.' Was he kidding?

Sugar and Spice

This was too good to miss. He didn't know the reason he had been sent out to Bosnia was that his predecessor had flipped with the insanity of the constant gunfire. He had gone out into the street with his 9mm pistol and discharged an entire clip into the centre of town, towards the latest firefight, screaming:

'Keep the fucking noise down!'

He had quietly been sent home. We were callously indifferent to it all. We went up onto the balcony and watched the show. Somebody put on Hendrix, and we drank imported beer and played air-guitar. Man, we were living our very own 'Nam movie, seduced by the horror and the knowledge that we were ALIVE. War is intoxicating like that.

Sometimes, I get a flashback to my wars, the cocaine high of the excitement. Like the drifting smell of cordite after the explosion, nothing is quite the same the same as the moment, only a faint memory of an exquisite sensory buzz. The simple truth is war is addictive. When the bullets flew, I forgot who I really was and entered another temporal plane, where my body and society didn't matter because it could all be rubbed out in an instant. War is such a drug; such a palliative, such a way to forget.

I got truly hooked on it all. War didn't save me, it forced me into another form of denial.

Sugar and Spice

Before the dreadful war, Mario had been a novice monk. He had dedicated his life to God and to helping his fellow human beings. He was tall, with an open, almost beatific face, short, blonde hair, and a ready smile. The thing that impressed me most about him was his sense of inner peace and contentment. He had a light that was other-worldly. Something shone from within him that was hard to define, but I could swear you would sometimes see a physical light emanating from his body. I have spent my entire life searching for that contentment.

Many years later, seeking answers to questions I had not yet resolved to formulate, I went to stay for a short period at a Franciscan monastery. Within those hallowed walls, I met men who had forsaken all their worldly goods for a life of humble abstinence. A new initiate told me he had been a New York psychiatrist. One day, he had sat there in his office, after another multi-hundred-dollar consultation, and been hit right between the eyes by the question,

'What is this all about?'

He had no idea where the question came from, or who had asked it. He was a millionaire, with a vast penthouse apartment, suitably wealthy friends, liked and admired by his peers, enjoying the sort of minted lifestyle that you only ever see in adverts. Yet none of it had satisfied his soul. That day, he changed everything. He sold all his worldly possessions and swapped his Upper-East side life of pampered opulence for a monk's habit and a bare cell.

In doing so, he had found a spiritual peace that, to him, was worth more than all the money in the world put together.

His monastery, Greymoors, sits high above the Hudson River, in New York State. Every summer, the monastery opens its gardens to Appalachian Trail thru-hikers. In 2001, a decade after Bosnia, I was one of those hikers, like most of my fellow travellers, on a personal search for peace. My internal struggle to break free of my earthly construct, to let loose the true person within me, had reached another of those over-whelming crescendos that had made me suspend my new-found life as a Parachute Regiment officer for the strictures of a wilderness mountain range. That year, I hid from myself by walking the length of America on its mountain tops.

By the time I reached Greymoors, I was 1,500 miles into my personal odyssey of self-discovery. On that trail, I found more internal peace than in the rest of my life put together. The mountain didn't care who or what I was, the rock simply existed. The mountain said:

'Climb or don't climb, it matters nothing to me. Either way, I will still be here when you are gone, as I have been here for thousands of years before and will be for thousands of years to come.'

Confronted with the eternal majesty of nature, I had my first inkling of what I had to do. We are only here for a very short period, mere pinpricks in the vast tapestry of existence. Who cares what anybody else thinks? We only have one chance to contribute, and to expedite that chance we must find a personal nirvana before any of that joy can be spread amongst our fellow human beings.

At Greymoors, no matter how I tried to goad an argument from my Franciscan brother, he had an answer. Even the complicated ones, like how a sip of wine and a piece of bread can literally become the blood and body of Christ. While he acknowledged the implausibility of that miraculous transformation, his answer was always,

'You either believe or you don't. I choose to believe.'

No matter what I said, he would just smile at me, and steeple his hands. In his own mind, he was content. How I longed for that self-awareness.

Before I left Greymoors, I went to the chapel, got on my knees, and prostrated myself before God. I asked him why I had been made so different, why I was forced to live this lie. Why I could not be the woman I am. Was my entire life to be a cruel joke? The laughs had dried a long, long time ago. What could I do? How could I make this happen? How could I construct physical and emotional change? I didn't have the courage to bring Abi to life. Would God help?

In response, all I received was silence. There was no earth-shattering moment, no revelation from above, just the stillness of the air in that room. I left frustrated.

God had given me an answer, though, in meeting that nameless Franciscan monk. The answer was moral courage: the courage to abandon everything else and seek enlightenment. Courage comes in many forms. We reward the physical kind with medals and certificates. Moral courage is rarely rewarded. It is the kind of courage that Nelson Mandela showed in refusing to acknowledge apartheid, at the cost of his physical imprisonment. It is the courage to set aside a million-dollar practise for the austerity of a monastery. It is that inner vessel that provides the sustenance and provision to follow a course of action, no matter the consequence, in the true and sure conviction that that course is right.

One day, I would have to find that courage too if I was ever to be me. Writing this book is proof I did find that courage. Eventually. I am no longer accepting the things I cannot change. I am changing the things I cannot accept.

Nearly ten years before Greymoors, I was but a neophyte taking her first steps: which is when Mario came into my life. He had that Franciscan light of certainty and moral courage too, although I did not realise it at the time, but which he was to bequeath to me. Mario was the first person I ever met that had found himself.

Despite surrendering to God, when war came to visit Bosnia, Mario had joined the Croat army, to defend his homeland. Mario would become my guide and mentor, across the front lines of Travnik, to the centre of fierce and vicious fighting. I met him in Vitez, a nearby village, at Croat headquarters. He was a lieutenant in the local militia. When I first saw him, he was clad in a long greatcoat, backing out of a doorway, exclaiming loudly at whoever lay unseen within. He turned and smiled at me: and lit my soul. He agreed to be my tutor, to show me why this war was being fought. We spent several days together, discussing the war, what had gone wrong.

Mario despaired at the motivations of those who had sought conflict. More than anything, he wanted peace. He worried about how the war had changed him. We drank a lot of slivovitz, and our conversations ranged far into the night. We sat around the dim light of a candle, in a cellar, mere yards from the front line. With the sounds of muffled explosions reverberating round our subterranean womb, he told me of God and courage and self-determination. Despite it all, my camouflage of dark clothing, camera and body armour, my inner-self found her way out to revel in his stare. I can still see his face, hardly lined, his angelic eyes and his mop of unruly hair, and wondered as I unwittingly fell in love with this unlikely soldier. My corporeal body remained within its earthly constraints, but the person within stirred as never before.

Sugar and Spice

Vitez lived on a knife-edge. The Serb front-line was only a mile away. The Muslim enclave, mere yards down the street. Mario in the middle. Trust had disintegrated. This battle was for survival.

High above the township, trenches wound their way in a random zigzag across the hills. No UN soldiers ever saw this battlefield. On Christmas morning, 1992, I willingly followed Mario into those uncharted waters. The line of fortifications Mario took me to see had been dug by an army of volunteers, to defend the very soil they had been brought up to tend and cherish. This war was unseen, between neighbours and former friends.

Mario and I toured the front-line together, amidst a blessed silence. Snow fell gently on the country, soft flakes that gently dissolved as they hit the ground. Together, they formed a thin sheet of icicles, quite translucent, sparkling in the weak winter sun.

I was laden with camera equipment. Mario shared that burden, as we climbed higher and higher, above the low-lying fog, into the sunlight above.

The trenches were filled with small groups of volunteers, clad in a ragman's mishmash of discarded camouflage. Many wore ordinary town shoes; they could not afford boots. One wore a bright yellow sombrero. Some were armed with assault rifles, some with shotguns. The Croat army was an army of the people. Above Travnik, the Croat army was merely a group of volunteer amateurs, nothing more. This was no organised military, no matter the strut of its members.

Facing them, a couple of hundreds of yards way, was the might of the professional Serb armed forces, lavishly armed with the contents of Tito's armouries. Their daily amusement was to launch an indiscriminate barrage against Travnik town in the valley below.

As we walked, I asked Mario why he fought. In all our animated discussions, until that day, we had never talked of vindictive violence or aggression. He walked and talked with the economy of masculinity, leaving sentences unfinished, a mere glance towards me silencing my thoughts. The man could see deep within my own soul. As much as he was a victim of his circumstance, it seemed to my fevered imagination that he saw the root cause of my own dilemma.

Wordlessly, he beckoned me to follow him a little further down the line. He stopped and asked me to look across no-man's land, to point out what I saw. In the middle of the expanse of snow-covered field, I saw a ruin, broken walls, a caved-in roof, marked with bullet-holes and shrapnel scars.

'See that ruined house?' he asked.

I nodded quietly.

'That is my home. I lived there. That is why I fight.'

In Bosnia, this man of God had turned warrior simply to protect those he loved, and in the doing so, had killed his fellow human being, in direct defiance of the very scriptures he had dedicated his life to learn and preach. Mario was not alone. His fellow soldiers were not professionals. They were simply people doing what they thought was best to protect the homes they lived in.

Mario was conflicted by what he had been asked to do. We spent hours after that moment, sitting in those trenches, discussing the barbarity of man, the agonies he faced each day, and the family and friends he had lost. There are precious few rights and wrongs in war. Death is death. The glory belongs to the storybooks. The reality is more sordid in its petty detail.

Mario saw through me, through that hard exterior, to the person within. He was a kindred spirit who was both gentle and understanding. On Christmas morning, drawn together, we stood looking at the remains of his house. He put his arm around my shoulder, while I tenderly circled his waist and we turned and smiled at each other. Nothing was said, but our eyes spoke the truth. In a different world, maybe we could have found each other. In what form, I do not know, but our spirits locked in an embrace that day. In his world, of hate and battle, we were but a brief encounter on a hillside pocked and ravaged by death.

Mario took me down to his headquarters. The weather turned, the skies darkened. He told me he had to check his men were alright. He left with their Christmas ration of cake on his back, a box of cigars clasped in his hands. One human treat for those afflicted with the task of living in those hastily dug subterranean shelters. I watched him slowly tread back up that hillside, until his figure was lost in the tendrils of fog.

High on the hills above Travnik that evening, Mario was shot and killed by a Serb sniper. The bullet hit him square in the forehead as he walked with his sack of Christmas gifts. He would not have known what had happened. He fell on the land he loved; his blood intermingled with the very earth he had been born on.

Nobody will remember Mario. I never even knew his last name. But I remember his spirit, his sweet soul, his inner light, his love, and our short days together. I still dream of him - and savour the moments when he visits me in my slumber. He and I had but a moment, but I will never, ever forget him, nor what he taught me; there are some moments in life where to back down is to destroy any life to come.

Every now and again, there can be no compromise. Such was my story in the years to come. I could no more find compromise with the girl I have always been than fly to Mars. Abi wanted - and deserved - her moment, without her there was no future worth thinking about.

This was why Bosnia started the end of my relationship with Mary. I wanted Mario, deeply, to my core. As a woman. Not in the form the world still saw me.

Mary and I were comfortable together, but she was a sister, not a partner. In the end, our love of each other was essentially platonic. Deep, but platonic. Neither of us, for our own very personal reasons, could ever bridge the divide that body, sexuality and sheer desire could ever quite make whole, no matter how we both tried. That was the year we retreated to separate bedrooms. I'd tried to make that compromise in that time and place; television had helped me find yet another accommodation. Mary and I had found a temporary happiness, but that was built on sand too. I had met Mario and his loss reverberated around me.

Compromise, compromise, compromise.

None of it was satisfying. It was merely gradations of unhappiness. Sometimes dimmed, but never extinguished.

I am woman. I can't change that. I still had fifteen more years to travel before I realised there was no more compromise to be found.

BLACKPOOL, 2006

I threw all his clothes into the bin. Everything that had been that version of me went into the skip. All my jackets, trousers, shirts, shoes, under wear, sportswear, smart wear, casual wear, informal wear, sleep wear: everything, all of it. I wanted none of it.

I resolved that that Sunday would be the last day presenting as a man. Tomorrow, I would re-awaken as woman. I might not yet have the complete body, but my mind would take me to where I wanted to be. I would absorb the knocks; I could take the rejection and the pain.

For some months, I had been self-administering hormones bought on the black market. I had experimented with the dose. Two types: one an oestrogen, the other an androgen blocker. The oestrogen would start introducing girl power to my body, the blocker would stop that horrid testosterone. Bingo; double whammy of happiness. The joy pills came straight from Vanuatu, packaged as 'herbal supplements'.

The oestrogen made me instantly happy. I knew that. The day I had started on those pills was the first day I had felt truly content. My body began to smile. The anti-androgens were more problematic. They robbed me of any energy. I felt weak, feeble, and unable to focus.

Quite quickly, I became unable to achieve any form of an erection. Oh, bliss. I'd never wanted nor enjoyed that. Finally. I robbed myself of the potential to orgasm. Between the two, I became asexual, unable to find any physical reaction to sex. My genitalia became mere appendages, excess skin, and tissue, hanging there, obscene, between my legs. I had long abused those organs, taping them up between my legs, crushing them by crossing my legs. I hated them, for what they had done to my body, to my soul, preventing me from being me.

The loss of an erection was small beer.

For most of my life, during penetrative sex with a female, I had only been able to orgasm by imagining myself to be that female. I liked to lie on top, so I could dream of my partner fondling my breasts, feeling my partner inside me. Most time, I could not climax at all. I would make up excuse after excuse, but I was rarely capable of just throwing my feelings away. I so desperately wanted to physically be a girl. Physically touching the naked form of one brought forth a powerful yearning, not sexual abandon. It had been that way with Mary.

I had many encounters with men all through my previous life, some very tender. I've always found a certain type of rugged, masculine man attractive. That never worked. I was what the gay community would call a receiver rather than a giver. But nothing could make up for the fact that my body was wrong. As much as a partner enjoyed that body, it was the wrong body. Perhaps strangely, I regarded myself as heterosexual. I know now it was the desire to physically be a woman that I venerated; I adore the company of women. I love women's conversation, the expression of emotion, the sense of belonging. It is me.

Before I physically realised myself, the girls told me they liked me. I had no shortage of willing partners. Apparently, I was sensitive and a good listener. I rarely took them up on their sexual offers. In those mortally embarrassing moments that could not be avoided, I would either fake an orgasm, or will my mental image of womanhood, having sex, of my body being soft and pliant with my partner, as my curves were caressed.

My climax would be a guilty one. I would be happy I had finally achieved what my partner was willing me to do, suffused in the secret guilty knowledge that I had been untrue to her. I was never at one sexual congress with my partner, I was off in my own mind, living my own fantasy of a world I had longed for all my life.

That Sunday was the day that lie would end.

I phoned my mother, to tell her of my decision. I had told her of my childhood abuse at boarding school mere weeks earlier. She had slapped me. We had not spoken since.

This day, she took my call. I told her I was going to openly be a woman. The line went silent. Her voice, distraught with emotion, came back to me. She told me I would be condemning the family to disgrace. She could not live with me if I did this to myself. I told her I could not live with that body and that life anymore. If I did not do this, I would rather be dead.

She told me if I went ahead with this, I would be dead to her, and all my family. She would rather I died. Her religion and her deep socialised convictions over homosexuality as perversion trumped her role as mother. There had always been limits to her love. My decision was clearly well into hostile territory.

This was my Mario/Greymoor moment. I could either walk it back and accept the compromise that would ruin me; or make that stand for something so deeply ingrained in me as to be the foundation of my moral purpose. Compromise? I'd long since passed the time I could do that.

I had to choose, between a continued life as walking dead, or a re-birth that would kill everything else.

I chose rebirth. I chose me. I chose life.

I had done everything the world had asked of me for 44 years. Now, I wanted to do this for me. I was sorry, but that was my decision. It was time to show that Greymoor moral courage, to live my conviction.

Abi came first, for the first time.

She put the phone down.

Three days later, several suitcases arrived at my door. They were filled with everything my mother had kept of my life. Photographs, the odd piece of clothing, documents. She had wiped her home, shelves, cupboards, and her life of anything that might be of me.

My parent's house had been scrubbed clean of any memory of their oldest child.

With the suitcases came a letter. In it, on one page of hand-written text, my mother explained that she and my entire family would dis-own me. I was never to contact any of them again. She told me I would forever be a freak and an outcast. She wrote that she wished I had never been born.

That was the last communication my mother was ever to initiate with me for the rest of her life.

GLASGOW, 1994

Mary and I had been in separate bedrooms for several years. On the surface, we were the happy couple. Underneath, we were beginning to fray.

My innate dichotomy was beginning to come uncontrollably back to the surface again. Mary and I argued about my borrowing her clothes and make-up. I was wearing female underwear to work. It made me happy. Mary was embarrassed by my lack of control. I was breaking our compact. Now, I understand that. Then, I was too riven by my own mental ill-being to pay sufficient attention.

In turn, her own issues were beginning to realise.

Within 20 years, she would be committed to permanent care suffering from dementia. It is a terrible disease, and it would rob her of everything. Then, neither she nor I understood what was going on. There was the night I woke with a kitchen knife at my throat as she proclaimed me the Devil. There was the time on holiday in Turkey when she walked off and didn't re-appear for two days. She had no idea where she had been. Every day, little things would go awry. She'd forget to meet me or repeat stories in the same conversation. I didn't notice it, but little by little, you could see friends cough gently or cast glances. Whatever was eating her brain was slowly, piece by piece, day by day, robbing the world of the beautiful, stunning, vivacious woman I'd first seen that studio day eight years earlier.

Both of us went with it all. The change was so slow and incremental, we made our own internal adjustments without comment or evaluation. Whatever else we were, we had made an agreement all those years ago that was private to us. Nobody else. We soldiered on in our separate bedrooms with our own demons.

At work, I continued to be extremely successful, even if privately I was falling apart. I countered depression over my horrid physical form with ever more exotic trips abroad, ever more complicated film projects that I deep dived obsessively into to hide my own inner torments. Afghanistan, Belize, Angola (with the UN again), Barbados, the States many times, South Africa, Cannes Film Festival, Thailand, Kenya. The list was endless. I flew to Atlanta for eighteen hours filming, came back overnight on the red eye and then turned up at 0900 same morning on location for the first day directing a multi-camera series. The show was a lynchpin of the schedule. Several executives had put their budget and reputation on the line for it. I sketched my storyboard during the flight back from Atlanta on the airline sick bag, getting wazzed in business on the company dime. I could do that then. I had the energy. Nobody questioned me. The station indulged me. I always came back with a winner. Television came easily to me. I had the creative process down pat. Some concepts I developed myself, some I did over champagne in Rogano, my development office.

Of course, I was getting egotistical. I was out-growing what Scottish could offer me. The creative process was becoming too easy and the challenges less interesting. More seriously, the money tree was dying. Satellite and cable and Thatcher would soon end the monopoly. Revenues were falling, budgets were tighter. My expenses paid global travel-a-thon contract was in its sunset clause. I was in danger of becoming extinct. I didn't read the runes, maybe I didn't want to. The frustrations at work began to rise, as I had to fight for shows that a year earlier hadn't even been questioned. My expenses (always a legendary television fudge) started to be examined. I didn't like the attention one little bit.

Still, I had Mary. We both had Rogano. Mary didn't have much of a family. As far as I was concerned, neither did I. We completed each other.

Mary had met my mother. A one-time deal. Disaster: I wasn't close to the family, for all the reasons explained. My father had come back to Aberdeen after an extended period in London. I wasn't exactly overwhelmed by the reconciliation. In all those years, I'd once gone up to Aberdeen for Christmas for a day, and then for my brother's wedding, where I'd stayed in a hotel. I'd phone once a week for an hour, out of duty. I had literally no reason to go to Aberdeen. My mother and father came down to

Glasgow to meet Mary, who had so obviously captured my heart. We'd gone to Rogano, as ever. I got to be showbiz camp there with the overwhelmingly gay staff. Both Mary and I viewed it as nights on stage. One disapproving glance from my mother at my cabaret and all those childhood tropes of perversion came flooding back. I became so awkward; I spilled my glass of Bollinger all over my mother's dress. I don't remember speaking to my father at all. Mary took my side, held my hand, which I loved her for. Which marked her with my mother as Cruella De Ville marks Dalmatians.

After that dinner, I was very depressed and withdrawn. Mary and I both loved the film 'Out of Africa'. Both of us saw ourselves as Meryl Streep. Both of us were very keen on Robert Redford. His character in that film reminded me of Mario's strength. I'd already been filming there and had raved about it on my return. After our misstep in Rogano with my mother, the ship was off kilter again.

Mary, bless her, said,

'Let's go to Kenya and get married...' Just like

Meryl did.

Why not?

Sugar and Spice

In those days, neither of us thought that much about these things. Life was libertarian fun. Mary went off and researched outfits for us both while I booked a wonderfully exotic private safari to Treetops, the Masai Mara, Karen Blixen's old club in Nairobi, a week on the beach down near Malindi, a plane ride over Lake Naivasha and a balloon ride by Mount Kenya. That's how we rolled. All in. Prep done and dusted within a fortnight, then sat drinking champagne in business at 40,000 feet.

We resolved not to tell anybody, including my family.

I'd been to my brother's wedding the year before and had squirmed as my parents had taken over the entire event, to the extent of inviting their own work colleagues, many of whom had never met my brother. My mother even wore a pale cream dress on the bride's big day. My brother had his own fist windmills with my father and immigrated to Canada a couple years after his wedding. I've not spoken to him in 30 years, no idea what happened to him. I did get a hate filled letter when I became openly me, so I'm not exactly desperate to find out. However, his relocation is a mark of how estranged we all were from the norm. I'd seen what had happened to his nuptials. I wasn't going to let that happen to mine.

The Kenya safari was everything we hoped for. Utterly magical. We marvelled at elephants, fed giraffes, ran from the monkeys, and stared at the crocodiles. We took our balloon ride in the pre-dawn and flew over a pride of sleeping lions. When we landed, we married in the bush as the hot African sun warmed the plains. We flew to Malindi and ate our wedding dinner on the beach being serenaded by a gospel choir of wonderful African ladies.

Viv Richards, the cricketer, and I had filmed together on a previous trip. He gifted me use of a cottage in a hotel he co-owned, right on the beach. As the ocean waves gently lapped just beyond our private balcony, we nestled together under our pristine mosquito net, in our rose-petal strewn bed.

I told Mary I loved her unconditionally.

She told me,

'You love me more than I can ever love you.'

Wow. That was a moment. Honest, looking back on it, but quite the sabre thrust all the same. Unpacking it, she could see the future much more than I. By an awfully long mark too.

On my side, I was saddled with being me, yet unresolved. At least part of me had got married because I was determined to make a success of my relationship, to not repeat my parent's unhappiness and the pain that had inflicted on me. It wasn't just love that drew me to accept marriage. I was holding on sinking wreckage.

On Mary's side, she knew I would leave her one day for me. She realised before me I couldn't go on forever as I was in that form. She'd helped me, hidden me, encouraged a compromise, but it was self-evident that couldn't last. She also knew, but hadn't told me, that her family had a history of dementia. It killed her father and her sister. In both cases, the disease had started to visibly show at 50. Mary was 51. I was in denial that she wasn't well, but she knew it was coming.

So, she put a time limit and an emotional limit on our marriage.

For a year, it was alright. We went onwards. We slept in the same bed for a bit. We needed that emotional re-assurance, but the egg timer was nearly empty.

In no small part accelerated by the fury my family exhibited towards me. I had defied them and eloped. I asked them all to a celebration dinner in Glasgow as a compromise. Every single one of them - mother, father, brothers, aunts, uncles, cousins - refused absolutely to make the trip. It was the first decision I'd made in my life entirely independently of them. They hated me for my individuality. Mary hated them right back. She was ferocious in her defence of me. I really did love her for that. She stood by me. She gave me strength. I chose her over my family. Unconditionally.

I should have listened to her words on our wedding night.

TELEVISION – THE END GAME

1995. The year I left Scottish Television. The end of the longest period of employment in one place I've ever had. The company was in the throes of fundamental change. Within five years, a staff of 1200 was laid off or made redundant, to be replaced by contract workers. The big network shows disappeared, the series I worked on got smaller and smaller in scale and then weren't made at all.

I had a couple of last hurrahs, social conscience stuff that appealed to my left-wing beliefs. Glasgow had awakened my interest in politics. I joined Labour and was heavily infused with the whole Blair Brown spirit of change. In Glasgow, there wasn't much debate. The city, like all great industrial conurbations, leans leftward as a rite of passage. To live there, the reason and justice behind the labour movement is self-evident. You only have to walk the streets of the crumbling sink estates of social housing to become impassioned about changing the lot of the working class.

I made a couple of series that took troubled young people off the streets and offered them a chance to make the television they wanted. We called them 'VJs'. The union folks were embittered by it. Another agreement broken. But I was very passionate about the whole concept.

Several went on to very successful careers. Working on the series had given them stability in chaos. Giving them that opportunity was very personal. A form of giving back if you like. Doing something within my power to put the success elevator back down to the ground floor for the next generation of troubled kid.

My last series was in the same vein. Taking kids from youth football and sending them to pro school for a week, where they got to work with the legends of the day. Hosted by Rangers' Davie Cooper, Celtic's Charlie Nicolas and Scotland coach Tommy Craig, the young talent got master classes from the likes of Scottish national team legends Ally McCoist and goalkeeper Jim Leighton. Davie, Charlie, and Tommy were a joy as human beings, perpetually still struck with the same naïve joy of kicking a ball they had known as kids themselves. Seeing them spark off the youth team was a meeting of the generations. It was wonderful to watch, so empowering to be capturing and delivering as a director. A lot of the director's art is artifice, in the creation of emotion. With this show, these personalities, and the game as the unifying device, it had its own wellspring.

None of the hosts had any television experience. I extemporised the whole thing on the spot. Improvised the script, shot the whole thing reality-style. If you gave the fellas written words, they were too self-conscious, tongue-tied, false and wooden. But give them thirty seconds to freely talk about the joy of kicking a ball, then their natural love of the game shone through. It was television gold.

We were working on a script link together and I turned to signal the crew to turn over the cameras, to capture the vibe. I turned back and Davie was on the ground, not moving. I thought he was joking around.

He wasn't.

Scotland's greatest wing forward had had a cerebral embolism. He was dying.

I gave Davie CPR and the kiss of life. I rode with him in the ambulance. Time slowed right down. I find that happens to me in crisis. I remember every second. How his skin turned clammy, the rise and fall of his chest as I breathed into his lungs. How I yelled at him not to give up.

I kept his heart and lungs going long enough to get him to hospital. I was the only one in the ER with him when they asked what I thought his wishes were. He didn't have family in Scotland, so I sat with him overnight in the ward, holding his hand, as the machines wheezed, and the doctors shook their heads. Ally McCoist came, and we held each other as the tears fell. I had to give a press conference to the dozens of crews and reporters that had assembled. Nobody else would do it. I was in the same clothes I'd worn when I had held him and massaged his chest and breathed my breath into his body.

He lay for two days before they turned the machines off. The Daily Record, Scotland's best-selling paper, ran the headline,

'Dear God, not Davie Cooper.'

100,000 lined the streets of Glasgow for Davie's funeral. I hugged his family and touched his coffin one last time.

I went to a bar and got really, really drunk. I spent all day there, as a succession of people came and went, joining in my bacchanalia of nihilism.

As traumatised by Davie as I was, I also mourned Mario and Eloise and Mary and my own tortured existence. In my head, my inability to restore Davie became mixed by my own self-pity and self-loathing at my inability to fix me. I had an enormous bow wave of unresolved trauma inside me that broke my internal dam of self-control when I began to process the immediacy of Davie's death. Davie's death was an allegory for my life: perpetually on CPR.

Not one person in Scottish asked me how I was coping. No referrals for counselling, no time off. Nothing. I went back to the edit suite and spent two months looking at footage of Davie and the others while I tried to cope. The show was a great success. Ratings were great. I was in all the papers.

None of it mattered. A man I liked and respected had died on my watch. I felt responsible.

I'd had enough of Scottish Television. It was time to geographise again. Make a new start, run away from all those issues again. Mary had gone freelance, she had nothing holding her to Glasgow. For some time, she'd been advising me that I needed a bigger stage. The classic route that I'd seen other directors travel, down to England for a few years, then back up to Scotland again in a promoted post.

I figured in her enthusiasm for me to move on, she shared that same ambition.

I was very ambivalent about crossing the border. England has always been a foreign country to me. I'd spent my time in the army being patronised by the posh boys for my accent and class. I'd gone to art school in London, but London takes money and my memories of then were of my face pressed against the window watching the rich people trough it while I stood shivering in the street.

Still, Mary and I were a team. I'd be going back down there with an ally. And I'd be making big money this time. My ambition clouded my judgement. My stuff was just as good as anything coming out of London. It just wasn't being seen there. Television is a cottage industry of connections and relationships. I felt I needed another stage if I was to push onwards.

It wasn't difficult to find another gig. I had a great reel, and a great rep. Anglia Television picked me up as a series producer/ director. I was off to Norwich. What was more important was they had a network deal with London for their current affairs output. My stuff would be seen in the capital.

I accepted with alacrity and started looking at property. Then I was hit with a bombshell: Mary told me she wasn't coming. She was staying in Glasgow. I had to go; the contracts were signed. We argued long and hard about her decision. I was bitterly, bitterly upset. Her disease took over her judgement. She'd gone back into her bedroom, started obsessively organising her life, locking her door, buying bags of expensive designer clothes, then hiding them, still in their wrappers. She stopped getting up in the mornings, not appearing until after lunch.

I was too young and too riven by my own issues to properly address this. She was incapable of confronting her own demons.

I went to Anglia on my own and sent my salary home each month to pay for a mortgage on an apartment that I never saw. I rented one room next to the railway line, listening to the trains pass in the middle of the night. The first week I was there, I had an acute asthma attack and was hospitalised.

Mary came once in the nine months I lasted at Anglia, staying for one night. In an act of desperation, I fronted with the head of programmes about the separation, and he agreed to offer her a gig. I thought that might help persuade her to join me. Over a breakfast meet he arranged in one of Norwich's posh hotels Mary refused point blank. She didn't just refuse; she threw it right back in his face. She went to the railway station and went back to Glasgow as I stood in tears on the platform begging her not to go.

The folks in Anglia were fine. The programmes were a little pedestrian, but I was doing everything right, building my portfolio as a series producer. Internally, I was falling apart. I had no money – I was sending most of my salary to Glasgow, the remainder on renting. I didn't have a car; I had a bicycle.

At the weekends, I'd go for monster bike rides round East Anglia and dream of owning a country pile.

I felt abandoned. Which was the reality.

That was the start of the lonely years.

I still don't understand why Mary refused to join her married partner. The charitable side of me thinks she was trying to send me off because she knew what was coming. The darker side of me says 'yes, but she took your money.' I'll never have an answer to that. I do know that I was badly, badly affected. I had put my love into one person, and she had let me down like everybody else in my life had already done.

I left Anglia and went to London. I got a job with Mirror Group Newspapers, at their media company called 'Live TV'. From the beginning, it was chaos. The interview was at their group headquarters in Canary Wharf. I got

Sugar and Spice

whisked up to the 22nd floor and shown into a corner room with a hugely impressive vista of London laid out below me. I sat there waiting for two hours before I lost my rag and walked the corridors to find somebody in charge.

Mirror Group was still in the throes of recovery from Maxwell. It had been taken over by a bunch of sacked executives from the Murdoch Empire who had a grudge to prove. They were to spaff thirty mill against the wall trying to re-create Sky. The foundation investment for the cable company called Live TV. None of them knew anything at all about television. Not a single thing.

They needed me.

I eventually emerged from that interview with a contract for a large proportion of the thirty mill. In return I sold my professional self-respect. I was appointed Editor-in-Chief. My oppo on the print side was Piers Morgan. While The Mirror has a long pedigree as a left-leaning newspaper, the Group had none in television. Nor did the bosses. I fought a long and ultimately fruitless campaign to try to instil some sort of professionalism in that company. Every time I thought I had made my point, they reminded me what they paid me and then did something else that was untenable. The operating model was a classically male toxic city boy mix. The C-suite got very rich, but the human management was awful.

I was able to establish my own headquarters in Edinburgh, where I set up a city station. I was back in

Scotland, 50 miles from Glasgow, in my senior role. I dreamed of buying a home in the New Town and being an Edinburgh laird. Again, I approached Mary about moving. Again, she refused. I bought my own place in Edinburgh and concentrated on work, still sending thousands every month back down the motorway to Glasgow for a home I never saw and a wife I never heard from.

I should have divorced then. Whatever we were was over. A marriage should be a partnership. I was doing all the heavy lifting with no reward or recognition. I didn't divorce. I kept on hammering away at the same failed project because Mary had once been good to me, and I couldn't admit my marriage was the same failure my parents had been. I couldn't keep the demons out of my head. As ever, in time of emotional distress, I retreated to Freeman's catalogue, my bags of clothes and the hidden me. My entire life was a pretence except for those secret moments.

The stations I set up were the first digital news network in the UK. I carried on my belief in putting the elevator down to the ground floor and deliberately hired socially disadvantaged folks with passion. There are still dozens of those alumni plying their way through television today because of the break I gave them. The bits I could directly influence were good. The news stuff I managed to put out next to the utter fluff the London boys controlled was great. I got another British Academy

Award nomination, as well as a host of other awards, for my technical innovation and programmes.

My former peers in Glasgow remained intensely jealous. I was invited by the British Academy to deliver a lecture at Scottish Television on digital television and the technical innovations I'd devised. I was very proud to be asked to come back by the Academy. They put flyers up all over the station. I remembered those lectures in the past as busy and exciting occasions. I felt like I was the prodigal child returning. On my night, the only person in the room was the man who had invited me. Row upon row of empty seats. Not a single person from the company I'd worked for eight years came to hear me. That hurt. It's the downside of the Glasgow character. They are awful at praising success and intensely jealous of personal advancement.

In the end, the Mirror Live TV Company went broke. The operating model was an utter fantasy. The management changed and I was given the chat. I had the classic newspaper exec three hours to clear my desk. They gave me a lot of money to go, but it wasn't a good moment. I'd put my heart and soul into making it all work. With that management, it had been a long, lonely struggle that ended in a failure I was powerless to alter. It wasn't my fault, but at the time I thought it was.

My reputation had taken a hit with Mirror. I was still known as a good programme maker, but Live's unedifying reputation as Stunt TV carried over onto me.

My next stop, and my final television job, was at Granada Television. I was appointed as a Channel Editor. Management once more, bit lower down the pecking order, but back in the mainstream. It wasn't Granada's fault, but my tether broke there. I hit my identity brick wall again.

SURGERY NIPS AND TUCKS 2008

There was a time, between the top half and the bottom half parts, when I was supremely dislocated. Look at me, and you'd see a very lovely lady. I was trim then, and Dr Suporn had done a superb job.

Naked, though, I still had the horrid physicality I had not yet disposed of. Paradoxically, I was to find that made me very popular with the men. Go to a certain type of bar and you'll find a whole subculture of supposedly straight men who are looking for somebody like I looked then. I didn't indulge, but it was truly bizarre.

I was changing mightily. My dress sense had originally been very 1950s big full skirts, then I'd moved into the whole Dallas/ Dynasty mother of the bride thing. Both looks were full on glam, which is what I thought being a woman involved. I refused to wear trousers for an awfully long time. To me, trousers were a sign of the past. I got stared at a lot. I'd still get stared at if I went to Tesco's looking like Doris Day.

Gradually, I found what works for me. Which is, strangely enough, just a differently cut version of the kind of jeans, Cuban heels, top and jacket I always wore before. A bit more sparkly, and the hair and make-up things are definitely more involved, but I'm back pretty much full circle now. I was always there if you took the time to look. That's part of finding yourself.

My biggest issues after the major interventions were getting rid of the last signs of the drugs I had been on. Testosterone had thinned my hair. I had a tiny Adams apple - scarcely a pimple, but still visible – with a flat ass, and a thick waist. Several more trips to Thailand and I had all those fixed. Call it the icing on the cake if you like.

In total I went through 36 different procedures. It has been a lot of surgery. I don't regret any of it. There's a whole gaslighting thing about transition being the act of surgery. That's nonsense. I was always female.

My body is my vessel for my soul. It is mine to use. I'm the only one who must live in it. I didn't arrive the second the scalpel came out. I was always in there. What the scalpel did was cut the bonds that tied me, unchained my bound feet. Surgery let me fly.

Surgery let me be me.

The hormone patch I take once a week keeps me there.

There's no other great secret to it. No psycho-sexual weirdness or mental therapy required. No religious conversion or secret rites applied. What happened to me was genetic but continually negatively influenced by society and culture.

I had a medical issue and medical science cut that problem from me. I am healthy now. I am happy now. I see life with such focus now. In that previous form, strung out on male hormones like a junkie, I saw nothing.

I don't know why society still has an issue with this. To me, it is entirely normal. No different from having a life-threatening cyst removed. Except for the fact it took 44 years for me to reach a self-diagnosis, because society didn't recognise the medical nature of the emergency. They thought me criminal and perverted. Nobody has yet asked the question scientifically. We acknowledge change in other arenas, like the effect of socio-economic opportunity or education. Nobody has ever properly researched gender, discovering the intersectionality of identity and society.

I think this will change. When I was young, smoking was entirely acceptable. We didn't understand carcinogens then. Now we do. It'll be the same thing with the DNA strand and gender. Maybe there will be a pill, like the one I dreamt of when I was young, that brings change without months in hospital.

I hope I'm still alive to see it. What a vindication of my struggle that moment will be.

GRANADA END OF DAYS

I led a channel called 'Men and Motors'. It did exactly what it said on the tin. Half an hour of fast cars, half an hour of men's obsession with sex.

The idea was basically a quick ham shank for the fella, vindicated by the scheduling fact that he could shamelessly justify it because after every 30 minutes of soft porn, there would be 30 on maintaining a Ford Cortina. The churn in the programming was key to the advertising model. To get the ratings hit, viewers must stay for 11 minutes. The more viewers, the higher the rate you can charge for advertising. Even if you only tuned in for the soft porn half hour, I calibrated each flesh reveal to an 11-minute rhythm of climax. I was very precise in that. Every viewer was a tick in the box, 11 minutes every time.

I hired a lot of top female glamour for the channel. Jo Guest, Katie Price, Linda Lusardi, Linda Nolan, Kelly Brooks, the list of models of the day on my channel was endless. I gave each of them their own shows and filled the rest with US bulk product I went to Hollywood to buy. There were rules on what we could show, a precise nipple count per half hour. No genitals, no intercourse. Just a lot of breasts and a lot of lingerie.

My intersectionality worked rather well. I understood what men wanted, but I also had an eye for lingerie and beauty. Within 6 months, I had tripled the ratings. My model was box office gold for Granada. I made them a lot of money.

My ideas gathered attention. I came up with a talent show creating a female band like the Village People. Straight from my old disco days. There was a nurse, a police officer, a teacher, a secretary, and a fairy Tinkerbell, all in suitably saucy attire, running the gamut of male desire from dominant to submissive. I ran adverts in Stage and filmed the whole audition process, the rehearsals, the search for a song. The prize was a recording contract for a single and an appearance on Granada. Thousands applied. It was the Spice Girls meets Opportunity Knocks. Nigel Lythgoe saw the show and optioned the format. That became 'Pop Idol'. Originally my concept.

Granada had an executive penthouse floor. I used to go up there for creative dinners with the head of programmes, who went on to run ITV. That was where I pitched what became 'Loose Women'.

I was gathering steam again, becoming hot creatively. Granada was taking over the whole network. I was in the right place at exactly the right time. Luck is basically creating opportunity. I'd done the hard yards. I was off and running in the biggest television company in the UK.

I asked Mary to come to Manchester, to be a married couple, try to recapture what I thought we had. Mary again refused to join me. I was still on my own, living in a rented room in Salford, riding my bicycle to work, sending all my money to Glasgow to pay for a beautiful apartment I never saw. I tried one last time. I persuaded her to visit. The one and only time in my year there she came to see me.

I set up a meeting in a very smart hotel with the Head of Programmes and the Head of HR. They formally offered her the position of stage manager on 'Coronation Street,' the most prestigious serial drama in the country. They did it as a personal favour to make me happy and keep me. She was certainly talented enough to do the gig. They tied the deal to a long-term and lucrative creative contract for me and a promoted position as Head of Development. Riches awaited us both.

Mary turned them down flat, walked out of the meeting and got on the train back to Glasgow. My deal was put on ice. Granada wanted to see what I would do before they committed themselves. She never came back to Manchester.

I did indeed love her more than she ever loved me.

I spiralled.

Just down the road from Granada is Manchester's very active and fabulous gay quarter. The drag bars there are wonderful. My Freemans habit crept back in; except this

Sugar and Spice

time, I was going to all the meetings. I was obviously male formed dressed in drag, but it was the only thing that made me happy. I hated myself for it, all those societal lessons of perversion and criminality. I started going obsessively to the gym. I got very, very fit, and very muscled. I started on creatine and other body supplements. They made me very angry, very aggressive. I didn't care. I was caught in the vice of self-loathing and my inner reality that I needed to be me.

I got a lot of offers in those days. I moved in showbiz circles with a lot of very attractive men and women. I was a boss, a good looking one, and a player in the industry. All the temptations of life on the road were there for me. I had been on my own for four years while Mary had stayed in Glasgow. We hadn't been together once in all that time. I wrestled for an awfully long time with that. In the end, I decided I had a right to be happy too.

It didn't solve anything.

I came up with a show format for a national 'Lady Motors' beauty series, mixing the driving and the sex halves of the channel, the prize being a presenting gig. We went round the country with a format of mucky off-road 4X4 trails, fast cars, dress up and chat. Again, thousands applied.

I needed a panel of judges. One of them was Chris Ryan, the SAS hero from Desert Storm. His autobiography was on the way up then. His agent went low financially, just for the exposure. He fitted the demographic for the audience. Chris was in.

Ryan had the same effect on me as the Parachute Regiment officer all those years earlier had had. I got to know him quite well, staying with his family in Hereford, hiking the Brecon Beacons with him. He was good to me at a time that I was obviously lost as a person. There is a sensitivity to him that makes him different from a lot of the other SAS folks I have worked with. Of course, being good to me opened media doors for him. He liked what I offered as much as I like to think he liked me as a person. I did open doors for him. He was fine at what I needed him to do on the telly. From my perspective, being with him re-awoke the Airborne dream from all those years earlier. It was a symbiotic relationship, but he re-awoke a dormant ambition in me.

I figured if I could be like him, I might finally be able to nullify who I am, be rid of the stain of shame my family had inculcated in me. It sounds crazy, but I was crazy - with self-imposed and entirely unnecessary guilt.

I resolved to go back to the army, this time to fulfil unfinished business and join The Parachute Regiment.

Which is about as big a 180-degree hand brake life turn as I could do. I was 36, going great guns in a top media job, with much more to offer. All I had to do was stick at it. A balanced person would have got a divorce, met somebody else, ridden the wave. It's what I would do now. I'm me now. I am happy in my form. My soul has found its expression.

I wasn't balanced then. I was living as somebody else. I hated myself for the duplicity of it. I was in a cul de sac of grief, loneliness, rejection, and shame. In response, I didn't just geographise, I turned the kaleidoscope inside out.

Once more, I took another bag of Freeman's clothes out to the bin.

I walked out of Granada Television and a glittering media career without a backward glance, armed with nothing more than an ambition to be a paratrooper. I was done with television.

Utterly mental, but that's precisely what I did.

LONDON 2007

The dining room was open plan, built as an extension to the Victorian terraced home. It was terribly stylish, in that sort of Norwegian IKEA-influenced way that the trendy set see as an interesting addition to the adornment of the original building. All straight lines and effective insulation, walls of glass and steel, slate floors, and clean pine furniture.

The conversation centred around IKEA too. The best buys, the best build. How Conran's stuff seemed so over-priced. And family, competitive family – how the children's education was just sooooo expensive:

'It really is going to be a toss-up between the Algarve and summer school this year.'

My hosts were perfectly reasonable people, products of much of the same upbringing as my own could have been, had I not been born the way I was. The same second division public school, same start in a sensible occupation, same marriage to a sensible type. They were contented with their lives.

My life had never really started.

Somehow, somewhere, our paths had gone radically different routes.

I wasn't a bank manager, or an accountant. I was a wounded war hero. An officer in The Parachute Regiment.

I thought of Afghanistan. I'd been back three months, three months of painfully putting my head and body back together after the bomb. The end of two years away at the front, of trying again and again to persuade myself I could be an Airborne officer in the body I had suffered all those years. The officer bit wasn't the issue. It was that body, every time, the same problem. Being me, trying to hide being me, being ashamed of being me, being me. No matter how hard I tried to find a way out of the maze, I always came back to the same place.

I am me.

I had done everything the British Army asked of me: four extended operational tours, three different wars. Staff jobs, command jobs, exercises, training courses, operations, wars, leading, commanding, ordering, shooting, wounding, killing. Airborne forces, Special Forces, other country's forces. I had done everything the British Army asked of me.

Finally, to find myself in Northern Afghanistan as part of a CIA team supporting Afghan Special Forces.

That's when it went wrong.

I took one too many chances, ran out of lives. Got too close to the folks who wanted to kill me. I remember a big explosion, trying to get to my feet again, and failing. They put me in hospital. Then they sent me back to the UK.

Everybody was very nice to me, but they made it clear my days in the frontline were over. My Lawrence dream had burned itself out. I had burned myself out.

The nice, normal people in London at the dinner party asked me about being in the suck, deep in the heart of war, in that concerned civilian kind of way:

'Gosh, it looks terrible on the news, what's it like to shoot somebody?'

The women leaning forward, the sexual arousal clear on their faces. The men, leaning back in their chairs, pretending to share in the feelings and emotions of a warrior, too inculcated in their gender role to understand the reality of the horror.

None of them had been there. None of them could understand.

If you'd never been there, you could never explain it. If you had been there, you wouldn't have to.

To smell and taste one's own fear, the adrenalin shakes as the bullets fly overhead. All I had to do was reach up to touch them....and if I had, all the pain would have melted away....

I looked at them as they all dissolved away, to only see my real soul, as she gently touched me on the shoulder. I could not fight her anymore. My time as that other person was over.

I heard myself say, 'I'm sorry, I can't do this anymore.' I stood up and left, walked out without a goodbye. Not a word to these ordinary people, who had been kind enough to invite me into their home. Who may as well as been Martian for all that I could relate to them.

The next day, my entire life went in the bin. I was resolved to live as the woman I had always been.

That same day, I told my friends. I told my family. I told The Regiment. I told the Army.

A week later, The Regiment and the Army fired me. My family disowned me. Somebody leaked: the shock value news of my military dismissal over my gender was spread on the front cover of every paper in Britain.

THE PARACHUTE REGIMENT

Nine years earlier, I had pulled a full Bette Davis and flounced out of Granada Television. I was off to be a paratrooper.

A dream that came to rather a sudden and screeching halt. I was 36, well past my military sell-by date. I was a decade too old for the Regular Army. Too old too for reserve selection, which had a bar of 34. This wasn't going well. I might want, but the army was in no mood to give. I couldn't see where this was going to go. I hadn't done any effective planning at all.

Most folks would have gone right back to Granada and pleaded insanity. I didn't: I had a dream.

The best way to change the future is to create it.

I did have a ton of professional experience as a journalist and film maker. I'd been on three missions, to Desert Storm, Bosnia, and Angola. Fortunately for me, at the turn of the millennium, the army had woken up to the existence of the internet and the possibility of weaponising the media. There was a sudden interest and desire to recruit folks with professional skills to create and deliver information operations. The age waiver for that skill had exemptions.

I had to make my own route to market, but if I could pull it off, I had the moxie they needed.

I made an enquiry, found a sponsoring Manchester-based line infantry regiment, and got in as a qualified over-age candidate to the reserves, specifically to deliver information operations. It was tight, another elevator pitch moment, but basically the same selling exercise as I'd done to get into art school. That bit worked, the next was not so easy. I'd been in the private sector too long. I'd forgotten the army had its rules. I wanted to be a paratrooper. The army wanted me to deliver information operations, not jump out of planes.

I'd have to square the circle. I needed to tickle the trout.

They made me go back through Sandhurst again, this time on the course they put the nurses, padres, surgeons, and lawyers through. It was simple enough. There was a gentility to it all, almost apologetic sergeant majors in charge. I cruised it.

Then came the harder part. Courses cost money. The army needs a reason to send you on something as hard and as arduous as Parachute Regiment selection. They want to know there's value at the end of it, a reasonable chance of utility in the investment. The selection process, known as P Company, offers the hardest, most physical tests in the conventional army. Twenty-year-olds are broken by it. I was 36. Positively ancient. Utterly impossible for me to succeed, according to the army.

I pulled another elevator pitch. I wrote to the commander of the Airborne brigade, extolling the advantages of having his own information operations officer on call if he'd just support my bid to be a paratrooper. I didn't tell him how old I was. All highly irregular. Luckily, the man in question was an out the box type, and he sent me back a carefully qualified note that he agreed it would generally be a good idea to have a qualified information officer, without specifically recommending me. His letter was senior enough for me to roll with it, the writing vague enough to cover him from responsibility for me.

Fortunately, the sergeant major loading the candidates on P Company was sufficiently impressed by my general's recommendation that he gave me a slot. I pulled off a full 360 spin of subterfuge. My success came with consequence. I marked myself by my ambition and intelligence before I even began. The army expected me to wait my turn. I had no time left to wait. I used the system for my own advantage. When they found out, the army didn't like that.

I worked my magic by exploiting the army's tribal stovepipe mentality. Nobody understood my full plan but me. I carefully let each of them see just enough to be attracted by me. I was one step away from winning my Regimental maroon beret. All I had to do was drag my 36-year-old body through the toughest test the army has to offer. The Regiment says P Company is 70% mental, 30% physical. You must want it. No matter how fit, there comes a point where the body gives up and the mental will takes over. You must want it.

I wanted it.

I'd given up everything for the chance. My only chance. If I didn't make it at 36, I wouldn't make it at 37. My motivation was quite clear. This was my Lawrence moment in full Yentl disguise. On the other side, I believed I could quiet my demons. I believed the needless guilt I felt over who I am would somehow disappear and I'd be free of all the pain.

I really wanted it.

Sugar and Spice

'P' COMPANY

Pegasus is a winged horse, sired by Poseidon, which bore the rider Bellerephon in his fight to kill the Chimera. Bellerephon fell off trying to ascend Mount Olympus. Pegasus was stabled by Zeus and carries his thunderbolts.

Pegasus flies into battle.

Pegasus and Bellerephon are the symbols of the British Airborne. The selection process, known as P Company, stands for Pegasus Company.

To win my maroon beret, I would have to complete 8 tests in 5 days. Each of the tests are based around lessons from the Regiment's campaign at Arnhem. I was about to re-enact my 'Bridge Too Far' sense memory.

P Company is the only selection in the army that every rank does together. Candidates are scored by a team of sergeants. It is not enough to be physically fit enough to pass selection. All candidates, particularly officers, must show what is described as 'Airborne spirit', commonly known as the stuff of leaders. The job involves jumping out of a plane, most likely at night, to seize and hold a strategic objective until relieved, regardless of chaos, confusion, death, or injury. The tests are designed to mirror that shock of intense combat. This swift delivery of violence is what makes the Regiment different. The parachuting part is merely the means of delivery. It is the ability to deliver and maintain overwhelming directed aggression for the duration of the mission that marks the paratrooper. The Parachute Regiment are shock troops.

The Parachute Regiment does not give up.

Ever.

Entrusted with maintaining that ethos is the job of P Company. They are the sole arbiters of who is chosen to carry on the Airborne tradition. There is no other way of entering The Parachute Regiment.

Unlike every other unit in the conventional army, you cannot be posted to The Parachute Regiment. You must earn the right to be there by first succeeding in a series of tests every single paratrooper has also passed. This is the significance of P Company. This is what make The Parachute Regiment so special.

Less than half of those who apply will ever pass.

I arrived in the usual welter of running and shouting and creating order out of disorder. We were lined up in a dark corridor and shouted at some more. Private soldiers wore a green T-shirt, non-coms a red T-shirt, and officers a white one. Officers would, by common understanding, be marked harder and required to deliver more. This is the job of officers. There are various types of officers. The Regiment requires more of the immediate currency of inspiration, sweat and selflessness. I wore a white T-shirt.

None of us had names. On our T-shirts were numbers. Throughout the course, we would be known by those numbers. Unlike other Regiments, we were not acknowledged by name. We had not earned the Regimental right.

The sergeant in charge pointed to a shrine made of a maroon beret, the insignia of blue wings, the insignia of a qualified paratrooper, surmounted by a miniature of the flag of the Regiment. He invited us to think for a moment what those symbols meant to us and how much we would each be willing to give to win the right to wear them and be called 'Airborne'.

He asked us all to put our right arm in the air and to lower it as he called out an age.

'Under 25.' Half the arms went down.

'26, 27, 28, 29, 30.'

There were 4 of us left. He looked at us and said, 'your chances of making it have now halved.'

'31, 32...'

Mine was the only arm left.

'33, 34, 35, 36.'

I put my arm down. He looked right at me and said, 'No chance. Go home now.' I replied:

'Go home now...Sir.'

P Company or no, he had irked me. He acknowledged my rank – and couldn't help but add, 'We'll see tomorrow if you're worth it...sir.'

Now that really put me in the mood. I'd been nervous beforehand, but the gauntlet was truly cast. Perhaps that was what he intended. The Regiment is such theatre. They have a very Olivier sense of the dramatic. The Regiment is as much attitude as practicality. I came out of the traps the next day with a determination firecracker lit in my ass.

Six of the 8 tests are variations of running very fast within various times over varying amounts of miles whilst laden with various heavy objects. Rucksacks, rifles, helmets, stretchers, tank tracks, scaffolding poles, telegraph poles. They are all the same rhythms on a theme of war.

Each event requires a huge degree of cardio fitness burn. The hurt is how the candidate deals with repeatedly expending so much physical burn in such a short period of time. The burn hurts. A lot. And then hurts some more. Candidates must show they love the hurt and joyously welcome the chance for more burn. This is the grunt: the desire to win the beret, to be worthy of the Regiment. The tests reveal whether you can overcome the burn and the hurt and grunt for more.

Never, ever give up. There is always more within you.

As an officer, you must not only excel but give of yourself, by example and encouragement and ignoring your burn and hurt by encouraging the grunt in others. This is how officers are marked.

Collectively, this is Airborne attitude. This is how The Regiment wins battles.

A lot of candidates can't handle the burn. Can't deal with the hurt. Don't have the grunt. They do not win the maroon beret. The wearing of it is not a gift. It is earned.

I adored it all.

All those years of disappearing into myself when I was being battered senseless served me well. I didn't care about the hurt. I'd been there before. I didn't care about the burn. I'd trained hard for it. As for the grunt, I literally had nowhere else to go. If this was what they wanted, they could have everything I had to offer. And then some. I had something to prove. I was going to pass. On bloodied stumps if I had to. I put my heart and my body on a platter and offered it to the Airborne shrine.

I found my calling. Right time, right place, right person, right officer.

On the 2-mile race, I gave my squad place to another and still beat the instructor home. On the log race, I led from the front, dragging a fallen comrade until he quit with rope burn, and still won by a quarter mile. On the stretcher race, I volunteered for extra duty in the carry and still brought my team in first. On the distance marches, I dropped to the back to grunt on the stragglers, running back up to the front each time they dropped. I screamed, yelled, exhorted, and gave all of myself. I was everything they wanted.

Six down, two to go.

No matter how much the staff tell you otherwise, the remaining events are the ones you must excel in to pass selection. The others are appetisers.

The first is known as the trainasium.

This is an assault course on stilts, 30 feet in the air. The idea is to assess whether you have the stones to jump out of an aircraft when faced with the nothingness of the sky. In The Regiment, you cannot refuse in the door. The mission is all. You must go. You must jump. Officers are always the first out. We lead the way by example.

To fail to complete the trainasium is an instant course failure. To show hesitation for a split second is an officer course fail.

I am hesitant to climb a step ladder. Six feet off the ground, I get dizzy. This is not good mental preparedness for the trainasium. I needed to find extra grunt.

Thirty feet up, there are a series of balance planks to leap over, followed by a full-throated leap into a cargo net, which you must catch in an approved manner with an outstretched arm. I closed my eyes and ran. I was so busy running blind I forgot to outstretch an arm and cannonballed into the net like a Warner brother's cartoon Coyote. Critically, I hadn't hesitated. Amidst much laughter at officer maladroitness, they gave me one more attempt. I closed my eyes, ran, and stretched. It wasn't elegant, but I caught the net and very dizzily clambered down.

I would enjoy the actual parachuting, considerably higher up than mere feet off the ground. Even now, I can close my eyes and remember the stillness of standing in the door as Number 1 in the stick, while the slipstream wizzed by. The tumble of going upside down in the chaos of exit, followed by the quiet of the wind as the parachute billowed above me. That was joy. The trainasium was not.

One to go.

The last event would change how the world saw me for the next decade.

This is called 'milling'.

Milling is the cachet event. Before it begins, candidates are lined up against a chosen opponent, told to look deep into each other's eyes and yell, 'Kill, kill, kill.' The Regiment is big on human drama.

Essentially uncontrolled and inelegant boxing, milling is the event where you square off against your opponent wearing heavily weighted gloves and have at each other. Skill is not required, indeed were you to show anything like boxing ability the candidate would lose points. The test is not skill based. The concept is that on a given command, candidates turn into each other and go windmilling until told to stop. This shows a lack of fear and an ability to deliver unbridled aggression under orders. As you wait for your turn, the other candidates form a human ring and push the candidates back into each other if they break or fall.

Milling is primeval. In my opinion, it is the most significant test of them all. How the candidate deals with the stress and the subjugation of fear to keep pressing on, no matter the cost or the pain, is the one test that reveals the soldier to be. It is not a test of skill that can be taught. It is a test of the soul. It is a competition. Candidates fight on until there is only one undefeated champion.

The point of being an officer is to lead. Milling is a demonstration of intent. It shows selflessness. It is very important that no favour is shown to the officers. The Toms (as soldiers are known in The Regiment) must see you took the same licks as them, showed the same

Airborne spirit as they had. This egalitarianism is a keynote of difference within The Regiment.

We train together. We jump together. We fight together. We die together.

Milling is an opportunity for the staff to test the officers. Candidates are evenly matched by height and weight. In the case of officer candidates, the staff pick the fiercest and toughest soldiers and tell them if they don't knock the officer out, they'll fail the course. What you get is a soldier so fired up against the officer, they come out of the traps like the bull at Pamplona.

In my case, I was paired with Lance Corporal Love of the Royal Horse Artillery. L/Cpl Love had run into a shovel at an early age. His face was a granite wall. As we were 'kill, kill, kill' mid-moment, he proudly told me he was a London middleweight ABA champion. Love was his name, not his nature.

There's no place to hide in the milling. At the given command 'Box!' I turned and gamely wind-milled. I have a vague recollection of Love's rictus smile before the darkness. He knocked me out in 12 seconds flat.

I don't remember anything after that. I was told later that they wiped the blood off my face and slapped me into consciousness. I was helped up, loudly proclaimed, 'I'm fine, Colour Sergeant, let me at him,' and then fell back into unconsciousness. This was greeted with much hilarity and smiles. L/Cpl Love went all the way to the final bout where he was knocked unconscious by a human sledgehammer.

I don't remember this as I was on a stretcher. When I came round, my white T-shirt was bright crimson. The medic told me my nose had been well and truly broken. I had a choice:

Go to hospital to have it fixed, which would mean coming off the course and failing. Or he would fix it there and then and I could stay on the course.

An Airborne moment indeed.

I told him to do his worst. I was staying. No matter the cost. He took my nose between his fingers, yanked hard, shoved a tampon up each nostril to quell the river of blood, and pronounced me good to go.

Love was standing off to one side being treated himself for his injury in the final. I went over and congratulated him on his victory. That man was nails.

The staff noticed. My action was Airborne. I passed milling because I showed no fear, lived with the consequences, and showed leadership in my loss. That's what I loved about The Regiment. Every action could be a life lesson. All you had to do was be alert to it.

A day later, after more very fast running with heavy weights, I stood on parade with everybody else.
As the numbers were read out, the candidate stood to attention. The officer in charge then declared, 'Pass' or

'Fail'. A pass meant stay on parade, a failure meant march off and face in the other direction as the candidate had not met the standard and was not fit to look at those who were.

Pure theatricality, very profound.

My number was read out. I came to attention.

'Pass.'

I didn't cry then. Instead, I looked to find Love. He had passed too. We smiled at each other.

They came around with the maroon berets. We took off the green cap comforters we had been wearing and proudly put our berets on our heads for the first time. The company commander came over and told me I had secured the highest scored officer pass they had seen in the previous three years. He welcomed me to the Airborne.

At 36, I hadn't just done it, I'd smashed it.

A lot of dust got in my eyes.

Love and I hugged, got embarrassed at the closeness, and broke off to shake hands instead.

I went back to my room and looked at myself in the mirror. I lost my beauty on P Company. I had two black eyes and a nose that was less vertical than W-shaped in a diagonal criss-cross. For the first time in my life, I looked like a man. I cried a lot then.

My old history teacher's words came back to me:

1. Get fit, get really fit.
2. Get determined to succeed, get really determined.
3. Get used to ignoring 'no', get really used to that.

Yup – tick 'done that'.

It took 3 nose jobs and all of Dr Suporn's skill to undo P Company's mark.

I wouldn't change any of it.

I am the first woman to ever pass P Company.

AMBITION ACHIEVED

I had won a maroon beret. I wasn't yet in The Parachute Regiment. I belonged to another unit. I had another lap in my race to run.

After P Company, I went to RAF Brize Norton to learn to parachute. Using a series of mock-ups that must have been built 50 years ago, we were taught how to jump from a plane, how to get ourselves out of a jam if our parachutes didn't open, and how to appropriately land once our downward descent was done. I loved it all. The course photograph shows me grinning from ear to ear, lit up like a Christmas tree.

My old nemesis L/Cpl Love was there too. It was an emotional re-union. I was somewhat surprised to find several folks there who hadn't attended P Company, but who had been posted on the jumps course because they had specific skills. Medical officers, mostly. I had thought it was one size fits all. In the welter of being shouted at again, I pushed my surprise to one side and moved with the flow.

I didn't know how I'd react to standing on the edge of the precipice in mid-air. I was so determined to succeed I took a civilian jump course the week before Brize, just to be sure I could do it. That first jump was a very different experience from military parachuting. There's an enjoyment to be had from a civilian jump. A military jump is merely a means of delivery. Carrying 180 pounds of equipment and parachute, essentially one's body weight, jumping in a choreographed ballet with 80 other paratroopers all going out two doors at the back of a military transport plane, is an industrial act of physicality.

The Parachute Regiment sergeant who'd told me I was too old was there. He and I continued to see life differently. As much as I looked like Rocky after the milling, I couldn't erase everything about me. I was also from a different infantry Regiment. My manner, my smile, and my alternate regimental heritage seemed to irk him deeply. There is a certain type of man who is threatened by people from my community. He was one.

Nonetheless, as I landed on the last jump of the last day, I was overwhelmed with joy. I'd qualified. I knew on the drop zone, I'd get my blue badge of courage to wear, the embroidered parachute with the blue wings, the mark of a qualified paratrooper.

I watched the doctors who hadn't done P Company get their blue badge from my sergeant nemesis. I watched L/Cpl Love get his badge and applauded them all.

It was my turn.

The sergeant walked up to me and gave me a parachute badge without the blue wings, disparagingly known as a 'lightbulb' in the army. I felt the anger rise then. I'd done everything they had asked of me, and here he was, at the end, after all of it, marking me for my difference again.

He told me I wasn't in The Parachute Regiment and therefore not true Airborne. I asked him why the doctors, who hadn't done P Company at all, had been given the blue badge of courage. He told me they were different. They were just about Airborne, but I wasn't at all. I could see the discrimination and the loathing in his fat face.

I lost my temper. The others had to restrain me. They then had to restrain him. It was the first time since I had lashed out at my father that I felt the urge to kill. The sergeant was the same as my father; blinkered, biased, hateful, deceitful, and disgusting.

The RAF flight lieutenant running the whole thing led me away. He told me the staff there all hated the sergeant as the worst kind of angry, bigoted paratrooper. He suggested I let it go and ignore him.

I couldn't ignore him. Once again in my life, somebody had deliberately tried to denigrate and deny me.

I did what I've always done when faced with those obstacles:

I would no longer accept the things I could not change; I would change the things I cannot accept.

I wrote direct to the Parachute Regiment Regimental Colonel, the big enchilada, the man who can make stuff happen. I explained my case, explained my worth, my utility, and asked for a transfer. He took me on. Within two weeks, I had finally joined the Airborne. I was gazetted in The London Times.

I was a Parachute Regiment officer.

I wore my embroidered blue badge and my maroon beret and my winged silver Regimental insignia.

Just like Sean Connery. I'd done it. Aged 36, I had passed everything they asked of me. I had earned the right. I had fulfilled my dream.

Much later, I saw that sergeant again at Thetford Camp. He tried to walk past, ignoring me. I pulled him up, made him walk back to me, salute me, and address me as a Parachute Regiment officer.

Did he like that? I doubt it, but I don't give a fuck about his feelings.

I am the only woman to have ever been a Parachute Regiment officer.

Airborne. Utrinque Paratus. Ready For Anything.

WEARING THE MAROON BERET

I might have won my beret and become a very proud Parachute Regiment officer, but I was back at the bottom of the pile again. These were the days before the Twin Towers. The army was very much short of genuine excitement, and what little existed was very much in demand with a lot of names in the frame before mine.

I went on some of the nascent information operations support to exercises. I was bored and frustrated from the first day. The folks I worked with were mostly public relation types, very smooth, brilliantine haired types with posh accents who spoke a very plausible game but had little actual, real transferable skills. I found myself back shooting and editing newsreel inserts as inject points to delivering the exercise narrative. Most times, we didn't wear uniform. This wasn't remotely what I'd got into the army to do.

My salary was a 5th of what I'd earned in television. Too big a hit to keep going indefinitely. I had a small property portfolio that I sold to subsidise the whole thing, but I was living off those savings to keep the big apartment in Glasgow paid for. I needed some reward for the sacrifice. This wasn't the army's problem to solve. It was mine.

Screw the system.

I was Lawrence marking time before the desert. I needed to stick a cattle prod onto this. I was too short of time. The operational army is a young person's game, the Airborne even more so. I was already at the outer edges of the envelope.

I discovered the army had recently adopted a way to bring the reserves into the regular strength through a specific type of contract. The infantry was desperately short of qualified officers.

Forget supporting exercises. Geographise.

The officer who managed the postings was based in Glasgow. I knew him from Desert Storm. I invited him to Rogano. An expensive champagne dinner and a bottle of Laphroaig later, I had my contract and my posting. I created my own future.

I went to Cyprus as the officer commanding the reconnaissance platoon of a regular infantry battalion manning the green line separating the Turks and Greeks. The PR smoothies went nuts; they would have to do their own editing. I could not have cared less.

I enjoyed the posting. It was fun being back doing intelligence related stuff. We hid in hedgerows, painted our faces black and crawled about in the night. My Airborne qualification gave me a kind of ready brek glow of competence, and my maturity gave me protection in the mess from the sort of class-based crap I'd struggled with as a young officer.

I applied for every training course going. I went to jungle warfare school in Belize, walked and climbed my way to become a mountain leader, passed the physical training instructors' course and then went to the SAS, where I became a combat survival instructor.

I had a wonderful couple of years as operations and training officer with The Highlanders, a fine Regiment that had subsumed The Gordon Highlanders, whose badge I had proudly worn as a Combined Cadet. History came full circle. I taught young soldiers as I had once been taught.

None of this was conventional, in any way. I bought and gave away a lot of bottles of Laphroaig to get my way. None of it would support a career trajectory, but I wasn't after that. I wanted adventures, not security. I knew I was on limited time physically. My body was creaking, no matter how much creatine and body supplement I took.

Then the Towers came down.

That changed everything.

I was in the United States, on adventure training, thru hiking The Appalachian Trail, an epic mountain walk of 2,200 miles up the East coast of America. That last summer of peace was my summer of '63 moment. I found myself in the mountains at Greymoors Monastery.

I'd achieved my dream of being a Parachute Regiment officer. I resolved that summer to leave the army and become me. The internet had arrived, and I had gleaned the knowledge to understand what I had to do. I was ridiculously fit by the end and determined to change everything.

I would leave the army, leave Mary, return to television, re-start my career, get it all back together as me, in a new body, my soul ignited, my future decided. I had nothing left to prove to myself, or anybody else.

I was in a hundred-mile wilderness in Maine when 9-11 happened. I heard on my shortwave radio that the first Tower had come down. I wrote in my diary that a terrible, seismic event had changed the world. I climbed the last mountain, Mount Katadhin, with the surety of a mountain goat and a dread in my soul.

I called The Regiment. They wanted me back as soon as possible.

Ten days later, I was in Oman, training hard, with the expectation of war resounding in our ears.

A month later, the US and the Coalition invaded Afghanistan. My military Lawrence years began.

I put duty first. I'd taken the shilling, enjoyed the privilege. I had responsibility to my country, to my Regiment, to myself. It was time to repay the debt.

I put my dream to be me back in the band box, re-tied the ribbon, and shelved the whole thing on the uppermost shelf of my mind, right at the back, out of sight.

I went to war then.

I stayed at war for another 6 years and 4 long, arduous operational tours. I killed those who tried to kill me, to protect my country and our values. That was not me, but I was a soldier. An Airborne soldier.

I very nearly died myself in the fight. Then the Taliban ended my career. I came home. I'd gone as far as I could in that form.

I repaid my debt to my country, to my Regiment and to my soldiers, then repaid my debt to myself.

I told the army, the family, and all who knew me who I really am.

WHAT'S THE POINT?

It's nearly 2 decades since I announced to the world the good news of my redemption. There's another book in all the adventures I've had since. I'm still travelling that road. It'll be another dawn before I decide it's done. The writing of that can wait. I'm still figuring out the ending.

Of the folks in this volume, I tied off the ends. Some easily, some surgically, some messily, some still bleeding.

When I told The Parachute Regiment that I am a woman, they removed me from post and declared me medically unfit. The news screamed out in headlines in every major newspaper in the UK. I took the government to court for two and a half years. In the end, I won the right to be me.

I handed in my ID card and was issued another in my name and true gender. I became the first and only female Parachute Regiment officer. You can't be in the Regiment without having passed P Company. The army acknowledged that day I was the first woman to pass P Company.

That very same day, I resigned.

My fight was done. I'd earned every victory I ever wanted.

The army changed the regulations to allow people like me to serve. I won that for my community.

I walked out without a backward glance. I had too much in my future to look at the past. Except to wonder at how far I had travelled.

My days in the army were over.

I told Mary what I was going to do. She looked at me and said I had waited long enough. She loved me enough to say that.

The State forcibly divorced us in 2007. Same sex marriages were illegal then. Whatever we had had was long since gone. In all my time in the army, I only ever saw or heard from Mary on the odd occasions I came back to Glasgow. In all my operational tours, she never sent me a single care package or card. All through those years, I continued to steadfastly pay for that flat in Glasgow. It had been bought out of love. It became a bit of a talisman, an investment in the past that sustained me. When I became me and we were divorced, I was seized by a sense of guilt and signed it over to her. On the proviso she would make me her heir in her will, and it would return to me on her death.

Mary met somebody else, and I wished her well. We still spoke with the familiarity of family.

In 2014, a friend of Mary's asked to meet me in a bar in Glasgow. She told me that Mary had finally succumbed to dementia and been committed. Mary's last responsible act had been to appoint her friend as executor and legal guardian. The meeting was to tell me I had no legal right of visitation or involvement in Mary's affairs.

Mary's friend now controlled everything.

The flat I had poured so much love and money into for decades was sold by the executor to pay for Mary's care.

I was granted 24 hours to remove my personal items before it all went to house clearance.

Over 25 years of hard work and money and sacrifice and memories came down to 6 pictures, a coffee table and sideboard salvaged.

I am not allowed to visit Mary. She is still alive. Mary is not her real name; it serves no purpose to reveal it.

She no longer participates in her world. She remains in mine as a conflicted memory shorn equally between anger, disappointment, and love.

When I told my mother and father of my decision, they spent a week making drunken telephone calls telling me I was an utter disgrace and a failure to my country and to them. They then sent me everything they owned of me, pictures, mementos, memories.

In truth, they had long been little more than a cipher. In all my years in the military, throughout every war, they had never been in touch. Not even a single card. On my last tour, my father had phoned Mary to ask why he hadn't heard from me for years. She told them I was in Afghanistan. He had no idea.

When I made my decision, my entire family joined in. Every sibling, aunt, uncle, and cousin. My life with them literally ended. Some went to the trouble of writing hate-filled letters, most simply refused to speak to me.

My aunt told me I had mortally sinned and was prepared to speak to me via telephone but could never, ever meet me again. I told her if that was her position, I'd never speak to her again. Which is how it has been ever since. I'll not change that either. I am me and I'll not compromise any longer.

In 2019, I received a phone call from a lawyer. She told me my mother was dead. She told me my mother had died 6 months earlier. They were only calling to let me know as informing her oldest child was a legal obligation to allow them to wind up the estate. I was written out of the will, and I know nothing else. Not how she died or what happened to her remains.

My mother was implacable.

Same with my father.

My brother wrote to tell me I was sick and a pervert.

I have had no other contact with any member of my family since I first made my public announcement. They chose that.

The news of my announcement was made in every paper in Britain. The juxtaposition of paratrooper and woman made for sensational headlines. A television company made a film about my journey that went around the world. It's still on You Tube: 'Sex Change Soldier'. Dreadful title. I was interviewed by journalists from as far away as Japan and Australia.

Not one of the people I had called friends reached out to me. Not one of the officers or soldiers I had served with. Not one of the television folks I had known.

I lost everybody.

I've reconciled with precisely 6 people from the four and a half decades the world saw somebody else during the 15 years of being me. Everybody else in my life is from the timeframe of the reality of who I now am.

I don't miss any of those so-called friends. Love should mean never having to apologise. And I have nothing to apologise for. If they didn't care enough about me to reach out at my time of greatest need, they don't deserve to share my success. No-one can demean you without your consent. They do not have my consent.

Always be a first-rate version of yourself, not a second-rate version of somebody else.

WOMANHOOD

Was it all worth it?

Oh, yes. In aces, spades, diamonds, hearts, and clubs. The best way to predict the future is to create it.

After the army, I went into a holding pattern as a police officer. I patrolled the streets of Glasgow as Abi. It was my first openly female job. The first time I had to confront an angry man is the moment I found that Abi the gentlewoman was not that different from who I had been before.

I loved the moments when I genuinely helped make people's lives safer and more stable. I did not love the macho culture, the open misogyny, and the transphobia.

I left after 3 years to go back to Afghanistan. Which might sound strange, given that I'd been medevacked from there a few years earlier. It was an invitation from the United States of America that drew me there. The land of Elvis offered me the chance to work with their army.

I adored every second of it. That story is in another autobiographic volume, 'Lord Roberts' Valet'. If you've made it this far with this one, go buy it now. I stayed in Afghanistan with the Americans for 4 years.

America was my second chance. I took my new body on the road and proved the old gal didn't just still have it; she was way out in front.

In 2012, I fell in love with a US Army Ranger. In Kandahar, Afghanistan, we had a very deep, torrid, and emotional love affair. I allowed him inside me many times. I felt that feeling that I had always longed for in my previous life, where he lost himself in me and the softness of my body caressed his hardness.

Dr Suporn was as good as his word. My orgasms are immense.

I adore every second.

The gift that America gave me in Afghanistan allowed me to create another career as a diplomat. I've spent the last decade criss-crossing the Middle East, Central and South Asia, and Eastern Europe. I went back to television too. I made several films and won several awards. This time as writer and presenter. I allowed my star to shine.

I adore every second.

You see, I'm happy now.

Now that I'm happy, I have the bandwidth to make other people happy too. It really is that simple.

In 2019, I flew from Kabul to Washington for the retirement of a dear friend of mine, a 3-star general officer in the US Air Force. All the military chiefs of the United States were there.

At that ceremony, my friend gave a speech to the assembled dignitaries. He singled me out for my professional skills and diligence. He praised my example, my kindness and my compassion, my bravery as a woman. I received a standing ovation from every single service chief that the United States possesses.

The celluloid country I had adored as a child sat in the dark of a cinema realised all my dreams and ambitions. Not just fantasy, hard reality.

That moment, after a lifetime of struggle, battles, and despair was my Everest summited.

I went to Memphis then. I went to Graceland. I went to Elvis Presley's home.

I'd always avoided it. Emotionally, it terrified me. So much of my childhood loss was wrapped around the axle of dreaming Elvis would come save me.

I booked a private tour of the estate. I was in tears before I even got through the gates. In the house, there was just me, the guide, security….and The King himself.

I swear to you, he walked beside me. He nodded his gorgeous head, smiled his gorgeous smile, shook his shaky leg, and told me it was all going to be OK, forever more. He would never leave me.

Sugar and Spice

I'll write down all those stories from the past 20 years someday. The years in Afghanistan, Ukraine, North Macedonia, Azerbaijan, Kazakhstan, all the other postings and adventures.

This volume is done now. All that was is no more. Merely stardust memories. Some dark, some not so. All are opaque and disappearing from the light.

I wrote this to remind myself of where I came from, what I endured, and what I've become. I wrote this as reply to the lies that are still told about my community and were told about me.

I wrote this as a beacon for every other young, troubled soul who is out there searching for answers as I did.

I wrote this to make a difference.

I am the first female officer in The Parachute Regiment.

Airborne. Utrinque Paratus. Ready For Anything.

I AM WOMAN.

Hear me roar.

Sugar and Spice

Memories

Mama

Desert Storm

Sugar and Spice

Mario. He was killed later that day.

Iraq

Sugar and Spice

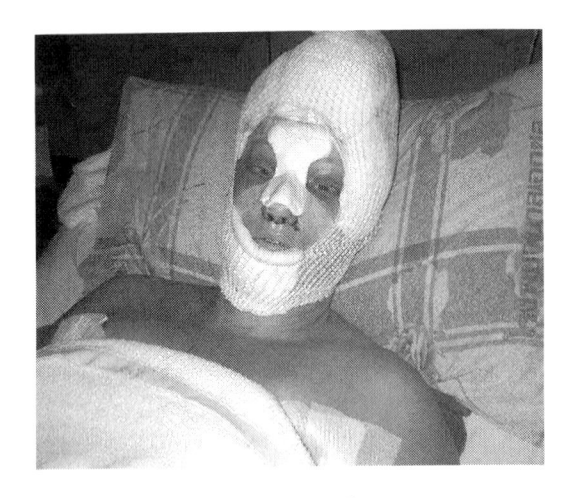

Thailand

Afghanistan

Sugar and Spice

Filming at the White House

The US Embassy in North Macedonia

Sugar and Spice

Memphis, Sun Studios,

Where Elvis Stood Thank-ya very much. Uh huh.

For mama.

Thank-you to those souls who had the conviction to acknowledge me, to accept me, to adore me.

All we need is love.

Sugar and Spice

Copyrigt

AbiAustn 2023

Printed in Great Britain
by Amazon